DATE DUE

DEMCO 38-296

Understanding
CAMILO JOSÉ CELA

UNDERSTANDING MODERN EUROPEAN AND LATIN AMERICAN LITERATURE

JAMES HARDIN, *Series Editor*

volumes on

Ingeborg Bachmann
Samuel Beckett
Thomas Bernhard
Johannes Bobrowski
Heinrich Böll
Italo Calvino
Albert Camus
Elias Canetti
Camilo José Cela
Céline
José Donoso
Rainer Werner Fassbinder
Max Frisch
Federico García Lorca
Gabriel García Márquez

Juan Goytisolo
Günter Grass
Gerhart Hauptmann
Christoph Hein
Eugène Ionesco
Milan Kundera
Primo Levi
Luigi Pirandello
Graciliano Ramos
Erich Maria Remarque
Jean-Paul Sartre
Claude Simon
Mario Vargas Llosa
Franz Werfel
Peter Weiss

Christa Wolf

R

UNDERSTANDING

Camilo José

CELA

LUCILE C. CHARLEBOIS

UNIVERSITY OF SOUTH CAROLINA PRESS

Copyright © 1998 University of South Carolina

Published in Columbia, South Carolina, by the
University of South Carolina Press

Manufactured in the United States of America

01 00 99 98   5 4 3 2 1

Library of Congress Cataloging-in-Publication Data

Charlebois, Lucile C., 1951–
   Understanding Camilo José Cela / Lucile C. Charlebois.
      p.   cm. — (Understanding modern European and Latin American
   literature)
   Includes bibliographical references and index.
   ISBN 1–57003–151–7
   1. Cela, Camilo Jose, 1916–   —Criticism and interpretation.
I. Title. II. Series.
PQ6605.E44Z625 1998   96–51296

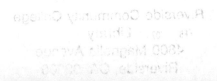

For Francisco

CONTENTS

EDITOR'S PREFACE

Understanding Modern European and Latin American Literature has been planned as a series of guides for undergraduate and graduate students and non-academic readers. Like the volumes in its companion series *Understanding Contemporary American Literature,* these books provide introductions to the lives and writings of prominent modern authors and explicate their most important works.

Modern literature makes special demands, and this is particularly true of foreign literature, in which the reader must contend not only with unfamiliar, often arcane artistic conventions and philosophical concepts, but also with the handicap of reading the literature in translation. It is a truism that the nuances of one language can be rendered in another only imperfectly (and this problem is especially acute in fiction), but the fact that the works of European and Latin American writers are situated in a historical and cultural setting quite different from our own can be as great a hindrance to the understanding of these works as the linguistic barrier. For this reason the *UMELL* series emphasizes the sociological and historical background of the writers treated. The peculiar philosophical and cultural traditions of a given culture may be particularly important for an understanding of certain authors, and these are taken up in the introductory chapter and also in the discussion of those works to which this information is relevant. Beyond this, the books treat the specifically literary aspects of the author under discussion and attempt to explain the complexities of contemporary literature lucidly. The books are conceived as introductions to the authors covered, not as comprehensive analyses. They do not provide detailed summaries of plot because they are meant to be used in conjunction with the books they treat, not as a substitute for study of the original works. The purpose of the books is to provide information and judicious literary assessment of the major works in the most compact, readable form. It is our hope that the *UMELL* series will help increase knowledge and understanding of European and Latin American cultures and will serve to make the literature of those cultures more accessible.

J. H.

PREFACE

Camilo José Cela's complete works consist of twenty volumes of short and long novels, plays, essays, and short stories, to which his most recent autobiography, other works of prose fiction, and newly collected essays have not been added. Given his extensive literary productivity, of which the novels constitute a major portion, this study will be devoted exclusively to his ten most acclaimed novels in the chronological order of their publication (with the exception of *La catira* [The Blonde], *Nuevas andanzas y desventuras de Lazarillo de Tormes* [New Adventures and Misfortunes of Lazarillo de Tormes], and *Tobogán de hambrientos* [Tobogan of Starving People]).

I have quoted directly from those novels that exist in English versions, relying on my own translations for the works that do not. In those instances in which the translation does not provide the necessary accuracy, I have indicated the same in the appropriate note. Providing suitable English equivalents for the titles of Cela's works that have not been—heretofore—translated poses a serious dilemma. Wherever possible I have consulted with translation experts and have indicated (parenthetically in the "Chronology") instances in which Cela's neologisms exhibit his ingenious playfulness with the Spanish language, thereby rendering foolhardy attempts at translation. All references to works that do not pertain directly to Cela are accompanied by complete bibliographical citations in the corresponding notes and are not included in the bibliography that appears at the end of this book.

Since the scope of this study does not lend itself to the presentation of a complete bibliography on Cela, two factors have determined the selection of the studies that appear in the bibliography—namely, those that are most relevant to the novels that have been studied in this book and those that represent the best (and oftentimes most up-to-date) criticism on Cela and his work. Special issues of journals dedicated exclusively to Cela are indicated separately in the bibliography. I have grouped in a heading by itself ("Travel Books") those works of Cela which constitute a subgenre that cannot be classified strictly as fiction or nonfiction. Finally, I have included under "Selected Nonfiction" some of Cela's pertinent essays which have been quoted in this study.

It is important to note that three significant works and one book review (of *La cruz de San Andrés*) have been published since completion of the manuscript for this volume. Those works are cited here with the desire of fostering ongoing Celian scholarship: Valerie Miles, "Camilo José Cela: The Art of Fiction CXLV," *Paris Review* 139 (Summer 1996): 124–63 [an interview with CJC]; Janet Pérez, "Text, Context and Subtext of the Unreliable Narrative: Cela's *El asesinato del perdedor*," *Anales de la Literatura Española Contemporánea*

21.1–2 (1996): 103–18; Manuel Ramiro Valderrama, *El énfasis en la prosa de Cela. La repetición como procedimiento conotativo* (Valladolid: Universidad de Valladolid, Secretariado de Publicaciones, 1995); and Janet Pérez, review of *La cruz de San Andrés, Anales de la Literatura Española Contemporánea* 21.1–2 (1996): 161–62.

Most specifically, I wish to acknowledge Juan Loveluck's steadfast support and encouragement. At a time when change and transition in my life caused otherwise encouraging voices to become silent, his was strong and true. Although Isaac Lévy did not warn me that I would never be the same after undertaking the study of Cela, I am most indebted to him for having reawakened in me an interest that had long been dormant. To the many individuals who, in familiar Celian fashion, amble about in my own dark space of existential confusion and uncertainty, I extend the most heartfelt expression of gratitude: Francisco, Leon, Ton, Suzy, Silvia, Sara, Josep, Juan, John, Alma, Noëlla, Louis, Thérèse, Marie Jeanne, Jean Joseph, Jean, and Frankie. A special word of thanks to my cousin and friend, Frank, who, at the time I was working on *oficio de tinieblas 5,* shared personal insights about our family that led me to a new level of awareness about Cela. I also want to recognize Nelson Orringer's unwavering confidence in my work.

I wish to acknowledge the University of South Carolina and the SPAR grant that enabled me to begin the research for this project. For the endless assistance that I received in the preparation of this manuscript, I also want to thank Laura Shull, Eric Roman, and Mary-Lou Sonefeld.

CHRONOLOGY

1916   Born in Iria Flavia, Padrón (La Coruña), 11 May.

1919   Travels to England.

1925   Family establishes permanent residence in Madrid. Graduates high/ secondary school and begins university studies.

1934   First bout with tuberculosis. Meets and becomes friends with Pedro Salinas at the University of Madrid.

1936   Writes *Pisando la dudosa luz del día* (Treading the Dubious Light of Day, later published in 1945). First poem, "Amor inmenso"(Immense Love), is published in *Fábula de la Plata.* Caught in Madrid when the Civil War begins.

1937   Drafted into the Nationalist army and serves in the Twenty-fourth Regiment of the Infantry of Bailén (Logroño).

1938   Second poem, "Himno a la muerte" (Hymn to Death), is published in *Fábula de la Plata.*

1939   Wounded and discharged on 30 May while recuperating in the military hospital of Castellón (Logroño). Returns to Padrón and later to Madrid.

1940   Begins to study law and to write *La familia de Pascual Duarte (Pascual Duarte and His Family).* First prose publications. Begins to frequent the Gijón café tertulia where he reads parts of *Pascual Duarte.*

1941   First short story, "Marcelo Brito," is published in *Medina.* Second bout with tuberculosis.

1942   *Pascual Duarte* is published, and his friends gather to pay him homage at the Nacional café (Madrid).

1943   *Pabellón de reposo (Rest Home)* is published and the second edition of *Pascual Duarte* is seized by government censors.

1944   *Nuevas andanzas y desventuras de Lazarillo de Tormes* (New Adventures and Misfortunes of Lazarillo de Tormes). Marriage to María del Rosario Conde Picavea.

1945   First book of poems (*Pisando la dudosa luz del día*) is published and also *Esas nubes que pasan (*Those Clouds that Go Past [and Disappear]) and *Mesa revuelta* (Hotpotch).

1946   His son, Camilo José Cela Conde, is born. Cela begins his walking tour of the Alcarria region of Spain.

1947   *El bonito crimen del carabinero y otras invenciones* (The Tidy Crime of the [Armed] Policeman and Other Tales) is published.

1948   *Cancionero de la Alcarria and Viaje a la Alcarria* (Songbook of the Alcarria) and *Viaje a la Alcarria (Journey to the Alcarria)* are published.

1949   *El gallego y su cuadrilla y otros apuntes carpetovetónicos* (The Galician and His Troupe and Other [through-and-through Spanish] Notes) is written and later published in 1951.

1951   *La colmena* is published in Buenos Aires.

1952   *Del Miño al Bidasoa* (From the Miño to the Bidassoa [Rivers]), *Avila, Timokó el incomprendido* (Timoko the Misunderstood), *Santa Balbina, 37 o gas en cada piso* (37 St. Balbina [Street] or Gas in Every Apartment) are published. Rumors of an invitation by the president of Venezuela to write *La catira.*

1953   *Baraja de invenciones* (Pack of Tales), *Café de artistas* (Artists' Cafe), *La cucaña* (The Greasy Pole), and *Mrs. Caldwell habla con su hijo (Mrs. Caldwell Speaks to Her Son).*

1954   *Ensueños y figuraciones* (Daydreams and Imaginings) is published.

1955   *La catira* (The Blonde).

1956   *Judíos, moros y cristianos* (Jews, Moors and Christians), *El molino de viento y otras novelas cortas* (The Windmill and Other Short Novels), and *Mis páginas preferidas* (My Favorite Pages) are published. Founds the journal *Papeles de Son Armadans* in Majorca.

1957   Inducted into the Royal Spanish Academy. *Cajón de sastre* (Hodgepodge), *Recuerdo de don Pío Baroja* (Memories of Don Pío Baroja), *Nuevo retablo de don Cristobita* (Don Cristobita's New Tableau), *La rueda de los ocios* (The Wheel of [Those Who Possess] Leisure Time), and *La obra literaria del pintor Solana* (The Literary Works of Solana [the Painter]) are published.

1958   Meets and establishes friendship with Pablo Picasso. *Historias de España* (Stories About Spain) is published.

1959   *Primer viaje andaluz* (First Andulusian Journey) and *La rosa* (The Rose) are published.

1960   *Cuaderno del Guadarrama* (Guadarrama Notebook) and the first series of *Los viejos amigos* ([Good] Old Friends) are published.

1961   *Cuatro figuras del 98* (Four Imporatnt People of the Generation of [18]98) and the second series of *Los viejos amigos* ([Good] Old Friends) are published.

1962   *Tobogán de hambrientos* (Tobogan of Starving People) and *Gavilla de fábulas sin amor* (Bundle of Loveless Fables) are published. The Spanish edition of *La colmena (The Hive)* is authorized. The first volume of his complete works is published.

1963   *Garito de hospicianos* (Gambling Den of Hospiced [People], *Las compañías convenientes* (Advisable Companionships), *El solitario y los sueños de Quesada de Rafael Zabaleta* (The Recluse and Quesada's Dreams, by Raphael Zabaleta), *Toreo de salón* (Armchair Bullfighting), and *Once cuentos de fútbol* (Eleven [Short] Stories About Soccer) are published.

1964   *Izas, rabizas y colipoterras* is published (Impossible to translate, this work is subtitled "Drama con acompañamiento de cachondeo y dolor de corazón" [Drama Accompanied by Joking and Heartache]. It also includes photographs taken by Juan Colom that depict various prostitutes, streetwalkers, and other such destitute Spanish women of the 1950's and 60's in Madrid. It is a deeply moving, poetic pictorial composition that ponders "life on the streets"). Honorary doctoral degree is bestowed on him by Syracuse University (U.S.). Second volume of his complete works is published.

1965   *Viaje al Pirineo de Lérida* (Journey to the Pyrenean Lerida), *La familia del héroe* (The Hero's Family), *Nuevas escenas matritenses* (New Scenes from Madrid), *Páginas de geografía errabunda* (Pages about Wandering), *El ciudadano Iscariote Reclús* (Citizen Iscariote Reclus), and *A la pata de palo* (To a Wooden Leg) are published. Cela's first play, *María Sabina,* is published.

1966   Moves to his new house in La Bonanova, Palma de Mallorca. *Madrid.* Series 3–7 of *Escenas matritenses* (Scenes from Madrid) and volumes 3–4 of his complete works are published.

1967   *Viaje a USA* (Journey to the USA) is published. Celebration in Madrid in commemoration of the twenty-fifth anniversary of the publication of *Pascual Duarte.*

1968   First volume of *Diccionario secreto* (Secret Dictionary) and the play *El carro de heno o el inventor de la guillotina* (The Haywain or the Inventor of the Guillotine) are published.

1969   *San Camilo, 1936, La bandada de Palomas* (The Flock of Pigeons), and *Al servicio de algo* (In the Service of Something) are published.

1970   *María Sabina* is performed in New York. *Barcelona* is published.

1971   *Cinco glosas a otras tantas verdades de la silueta que un hombre trazó a sí mismo* (Five Glosses of So Many Other Truths about the Silhouette that a Man Drew of Himself), *La Mancha en el corazón y en los ojos* (La Mancha in One's Heart and Eyes and volume 2 of *Diccionario secreto* are published.

1972   *La bola del mundo: escenas cotidianas* (The Globe: Everyday Scenes) is published.

1973   *A vueltas con España* (Again. . . Talking about Spain), *oficio de tinieblas 5* (service of darkness 5), *El tacatá oxidado* (The Rusted Walking Frame), *Balada del vagabundo sin suerte y otros papeles volauderos* (The Luckless Vagabond's Ballad and Other Loose Papers), and nine volumes of his complete works are published.

1974   *Cuentos para leer después del baño* ([Short] Stories to Read after One's Bath) is published.

1976   *Rol de cornudos* (Catalog of Cuckholds) is published. Cela begins to edit his *Enciclopedia del erotismo* (Encyclopedia of Eroticism).

1977   Named by King Juan Carlos I to serve as a senator in the Spanish Parliament. Writes numerous newspaper articles in favor of Spain's transition to a democratic form of government.

1979   *Los sueños vanos, los ángeles curiosos* (Futile Dreams, Strange Angels) is published.

1980   Inducted into the Galician Academy.

1981   *Vuelta de hoja* (Next Page), *Album de taller* (Workshop Album), and *Los vasos comunicantes* (Communicating Vessels) are published.

1983   *Mazurca para dos muertos (Mazurka for Two Dead Men)* and *El juego de los tres madroños* (The Game of the Three Strawberry Trees) are published. Begins work on *Madera de boj* (Boxwood).

1984   Premio Nacional for Literature for *Mazurca.*

1987   Príncipe de Asturias Prize for Literature.

1988   *Cristo versus Arizona* (Christ versus Arizona).

1989   Awarded the Nobel Prize for Literature.

1993   *Memorias, entendimientos y voluntades* (Memories, Understandings and Wishes) is published as the second part of his autobiography. *El huevo del juicio* (The Egg of Judgment) is published. Awarded the "Andrés Bello" medal of honor by Venezuelan president Ramón José Velásquez.

1994   Two novels (*El asesinato del perdedor* [The Murder of the Loser] and *La cruz de San Andrés* [St. Andrew's Cross]) and a collection of short stories (*La dama pájaro* [Lady Bird]) are published. Awarded the Planeta Prize for *La cruz de San Andrés*.

1995   Participates in a conference ("The Nobel Laureates in Literature") in Atlanta, Ga. Notified in late December of winning the Cervantes Prize for Literature (Spain's most prestigious literary award). Receives from King Juan Carlos I the Cervantes Prize in an official ceremony that is—apparently—boycotted by his son and previous Cervantes recipients for various reasons (among which are the belief that the award was too late in being bestowed upon him, while a few others vehemently opposed his nomination for the honor).

Abbreviations

AP	*El asesinato del perdedor*
CSA	*La cruz de San Andrés*
CVA	*Cristo versus Arizona*
H	*The Hive*
J	*Journey to the Alcarria*
M	*Memorias, entendimientos y voluntades*
MC	*Mrs. Caldwell Speaks to Her Son*
MTDM	*Mazurka for Two Dead Men*
odt	*oficio de tinieblas 5*
PD	*Pascual Duarte and His Family*
RH	*Rest Home*
SC	*San Camilo, 1936*

Understanding
CAMILO JOSÉ CELA

Introduction

In *Rojos y rebeldes* (Reds and Rebels) Shirley Mangini discusses the culture of dissidence during Francisco Franco's dictatorship in Spain (1939–75), and argues that literature is virtually the only reliable source of information concerning that country during the more than three decades of unrelenting and inescapable censorship imposed after the Nationalist victory in the Spanish Civil War (1936–39).[1] Camilo José Cela turned twenty years old when the civil strife broke out in his country, and in 1942 he wrote *La familia de Pascual Duarte (Pascual Duarte and His Family)*, the first novel that was published in Spain after the war ended in 1939. In the thirty-three years of Francoist rule that followed, Cela came of age as one of his country's most important writers, publishing well over two-thirds of what now constitutes his entire literary production.[2] In 1956 he founded the journal that was to bear the name *Papeles de Son Armadans* in honor of the neighborhood in Palma de Mallorca, in the Balearic Islands, where he lived at the time; given the repressive climate that pervaded all aspects of life on the Continent, in Spain in the 1950s and 1960s *Papeles* quickly became a major clearinghouse for the publication of all types of creative and critical works by international writers and artists.

To speak of Cela's literary opus is, then, to immerse oneself in contemporary Spain, for Cela continues to write. In 1983 he published *Mazurca para dos muertos (Mazurka for Two Dead Men)*, a novel that went through eighteen editions by 1990 and earned him the prestigious Premio Nacional for Literature. One year before being awarded the Nobel Prize for Literature in 1989, Cela wrote another novel, *Cristo versus Arizona* (Christ versus Arizona). In February 1993 he published the second part of his autobiography, *Memorias, entendimientos y voluntades* (Memories, Understandings, and Wishes), and one month later his work *El huevo del juicio (The Egg of Judgment)* brought together under one title 120 of his previously unpublished essays.[3] In addition to his continued work on the long-awaited novel *Madera de boj* (Boxwood), in 1994 he published *La dama pájaro y otros cuentos* (Lady Bird and Other Short Stories) and two other novels, *El asesinato del perdedor* (The Murder of the Loser) and *La cruz de San Andrés* (St. Andrew's Cross). Six of his works have been translated into English: *Pascual Duarte and His Family*, *Viaje a la Alcarria (Journey to the Alcarria)*, *La colmena (The Hive)*, *Mrs. Caldwell habla con su hijo (Mrs. Caldwell Speaks to Her Son)*, *San Camilo, 1936*, and *Mazurka for Two Dead Men*.[4]

1

Cela was born Camilo José Manuel Juan Ramón Francisco Santiago de Cela on 11 May 1916 in the small town of Iria Flavia, not far from what is known on the Iberian Peninsula as *finisterre* (land's end) in the Galician region of Spain. His ancestors include a great-grandfather who was governor of Parma, Italy; an English candle factory owner; and a distant relative who supposedly descended from an old family of British pirates; not to mention another relative, Juan Jacobo Fernández, who was reputed to have been beatified in the Roman Catholic Church on 10 October 1926 by Pope Pius XI (*La rosa* 23–24). Although immensely proud of his three bloodlines, Cela proclaims himself unequivocally Spanish. His father, Camilo Cela y Fernández, worked as a customs official, and, since his mother, Camila Emmanuela Trulock y Bertorini, had many close relatives in England, Cela began to travel at the age of three, when he first visited the British Isles. He also accompanied his parents on their trips throughout Spain and lived in Barcelona, Vigo, and finally Madrid, where his family took up residence when he was nine years old and where he himself lived until he moved to Majorca when he was thirty-eight, returning in his later years to the mainland, where he established residence outside of Madrid in Guadalajara.

His schooling was traditionally Catholic. He graduated high school in 1933 and shortly after graduation fought his first bout with tuberculosis, from which he recuperated initially in a sanitarium in the nearby mountain area of Navacerrada, then once again in 1941 in the Hoyo de Manzanares sanitarium in the Guadarrama mountain range north of Madrid. Cela boasts of his numerous unsuccessful attempts to secure a college degree at the University of Madrid, where, desirous of taking courses in the humanities, he instead followed his family's wishes and in 1934 began the study of medicine and law, which he abandoned one year later. All his endeavors to find a suitable career, including studying to be a customs agent in his father's own Customs Academy in Madrid, were overshadowed by his literary interests. His friends included other budding Spanish writers and artists, such as Miguel Hernández, María Zambrano, Alonso Zamora Vicente, and Julián Marías. It is no surprise that his wandering into a literature class taught at the University of Madrid by the renowned Spanish poet Pedro Salinas (1891–1951) yielded a close mentor-tutee bond. In 1936, at the height of the aerial bombings that characterized the Spanish Civil War, Cela wrote a book of poetry entitled *Pisando la dudosa luz del día: poemas de una adolescencia cruel* (Treading the Dubious Light of Day: Poems of a Cruel Adolescence), which was not published until 1945. For Cela, who never formally studied grammar, it was the fortuitous friendship between the student and professor which introduced him to a profession to which he devoted his entire life.

During his first period of convalescence from tuberculosis, Cela immersed himself in the tradition of Spanish letters, voraciously reading, among other things, the seventy-one-volume collection of works by Spanish writers which was published by the Biblioteca de Autores Españoles (Library of Spanish Authors). As his career began to flourish, Cela made it a point to distinguish, oftentimes harshly, between the institutionalized management of culture, which he grew to abhor, and the true Spanish aesthetes, who had a decisive influence on his own writing: "My thinking is that culture, in Spain, works when it is left to the creator, Cervantes, Quevedo, Goya, Larra, Bécquer, Ramón y Cajal, the ninety-eighters, Solana, Picasso, but it gets moldy and stagnant when the State protects it" (*M* 45).

Having barely turned twenty years old when the Civil War broke out, Cela found himself in Madrid, along with the other young men who in 1937 were among those replacements that were awaiting conscription. It was not, however, until he was transferred out of Republican-held Madrid and to Nationalist Valencia that he was drafted, on 4 December 1938, as a soldier on the side of the insurgents. His active duty in the war was curtailed by an injury he sustained when, lying unconscious after a bomb exploded nearby, he was hit in the chest by the shrapnel of a grenade. When he received the news that the war had ended, he was serving as corporal in a regiment of light artillery. His military duty ended on 30 May 1939, during the time he was recuperating in the military hospital of Castellón. Upon returning to Madrid and being reunited with his family, he, down to skin and bones, rejoiced in the fact that none of his loved ones had died during the war. His readjustment to what was a normal lifestyle in the days immediately following the war was, as one might expect, difficult.

In his recent autobiography he recounts that he had in mind killing himself shortly before New Year's Day 1942, when he took a pistol to bed with him. What ensued was a period of intense solitude and isolation, which he later came to cherish as indispensable for his future work as a writer. Cela's detractors insist on highlighting to this day the fact that he was on Franco's side during the war. They also sensationalize the short-lived job he had in 1940 as a censor. Given, however, the complexities of the Spanish Civil War and all that led up to it, in addition to Cela's age when it began, informed opinions concerning these matters require a conscientious reading of Cela's works and a careful study of that period of Spanish history.

The effects of his country's Civil War are far-reaching in Cela. Besides the almost constant allusions of one type or another to the war's impact on contemporary Spanish life, in 1969 he wrote *San Camilo, 1936,* a novel that many critics claim to be a fictive autobiographical rendering of the repercussions in Madrid of the uprising in Morocco which led to the three-year war. In that same year he authored another book called *Al servicio de algo* (In the Service of Something), in which he addresses the polemical issue of writers' responsibilities, stating—as he does time and again in other contexts—that Spain's youth and intellectuals were, regardless of the side they took, the real losers of the war. In one particularly insightful essay, written in defense of the controversial book *Descargo de conciencia (1930–1960)* (Discharge of Conscience), which was written in 1976 by Pedro Laín Entralgo, the well-known doctor, writer, rector of the Universidad Complutense of Madrid (1955), and apologist of the so-called Spanish "Generation of 1898," Cela refers candidly to the Civil War: "The drama of the civil war, with its heroes and its martyrs sown, with indiscriminate violence, in all zones, was not a movie about good and bad guys and, as long as it is not understood this way, we will always continue in the same bitter conditions that made the whole thing possible."[5]

Cela's rise to prominence was by no means meteoric. After the Civil War ended he too suffered from the economic miseries of his country. The previously noted publication of *Pascual Duarte* was preceded by another bout with tuberculosis. As he did during his first period of confinement, he continued to read the Spanish classics; cured for the second time, he knew that the rest of his life would be devoted exclusively to literature. In addition to provoking a polemic that continues to date, the 1942 novel also generated coinage of the much misguided term *tremendista* (tremendous/violent) to refer to the shocking style of its story line. Other novels followed, but none so powerful as the 1951 publication of *The Hive,* which Cela wrote on a small kitchen table in a dilapidated, rented country house in Cebreros, a hamlet in the Gredos mountain range northwest of Madrid. Ten days before his first and only son, Camilo José Cela Conde, was born in 1946 Cela presented *The Hive* manuscript to the censors for approval only to have it refused. Five years later *The Hive* was published in Buenos Aires.

After 1951 Cela's career as well as his public devotion and commitment to Spanish letters blossomed. Of significance at that time was an invitation by the Venezuelan government commissioning him to depict the country in a novel that was published in 1955 as *La catira* (The Blonde). In 1956 he published the first issue of the previously mentioned *Papeles de Son Armadans,* whose life span lasted until 1978. In 1959 Cela founded in Formentor (Majorca) the *Conversaciones poéticas* (Poetic Conversations) and a subsequent *Coloquio Internacional sobre la Novela* (International Colloquium on the Novel), both of which proved to be oases of free expression for writers, artists, and intellectuals whose work on the mainland was fraught with repression because of the regime's fanatical censorship. Despite the controversies that surrounded him, Cela was elected to the Royal Spanish Academy in 1957. While his popularity waned during the next two decades and his critics predicted that he had reached the pinnacle of his creativity, it is precisely the work of those years which attests to his constant innovative experimentation with form. In 1983 he resurfaced with *Mazurka,* which sold 180,000 copies in 1984 and 235,000 copies in 1990.

Given the fact that during his fifty-three years of literary productivity Cela did not write in exile, as did many of his contemporaries who left Spain during the Civil War or at the beginning of Franco's regime, his work serves as a testimony to the passage into twentieth-century democracy of a country that has been plagued with civil strife for the last four hundred years.[6] Cela has said repeatedly that his love of country and countrymen has been one of the great motivating forces in his life. He rejects, however, the "regional racism" advanced by some sectors of Catalonia, Galicia, and the Basque Country.[7] Cela repeatedly seeks a suitable definition for that complex geopolitical entity that the—rest of the—world knows as Spain. In many of his essays it becomes apparent that this almost obsessive speculation about his country, its history, and culture(s) is the alpha and omega of his literary career. It is perhaps for this reason that the articles he wrote in the 1970s and 1980s unmercifully censure historical myths because, in his opinion, they foster the intransigence that leads to civil wars and totalitarian regimes, of which Franco's hegemony is a prime example.

Nowhere is such reprehension so evident as in *Vuelta de hoja* (Next Page), a collection of articles written in 1976 (one year after Franco's death) for *Cambio 16* magazine. In one passionate essay entitled "A un pobre se le llama rico" (They Call a Poor Man Rich) he defines a Spaniard as someone who is so poor that he has "to count his pennies in order to make it through until the end of the month" (186), saying that "Spain, having been dragged along by some Spaniards, is broke because it has been living for many years without looking at its coffers and now, when it's time to pay up, everybody has to bite the bullet" (188). In "La difícil respuesta" (The Difficult Answer), an essay included in *El asno de Buridán* (Buridán's Jackass) and written in 1984, Cela once again attempts to define the Spanish psyche. He ends by saying that: "Maybe it isn't even clear what are, in reality, Catalonia, the Basque Country or Galicia or Andalusia or Castille, etcetera. Perhaps we do not know what we as Spaniards are going to be from this day forward, but it would be a good idea if such serious and profound questions did not lose their own meaning by way of adding to them even bigger doubts about what up to now we have been historically" (211). Such nagging queries about national origin, history, and identity are nothing new in modern Spanish letters. Cela inherited from his spiritual forefathers of the "Generation of 1898" abhorrence of the anachronistic rhetoric of imperialist grandeur which tainted Spanish thought from its sixteenth-century expansion into the Americas.[8]

Even though Cela, like his 1898 mentors, left the periphery of Spain to settle in the interior (Madrid), he derives much of his creative genius from his homeland of Galicia, a part of Spain which is known for legends and folklore. It is also the birthplace of gifted writers such as Ramón María del Valle-Inclán (1869–1936), in whom Cela found great inspiration. Much of Cela's prose fiction takes place between the coordinates of Castile and Galicia and in other parts of Spain, as is seen in the many travel books in which Cela's itinerant "vagabond" persona roams the northern, southern, and central highways and byways of his beloved Spain. Cela's ardent love of country is, however, most intense concerning everything Castilian, a fact that is aptly substantiated in Robert Kirsner's assessment of Cela's travel books.[9] In a fashion similar to that of the ninety-eighters, who also wrote essays based on their excursions through Castile, Cela's practice of note taking and direct observation of what he saw during his walking trips secured for him a place alongside other important Spanish novelists of the "realist" tradition such as Benito Pérez Galdós (1843–1920) and Pío Baroja.

The characters, places, and events that constitute Cela's works are, then, a tribute to the people of Spain. The defiant product of an orthodox Catholic mind-set that prevented Spain from taking its place in the European community, Cela's works defy the canonical rubrics of social acceptability and savoir faire by his bold, shockingly real, and often grotesque portrayals of humanity in its more graphic, agonistic, and downright ugly aspects of daily existence.[10] Whether in remote Spanish country hamlets, in Madrid, or in places like Venezuela and Tombstone, maimed and sickly characters abound in heartrendingly pathetic circumstances. Death, together with manifestations of human deprivation and existential questioning, is ever present, yet overriding this macabre dance of life is the will to go on, as Cela himself says in his recent autobiography: "la vida sigue" (life goes on) (*M* 86).

Having himself withstood the wrath of the censors and the scathing critical commentaries that followed the publication of *Pascual Duarte* and *The Hive,* Cela became adept at maneuvering his literary characters and the *fabulae* that surround them in such a way that numerous readings are possible, each of which reveals layers of criticism leveled at the injustices and atrocities that grow out of the hypocrisies of twentieth-century life and, more specifically, the impoverishment of a Spanish society whose ruling government proclaimed (until

Franco's death) vacuous prosperity for over thirty years. Consequently, Cela's signature traits entail such literary devices as the discovery of lost manuscripts, supposed eyewitness testimonies, introductory notes, prologues and epilogues, the use of bibliographical citations, and other paratextual materials, in what appears to be an authentic desire to convince the reader of the veracity and dependability of the narration. Of course, the Cela enthusiast, being much accustomed to these topics, realizes that they constitute an outwardly intelligent pretext for pure fiction while also poignantly remindful of the climate of mendacity that framed Spanish life for much of the twentieth century.

In his novels as well as his other works—essays, short stories, and travel books—Cela intertwines fact with fiction to such an extent that the reading process is often frustratingly disconcerting. He relishes framing events with a chronology of saints' feast days, a practice that Cela admits stems from old country folks' customs which he does not wish to give up but which the reader knows is directly proportional to his irreverent attitude toward all forms of institutionalized religion (*M* 230). To this end, in reading Cela, one is never certain of anything. His theater purports genre-based authenticity, yet his plays are more like readings of surrealistic poetry; his autobiographies read like a collage of fiction, fact, and history; his first novel appears to constitute the sincere memoirs of Pascual Duarte as he awaits death by execution, yet the textual gaps belie a parodic deconstruction of the traditional written confession; *Cristo,* which takes place in Arizona, is supposed to be a novel but resembles one long, ritualistic litany in homage to heroes and other legendary figures of the American Wild West; even his collected short stories and essays are difficult to recognize as such because they weave in and out of the prescribed norms of both genres. What you see is not what you get, as the outer layers, when peeled back, conceal a human emotion, suffering, and exuberance that transcend the Hispanic realm and define humankind in universal terms: life, love, death, and truth.

Cela has withstood the test of time. In 1963 Robert Kirsner wrote one of the few books that existed on the works of Cela, in which he said that Cela "creates literature out of the rough variegated fabric of Spanish life" (183). Thirty years later, in 1991, Darío Villanueva, one of Hispanism's most assiduous scholars, said that Cela, in stubborn dedication to his craft, had achieved the miraculous feat in Spain of being a born writer, a Spanish institution, and a writer of best-sellers.[11] Cela himself has commented frequently on the lack of esteem and outright hostility with which writers in Spain are, and always have been, held by the public at large. Notwithstanding such an indictment, Cela has patiently borne the insults of critics, censors, and colleagues alike.[12] Through it all, however, one factor has remained constant—namely, the enhancement of human freedom through literary creativity, as he eloquently put it in his Nobel lecture, "Eulogy to the Fable:"

> The architectural design on which we have tried to build successfully or otherwise the complex framework of our societies, contains the basic principle of human freedom and it is in the light of that principle that we value, exalt, denigrate, castigate and suffer: the aura of liberty is the spirit enshrined in our moral codes, political principles and legal systems. . . . For my part, I must say proudly that . . . the literary fable has always, and in all circumstances proved to be a decisive tool: a weapon that can cleave the way forward in the endless march to freedom. (16)

When news of the Nobel Prize was made public, reactions ranged from disgust to the euphoria of Cela's soundest critics, such as David William Foster, Darío Villanueva, John Kronik, Juan Antonio Masoliver Ródenas, and all the others whose articles appeared in a special double issue of *Insula,* one of Spain's leading and most well-established scholarly journals.[13] Cela has always engendered polemical discussions in academic circles and the public arena. It seems that this is something upon which he prides himself, his own demeanor reflecting nothing less, as is seen in his son's tongue-in-cheek account of his father's early years as a struggling writer in Spain and his move in 1954 to Majorca.[14] Cela was a good student of the *épater le bourgeoise* mentality of the early avant-garde writers and artists; he delights in scandalizing his readers, not, however, out of frivolity but as an attention getter and means of consciousness-raising concerning humankind's common needs and desires. Cela's characters eat, sleep, work, engage in uninhibited sexual license, kill, and die. Their actions as well as the literary molds within which they are cast insolently confront canonical protocol. Their names—usually accompanied by aliases—oftentimes sarcastically parody reality, while their life situations elicit pathos; in this way they are the artistic descendants of other characters in Spanish arts and letters who speak the harsh language of sixteenth-century rogues, Goya's eighteenth-century monsters, Baltasar Gracián's thwarted image makers, Valle-Inclán's twentieth-century deformations of reality (commonly referred to as *esperpentos*), and the painter José Gutiérrez Solana's (1886–1945) passionately stylized depictions of Spanish life.

Cela has devoted his whole life to the craft of writing, even during the brief period when he heeded King Juan Carlos's personal invitation in 1977 to serve as a senator in Spain's first democratic Parliament. Cela has cultivated every literary genre and has refused to box his works into a neat and tidy corner. In the frequently quoted prologue to his 1953 novel *Mrs. Caldwell,* he says that the novel is a genre that, in defiance of definition, admits under an assumed title anything that has been edited in booklike form for such purposes ("Algunas palabras," *MC* 9). Since 1942 each decade has witnessed Cela's continued commitment to change through stylistic experimentation. Even the first decade of his career saw the birth of four novels, a book of poems, collections of short stories, and his most well-known travel book, *Journey to the Alcarria.* This diversity continued over the years, with an increasingly audacious spirit of technical innovation, as is evidenced in such disparate works as his previously mentioned autobiography; the collection of ingenious character sketches that constitute the novel *Tobogán de hambrientos,* 1962 (Tobogan of Starving People); two plays of the theater of the absurd (*María Sabina* and *El carro de heno o el inventor de la guillotina* [The Haywain or the Inventor of the Guillotine]); novels such as *San Camilo, 1936, oficio de tinieblas 5* and *Cristo;* and three dictionaries of sorts entitled *Rol de cornudos* (Catalogue of Cuckholds), the two-volume *Diccionario secreto* (Secret Dictionary), and *Enciclopedia del erotismo* (Encyclopedia of Eroticism).

While Cela is known mostly for his prose writings, all of his works exemplify an ongoing love affair with the Spanish language. This attachment manifests itself in flights of linguistic virtuosity which give way to a register of terms, phrases, maxims, and colloquialisms that subtly invoke forgotten local customs and transmit the psyche of a people. In spite of the schizophrenic style of his later novels, all of his works proclaim absolute control on Cela's part. Critics often highlight the meticulousness with which he personally supervises every manuscript that goes into the publication of his complete works. Structure is of utmost importance and achieves a tirelessly balanced architectural geometry in his works. Repetitions are everywhere and contribute to a discursive style reminiscent of ceremonial litanies. Narrative voices and points of view appear in distinct levels of the fictive discourse, while spontaneous, short dialogues crop up out of nowhere and cut through narrative passages, thereby spurring on the narrative by means of the interjection of anonymous voices that ask simple questions regarding what is being told.

Cela's prose is an epiphany of twentieth-century fiction. It is a discourse that bristles with fragmentation and ambiguity, hilarity and profanity, iconoclasm and alienation. Oftentimes punctuation is totally suppressed, and hyperbole runs rampant. In works such as *oficio de tinieblas 5* semblances of traditional narrative logic fade into an amalgam of word associations that defy logocentric

9

analysis. Spanish myths such as that of the picaresque Lazarillo de Tormes, the Spanish Civil War, the discovery and colonization of the New World, and so forth are destroyed only to be recreated within the imaginary world of Cela's creative art. Interior monologues, soliloquies, and stream of consciousness characterize the split personalities of many protagonists. Family and societal dysfunction is commonplace. Fact is intertwined with fiction, literature is superimposed on art (and vice versa), historical fact is lavishly disseminated, and sarcasm is diluted by the pathos that allows the astute reader to discern the most salient feature of Cela's works: unabashed ridicule of all that is false, haughty, pretentious, and superficially contrived in the face of uncompromising understanding of the human condition. Of himself and his art Cela says that, in spite of the honors, titles, and full professorship that was granted him at the University of Palma de Mallorca in 1980, he is just a writer who has dedicated his entire life to literature.[15] In the years that he has devoted to his chosen profession he has striven to purify the one tool that has served him well—namely, the noble language of Castile, which he believes has enabled him to seek the truth above all else.

CHAPTER 1

Pascual Duarte and His Family

Published in 1942, *La familia de Pascual Duarte (Pascual Duarte and His Family)*[1] heralded two new departures for contemporary Spanish literature: the beginning of Camilo José Cela's literary career and an end to the hiatus in novelistic experimentation, which had been suspended because of the country's civil war. Many critics labeled the work *tremendista,* a term that Cela at first refuted and later defined as crude realism.[2] In November of 1943, shortly after the printing of the second edition, the book was recalled by the government censors and not released again for public consumption until two years later. To date it has been translated into thirty-three languages and has had more than eighty-seven editions in Spanish.[3] So controversial was *Pascual Duarte* that Pío Baroja, when approached by Cela to write a prologue for it, refused, saying that, if young Cela wanted to go to jail, he should by all means feel free to do so but that he himself did not have that desire. It was not until 1946 that the edition published in Spain by Zodíaco (Barcelona) was accompanied by a prologue written by Gregorio Marañón (1887–1960), a Spanish physician and an important man of letters. While it is obvious that Spanish censors and readers alike were not prepared for the harsh realities of the homicides and matricide that the novel discloses, the time was ripe, only three years after the end of the bloody Civil War, for the appearance of Pascual Duarte. He was, at first glance, the embodiment of those historical, social, and economic forces in Spanish society which culminated in the conflagration that claimed over a half-million lives. In evoking the sacrificial lamb that his name represented, Pascual was a fitting black sheep to raise public consciousness about Spain's ills.

Following in the footsteps of his literary predecessor, the Spanish rogue Lazarillo de Tormes (1554), Pascual Duarte has been the subject of countless studies, which oscillate between seeing him as a much maligned victim of forces beyond his control and an unscrupulous scoundrel for whom rehabilitation was a waste of time. Some critics have equated him with Camus's Meursault and with a modern-day Oedipus; others have cast him in the *machista* mold of the subculture of his Extremaduran roots, while still others confer upon him the political counterpart of a Republican who suffered the reprisals of Franco's early victory over Badajoz on 14 August 1936.[4] Pascual Duarte has engendered a literary feud that has raged for years.[5] As we shall see later, it is precisely because of the countless and strategically positioned textual ambiguities that Pascual's family and life still enjoy a wide readership. One has only to recall Pascual's opening line to appreciate the dynamics of opposing viewpoints that drive the novel: "I, sir, am not vicious, though I may have plenty of reasons to be" (*PD* 17).

On one level the story line of *Pascual Duarte* is rather simple. As told by Pascual himself in first-person narration, the novel's nineteen chapters represent his death row confession while awaiting execution by garrote in the Badajoz jail of Chinchilla in 1937.[6] While the narrator guides us through a deceptively nonchronological ordering of the events of his life in the small town of Torremejía and bearing in mind Pascual's disclosure that he has "not put [it] together like a novel" (*PD* 53), we read about his existence in the barren, economically deprived southwestern province of Extremadura. It is there where, as he wishes us to believe, his fate is cast, when he suffers the consequences of being born into a dysfunctional family of origin, two unsuccessful marriages, the loss of—at least—two children, a three-year period of imprisonment, the murder of his sister's and first wife's lovers, and the culminating matricide. Both of his parents were alcoholics who were given to vicious family brawls from which Pascual learned at an early age to distance himself to avoid bodily harm. As if to make matters worse, his mother was totally lacking in human warmth and maternal qualities. Pascual's siblings, Rosario and Mario, are also victims of their environment: Rosario left home when she was fourteen years old and became a prostitute in neighboring Trujillo, and Mario was mentally retarded. It is on Mario's grave on the day of his internment that Pascual seduced—by way of rape—his wife, Lola, who miscarried their first child upon returning from their wedding trip to nearby Mérida, when the horse on which she was riding threw her. One year later a second child, Pascualillo, died mysteriously of a "an ill wind" (*PD* 125); this plunged Pascual into the downward spiral that characterizes his life, a living hell from which he emerged thanks to the confession he wrote in jail before being put to death.

The threat to Pascual's manhood is the common thread that intertwines all the murders he commits. The first insult that is hurled at him comes from El Estirao (Ramrod), his sister's first lover, who accuses him of being like Mario, in other words, a poor excuse for a man. Although Pascual swallows the accusation without fighting, it becomes the "thorn stuck in [his] side" (*PD* 49) which festers and finally prompts him to kill his accuser, when Lola confesses that Ramrod is the father of her third child. On significant occasions during his life

Pascual vacillates between defending himself and staying quiet. This occurs early in the novel when he silently watches his mother's boyfriend, Don Rafael, kick and abuse the defenseless Mario. Although Pascual leads us to believe that he was too young to defend his brother, the astute reader is reminded that Pascual was twenty-four years old when the beating occurred. Before he ever reaches the point of killing Ramrod, Pascual appeases his frustration by stabbing to death the horse that caused Lola's miscarriage and by shooting his pet dog, Chispa, in whose gaze he senses the accusatory look of an inquisitor. Time and again from the end of the first chapter, in which the dog's death springs up out of nowhere after a typical day of hunting, violence abounds, Pascual constantly struggles over being labeled homosexual, and sacrificial blood overflows onto everything that he touches.[7] Perhaps the greatest irony of all is that Pascual is sentenced to death not for killing his mother but for the murder of the town's patrician, Don Jesús González de la Riva, to whom Pascual dedicates his memoirs and whose death is never mentioned in the confession.

Were one presented solely with Pascual's testimony, the reader's task in determining its sincerity would be greatly simplified. While it in effect *is* the story, this part of the novel is, nevertheless, embellished with a key hallmark of Cela's works: the inclusion of paratextual information that permits very different readings of Pascual's narration. Because these confusing documents immediately precede and follow the confession, they provide an ideal frame for a confession that is also unreliably contradictory. Those that come before it include the following (in order of presentation): the "Transcriber's note dated 1939"; a letter addressed to Joaquín Barrera López—a close friend of Don Jesús Gónzalez de la Riva—signed by Pascual Duarte on 15 February 1937 from the Badajoz jail; a portion of Joaquín Barrera López's handwritten last will and testament, dated 1937; and the aforementioned dedication of Pascual's manuscript. Following the last page of Pascual's account are to be found additional sources of information: "Another Transcriber's note"; two letters dated early 1942 which provide different points of view concerning the way Pascual faced his execution—one letter is from Santiago Lurueña, the chaplain of the jail and Pascual's confessor, and the other was written by Cesáreo Martín, a guard in the prison; and, finally, a comment from the Transcriber.

Each one of these documents abounds in ambiguities, contradictions, and textual gaps that mirror Pascual's tale of lament. The most important, though, belong to the Transcriber, because what we read as written by Pascual is the editorial work of this anonymous scribe who happened upon the convict's manuscript in a pharmacy in Almendralejo, another town in Extremadura not far from Torremejía. The Transcriber begins by saying that "the time has come to give the memoirs of Pascual Duarte to the printer," having decided that doing so earlier would perhaps have been premature because of the slow process that was involved in the "deciphering and organizing . . . due to the [Pascual's] bad writing" (*PD* 7). He later vows, nevertheless, to have served only as transcriber, not having corrected so much as a dot over an *i* in keeping with the style of the account. In the next sentence, however, he says that he took it upon himself to suppress the parts that seemed to him to be too graphic, assuring readers that they have been spared the "repugnant intimacies" of Pascual's life. Finally, he concludes by affirming that Pascual is a model to be imitated precisely for what he didn't do rather than for what he did. In more modern terms, then, the reader is advised to read deconstructively.

Equally intriguing is Pascual's letter to Don Joaquín Barrera López, the only friend of Don Jesús whose address Pascual says he remembers. In explaining that he wrote his public confession to ease his conscience, he apologizes for an otherwise poor memory and says that there were two parts to his confession: the one in print in the form of the manuscript about to be read—once removed by way of the Transcriber—and another part that, albeit worthy of preservation, is burdensome and better left unwritten and forgotten. He further states that he is bored with the hundreds of wordy pages that he has written and has, therefore, decided to leave it as is, open-ended, for Don Joaquín's imagination to *reconstruct* the last portion of Pascual's life. He confesses that what most bothered him when he started to write was not knowing whether or not he would be able to finish. Notwithstanding his hope for God's clemency, he recognizes the futility of asking for pardon. He believes that his life merely followed predetermined paths, teaching him its malice, to which his instincts proved stronger than his frail spirit. The last paragraph abounds in more contradiction as he beseeches Don Joaquín as follows: "Please accept, Señor Don Joaquín, along with this parcel of written papers, my apologies for disturbing you, and grant the plea of forgiveness I address to you as if to Don Jesús Gonzalez [*sic*] de la Rivahimself   "(*PD*11).

Don Joaquín's response immediately follows in the form of the fourth segment of his self-proclaimed will, in which he too is ambiguous about what we are to assume he decided to do with the manuscript Pascual sent him. In the first part of the statement he orders that the packet of pages which he has labeled "Pascual Duarte" in red ink be burned immediately without being read because of its scandalous nature; in the next sentence, however, he requests that, should the same bundle survive for eighteen months, it should be saved from destruction by whoever finds it and disposed of according to the discoverer's will— that is, provided that it not be "in disagreement with" Don Joaquín (*PD* 13).

This last line is followed graphically by a line of periods which represents the Transcriber's scissors; in this way the reader's curiosity is piqued by whatever else Don Joaquín (probably) said. Finally, we are left with Pascual's own dedication, which reads as follows: "To the memory of the noble gentleman Don Jesús González de la Riva, Count of Torremejía, who, when the author of this work was about to deal him a death blow, called him, with a smile, 'Pascual, my boy . . .'" (*PD* 15). Most intriguing is the use of the word *rematar,* which in Spanish exacerbates the meaning of the root word, *matar* (to kill), by way of the prefix. The interpretation is ambiguous, since it could signal the fact that Pascual either found him dying and, therefore, put him out of his misery by striking the death blow or that Pascual brutally killed him. The enigma grows when we realize that Don Jesús was smiling and that he called him "Pascualillo" (Pascual, my boy), leaving one to speculate about whether the diminutive was a sarcastic way of reminding Pascual of his social class or whether it was used endearingly as a form of address not uncommon in everyday Spanish usage. Moreover, the linkage of Pascual Duarte with the name of his eleven-month-old son, Pascualillo, fosters unconfirmed suspicions regarding the child's paternity by way of Don Jesús himself. While the unnamed *usted* (sir) who serves as the fictitious narratee of Pascual's confession could be Don Jesús (because of Pascual's dedication), there is no definitive textual documentation in the novel to confirm this.[8] Furthermore, the nature of the relationship between Pascual and Don Jesús is perplexing in light of Pascual's limited references to the count of Torremejía.[9] All this taken into consideration, this dilemma prepares the reader for the "systematic doubt" that emanates from the previously quoted first line of the confession.[10]

Given the ebb and flow of events that constitute Pascual Duarte's misguided life, an important rallying point is the last chapter of his memoirs, in which he describes the premeditated murder of his mother. After that everything comes to a sudden halt as he says,"I could breathe. . . "(*PD* 225), and we are then confronted with the first of the four remaining documents that further the hope of clarifying the hermeneutics of Pascual's confessional text. The Transcriber's voice again reverberates in an explanation of his unsuccessful scrutiny of the Almendralejo pharmacy for missing pages that would explain how Pascual spent his last years. Bemoaning the futility of the search, he says that one could assume that Pascual had again been remanded to the Chinchilla prison, where he must have been held "until 1935 or perhaps 1936" (*PD* 227). He further states that there is no way of knowing what Pascual did when the Civil War erupted in Badajoz. What is certain, he says, is that Pascual most likely killed Don Jesús at some point during two weeks of unaccounted-for activity after he got out of jail. He then warns that Pascual's manuscript is not as haphazard as its author would lead us to believe, for chapters 12 and 13 were written in the same purple ink with which he wrote the letter to Don Joaquín, proof for him that Pascual meticulously plotted every detail.

In a reference to the two previously mentioned eyewitnesses to Pascual's execution, the Transcriber says that he wrote to each one of them in an effort to secure more information. What follow are their responses to his written messages. Santiago Lurueña's letter is bipartite, dated 9 and 10 January 1942. In it we are told that Pascual Duarte's manuscript, together with the Transcriber's letter, was delivered to him on the same day—9 January 1942—by David Freire Angulo, the present chaplain of the Badajoz prison. He reveals that the infamous written confession reached him in the form of 359 typewritten pages. In the continuation of his letter on the tenth—having paused the day before to read the manuscript—he says that the part he read left him profoundly moved. Despite Pascual's hyena-like reputation, the cleric was gratified by the *lamb*-like meekness that allowed Pascual to commend his soul to God at the moment of his execution. Lurueña ends his letter in typical Celian tongue-in-cheek fashion, with a postscript lamenting not being able to provide the Transcriber with the requested photo of the notorious criminal.

The other communication is from Cesáreo Martín, the civil guard who swears to Pascual Duarte's hard-hearted criminality, citing the numerous confessions that Pascual made to chaplain Lurueña, each time cavalierly revealing different crimes that include Don Jesús and others which are not mentioned anywhere. He identifies himself as the one to whom Pascual made a final request that the priest remit his manuscript and letter to Don Joaquín, a task Lurueña routinely performed for all executed prisoners. Instead of corroborating the chaplain's firsthand testimony of how Pascual acted minutes before his death, Cesáreo Martín's recollection is that of a criminal whose intense fear brought on a fainting spell followed by shouting and stomping, spitting and kicking. In a similarly facetious manner the guard ends by requesting that the Transcriber send him two—instead of one—copies of Pascual's published memoirs, one being for another prison official (who will send payment for the book). The fourth and final part consists of a statement uttered by the Transcriber, who in effect has the last word: "To the testimony of these two gentlemen, what is there for me to add?" (*PD* 237).

And so one is left to ponder (some of) those happenings of his life which Pascual chose to commit to writing, keeping in mind that these have passed through at least two filters—Pascual's and the Transcriber's—before reaching their intended readers. Rearranged chronologically, Pascual's actions assume a noticeable pattern of behavior. The first incident is the seduction of Lola at his brother's grave site. When Lola later tells him she is expecting their child, Pascual, although apprehensive, experiences moments of satisfaction which enable him to view the world in the positive terms with which, for example, he recounts the happiness he felt in the Mirlo Inn in Mérida on their wedding trip. It is also during this episode that peculiar incidents emerge as foreshadowing devices—in this case, the old woman that was nearly run over by Pascual's horse upon entering the city. By its mere presence the ill-fated mare is also prefigured to die by the knife when Pascual learns that Lola's miscarriage was the result of having been thrown by the horse. As this was happening at home, the events in the local tavern forbode the horse's death. Amid the bravado of his drinking buddies, Pascual stabbed his friend Zacarías three times for having told a joke (about a cock pigeon thief).

One year after Lola's mishap Pascualillo's birth provided his father with eleven months of happy times. After the child's mysterious death Pascual began to suffer in earnest the ire of his mother, sister, and wife, the three fates whom he believed held his life in their hands. Constantly referring to them as witches, he silently bore their insults and assumed the role of scapegoat for the entire family's anger and loss. Nowhere else in the novel are the Transcriber's scissors more actively at work than in chapters 11 and 12, in which the conversations between Pascual and Lola reflect only his wife's affronts. Violence again looms as Pascual writes: "A man kills without thinking, as I well know, and sometimes without wanting to. A man hates fiercely, and the knife opens, and holding it open a man goes barefoot towards the bed where the enemy sleeps. . . . It takes years for hate to grow" (*PD* 143).

At this point Pascual leaves home and ventures to Madrid, hoping eventually to go to America via La Coruña (Galicia). While in the capital he stays with Angel Estevez and his wife, Concepción Castillo López, who show him that conflicts can be resolved with words rather than through violence, a revelation he never forgets. Once in Galicia his homesickness causes him to abort his trip to America, driving him back to Torremejía and Lola, who is expecting Ramrod's child. Upon forcing her to reveal the baby's paternity by promising her that nothing will happen because he wants only to know the truth, Pascual reacts so violently that Lola faints and (we are told later) dies. Whether or not the work of Pascual's hand or of natural causes, her death is added to Pascual's list, with Ramrod's soon to follow.

For this latter crime Pascual spends three years in the Chinchilla prison, from which he is released for good behavior and because of the benevolence of the prison warden Don Conrado. In retrospect, however, Pascual says that a worse fate could not have befallen him because freedom—and his subsequent return to Torremejía—sealed his destiny. The scene is reminiscent of the return trip from his honeymoon. In passing by a cemetery at night and overhearing other wayfarers talk about his imprisonment and his sister's latest boyfriend, Don Sebastián, the enshrouding gloom augurs more misfortune when, knocking at the door of his house, he hears his mother's gruff voice respond by asking what he wants. Once settled in again at home he is introduced by Rosario to Esperanza (Hope), who agrees to marry him. After two months of marriage his mother's presence in the same house is more than he can bear and on 10 February 1922—a poor memory notwithstanding, he remembers that it fell on a Friday—he commits the matricide that allows him to breathe freely for the first time.

The lingering question—and the one that has engendered the most critical commentary—is whether or not Pascual Duarte takes responsibility for his life. Although his memoirs constitute a confession, they are so laced with references to determinism that it is difficult to accept it as a sincere admission of guilt. How could Pascual possibly be held responsible for his actions when everyone around him led such ill-starred lives? Rosario made her appearance into the world as an ugly baby who slept in a crib that consisted of a shallow box with an old pillow for a mattress. So dismal was her home life that, it will be recalled, she became a prostitute, suffering constantly from venereal diseases. Needless to say, her luck with men was equally adverse. At one point Pascual sadly writes that she will never be a mother, an unfortunate reality given her nurturing qualities. His brother Mario not only dies by drowning in a huge jug of oil but is born retarded, never learns to walk, and has the nose of a rat. To make matters worse, his first tooth grows in the middle of his hard palate and has to be yanked out with a cord. He later suffers having his ears devoured by a pig in addition to being abused by his mother's boyfriend. One of the most moving passages of the entire novel describes Mario, whose "hind end (if you will excuse the word), broke out in a kind of rash like measles which took the skin right off on account of the pus from the blisters getting mixed with urine, and when they tried to cure him, the vinegar and salt hurt so much that the poor kid let out screams that would have melted the hardest heart" (*PD* 59).

Pascual's father, Esteban Duarte Diniz, abuses his wife and children, knows how to read, and sufers a tortous death. Having been bitten by a rabid dog, he dies insane and frothing at the mouth on the same day—6 January, the day of the Epiphany—on which Mario is born. Remaining forever nameless, Pascual's mother is a good match for her husband: she imbibes in wine, never bathes, is consumptive, and engages in licentious liaisons with men. According to Pascual, she has the temperament of a mythical basilisk. Whether viewed, then, from matriarchal or patriarchal points of view, neither male nor female escapes the ravages of life in the Duarte domain.

In essence we are confronted with two Pascual Duartes: the protagonist—and persona—of his memoirs and the author of the same. Both of them emanate from unique fictive times and places and speak different, if not altogether irreconcilable, languages. As he realized when he witnessed the verbal argument in Madrid between the husband and wife with whom he became friends, Pascual the protagonist hardly ever spoke because he did not know how. Pascual the autobiographer, on the other hand, learned to communicate with the elegance of a schooled thinker, as evidenced in his writings and the long philosophical digressions of chapters 6 and 13.[11]

Given the blatant plethora of intentioned blank spaces, black humor, sarcasm, and irony that characterize this novel, one is reminded of Cela's own words concerning his "poor puppet" Pascual. In commenting in 1951 on the numerous articles that had already been written about the character, Cela reasoned that they probably reflected his intention of calling things by their name—in other words, "when something smells, what one has to do, in order for others to notice, is not to try to smell the same foul air, but rather simply try to change the odor."[12]

In another essay, written in 1960, Cela states that Pascual Duarte continues from beyond the grave to speak words that originate in the "the criminal's deep sense of integrity." Cela insists that "it is not easy to apply the norm to something abnormal," thereby suggesting the anomaly of Spanish life in the early years of Francoist rule.[13] Furthermore, he is forthright in blaming society for Pascual's comportment, charging that everybody—who read *Pascual Duarte*—killed him, because it would have been too uncomfortable to keep him alive.

CHAPTER 2

Rest Home

When Cela says that *Pabellón de reposo,* 1944 *(Rest Home),* is the "imme-diate product of a bitter personal experience from which he learned a great deal," he is referring to periods of confinement in two different sanatoria in which he recovered from tuberculosis in 1931 and 1942.[1] In the "notes" he wrote to accompany the early editions of *Rest Home* he reiterates the fact that his novel is not, however, biographical but, rather, the product of an "aesthetic, more than a stylistic, concern," his own convalescence being the source of inspiration for this, his second major novel.[2] *Rest Home* was originally published in 1943 in serialized form in the Madrid weekly *El Español.*[3] It provoked harsh criticism because of its subject matter: the final months of life of seven terminally ill patients—four men and three women—who are dy-ing of tuberculosis. According to Cela, it was forbidden reading for the patients of all tuberculosis facilities.[4]

In the 1952 prologue Cela classified *Rest Home* as a "poem written in prose" which was especially poignant for him, given what he calls the bitter-sweet, almost hopeless, nature of its content (12).[5] Ten years later, having experienced firsthand the disapproval of many critics, he again wrote about *Rest Home* in the prologue to his 1953 novel, *Mrs. Caldwell.* In it Cela berates his critics and talks about *Rest Home,* stressing its passivity, thereby giving vent to his annoyance at myopic (critical) interpretations of the violence in *Pascual Duarte.* In *Rest Home,* he says, "nothing happens . . . there are no assassinations, no turbulent love affairs, no physical blows upon anyone, and only a minimum of bloodshed, enough for the reader to be sure that he is deal-ing with patients that are suffering from tuberculosis and not just rheumatism or people who have gone mad because of syphilis" ("Prólogo," *RH* 11). Al-though he refers to his characters as marionettes that resemble the pieces of a parquet floor, he also highlights the multiple points of view which emanate from their first-person narrations.[6]

Cela's deceptively mild-mannered words are examples of his tongue-in-cheek sarcasm, for it is commonly recognized that, before the discovery of streptomycin, death from tuberculosis was agonizingly slow.[7] To be certain, there is just as much death in this "pacifist" novel as in *Pascual Duarte,* as the seven patients are individually associated with death by means of the refrain-like presence (always in italics) of a redheaded gardener who, at the end of each chapter in part 2, appears pushing a faded green wheelbarrow. By symbolically carrying them away with no narrative explanation about who has died, his night-time appearances facilitate thematic as well as technical progression of otherwise negligible *action* amid such pallor, in which only the color red—of the patients' blood and the faded embroidery of the number 40 on their clothing—ironically hints at the vibrancy of life. In themselves the chaise longues that decorate the premises of the sanatorium symbolize the terminally ill. At the same time and on a deeper level are concealed those narrative techniques that unmistakably contribute to Cela's self-imposed goal of technical innovation; specifically, these include visual motifs (photographs and mirrors) and the manipulation of focal points; letters, diaries, and other written documents, some of which constitute the Cervantine *(Pascual Duarte)* "lost manuscript"; theatrical encoding and, along the same lines, the use of dramatic irony and unexpected, brief, anonymous conversations, in addition to cinematographic shifts from one fictive space to another; enigmas that defy explanation; and, finally, adherence to the *esperpento* principle whereby grotesqueness and deformation render a stylized appreciation of the darker side of humanity.[8]

Creative *life,* then, begins where flesh and blood end in the sanatorium. As the patients are constantly made aware of their alarming loss of control over spitting up the blood that marks the progression of their illness, we too are reminded of the metaphorical martyr's blood that in time produces its own heroes.[9] Of particular significance in *Rest Home* is that the invalids proceed from the suffering human beings whom Cela saw day after day when he was treated for tuberculosis. He insists, nevertheless, that they are thoroughly *literaturizados* (converted into literary figures), because a realistic portrayal would have been too cruel and shocking.[10]

Set in an unnamed sanatorium in a *locus amoenus* of the mountains from which Madrid can be seen, the action unfolds with masterful symmetry over the seven chapters of each of the two parts of the novel.[11] For the most part each chapter is devoted to one of the seven characters whose names (even among themselves) are the numerical designates of their hospital rooms. Presented (in both parts of the novel) in alternating male-female order, they are identified respectively as numbers 52, 37, 14, 40, 11, 103, and 2.[12] In addition to the uniformity of their appearance throughout the novel, their unique manner of expression is also constant; that is, numbers 52, 37, 14, 40, 11, and 103 keep different kinds of journals, while number 2 writes letters to his business partner in the stock market. Their interactions in the hospital are transmitted to us through their writings, and, with the exception of the brief *intermedio* (interlude/intermission) which separates part 1 from part 2, neither we nor the extradiegetic narrator are actual eyewitnesses to their confinement, as what little we know of them transpires during the summer and autumn months of the undisclosed final year of their lives.

As such, *Rest Home* is a network of different modes of discourse which are fused together and plotted on a larger narrative grid of which we become aware thanks to the different structural components of the novel. Specifically, these include the following: the previously mentioned *intermedio,* in which seven fast shifts of scenery flash before us (from the board of directors' room to the sewing room to the kitchen to a hallway in the hospital to a curious aside about an undisclosed romantic involvement between a woman and the hospital's doctor-director, and, finally, to the narrator's curious reference to his eleven-year-old cousin Anton's theory of relativity); various "notes" supposedly from Cela—the *author*—in which he makes reference to letters of complaint received concerning the publication of this novel; and the epilogue.

Cela has seen to it that what could have been expressed in facile third-person narration by an omniscient narrator is replaced by the patients' personal accounts of their suffering and, more significantly, those of the other patients in the hospital. In this way perspective becomes the determinant of a narration that is purposefully disjointed concerning biographical facts and personality traits. For example, it is from number 52 that we learn about number 37's romantic nature and the photograph of her boyfriend which hangs on the wall of her hospital room; in turn, number 37 writes that number 52 is a cultured man ten years her senior who writes poetry and has loaned her one of his books of poetry; she also makes us privy to hospital gossip such as the recent arrival of number 40, whose persistent cough is heard everywhere; number 14 makes comparisons about numbers 37 and 40; and so forth. In the first part of the novel the romantic involvement of the patients (numbers 52 and 37, 14 and 40) is similarly made known, while more somber facts, such as the deaths of numbers 14 and 73, are revealed by way of indirect cross-references. In addition to the cohesiveness that these otherwise unattractive characters bestow upon the narrative discourse, they are transformed into feeling human beings whose intense self-consciousness converts the monotony of daily existence into invaluable moments in time.[13]

Since we get to know them twice removed—on paper by way of their written accounts, which are passed on to us by the narrator—we feel privileged to read about their innermost longings, heartaches, and terror. Just as Pascual

Duarte's imprisonment allowed him to discover and express himself through words, the psychological and emotional solitude that these patients experience also enables them to put pen to paper and find solace in the act of writing. As Ilie puts it, the patient becomes the hypersensitive artist who is totally isolated from the rest of the world.[14] Nowhere is this more evident than in the second part of the novel, in which number 40, having become traumatized by her deteriorating physical condition, is denied access to the notebooks that she has meticulously been keeping; trying to convince her that she has confused them with other logbooks that she kept before entering the facility, the doctor convinces her that she never wrote anything during her stay in the sanatorium.

In reality, just as the dying gauge life according to death's measuring stick, absence becomes presence, as photographs and letters are reminders of healthy people and the world outside the sanatorium. Even the mirrors in patients' rooms bring to mind the absent self that has vanished before their eyes. Not only is the written word a means of bonding with absent ones, but it also unites them within the hospital, where direct communication is absent.[15] Number 103 receives letters of advice from her mother and keeps in a special box of Philippine ivory the letters sent her by her deceased sailor boyfriend—once known as number 73, when he was hospitalized in the same place; although the letter ironically arrives after his death, number 11 is cruelly rejected by the woman whose hand he asked in marriage; number 14 is told in a letter that his land has been severely affected by a drought; and number 2, the former director of the B.E.L.S.A. company, keeps busy with business correspondence. Cela also makes himself a part of the fictive world of *Rest Home* by way of metered interruption-responses to letters (of protest about his novel) from a friend and phthisiologist and his aunt Katherine Trulock, who, in turn, sends *him* a letter she received for him from his old friend W. L., who is also dying of the same illness.

The critics who have studied this novel recognize the important themes of human suffering, loneliness, and death. Love is equally important because it sustains the patients from day to day. Manifesting itself as both mundane and spiritual, it sparks enthusiasm in the patients. Number 52, for example, delights in remembering some things from his everyday world: old sardine cans, newspapers, couples strolling hand in hand, his old diaries, and a scrap of paper which he carries in his pocket and which bears the obituary of his beloved girlfriend, who died four years before in the north pavilion of the same sanatorium. At first his mention of "the young girl in Number 37" goes relatively unnoticed (*RH* 19), but, when she also makes reference to him (chap. 2), the stage is set for romantic involvement, as she recalls how they sat holding hands in her room in clear view of her boyfriend's picture, which was hanging on the wall.[16] Number 14's longing for number 40 follows along parallel lines (chap. 3), while number 11's romance deals with a tuberculosis-free woman who, it will be recalled, refuses to marry him. The female counterpart of young 14's absent love is number 103's sailor boyfriend, who died of a relapse of tuberculosis while at sea. Despite its ordinariness, the stockbroker (patient number 2) also has a love interest in a woman named Fifí (who is not his wife).

Because Cela's experimentation with technique would not allow him to structure his novel along traditional narrative lines, his treatment of the couples is unpredictable. On the one—and most obvious—hand, these people find imperfect, albeit momentarily satisfying, partners who end in death, rejection, or absence. Whereas the outcome of the romantic interludes provides ample motivation for the development of the story line, Cela engages our curiosity about two instances that go virtually unnoticed. In the first case there is a strong yet subtle suggestion that numbers 52 and 37 engaged in sexual relations (pt. 2). Indeed, although we are left to speculate about this, some incidental details engage our curiosity—namely, the two and a half hours they spent together in her room, the torn nightgown she hid in her closet after he left, and her (later) recollection of his Herculean "naked torso." In addition, one of the last lines that number 37 writes before dying states that "[she does] not mind dying at all, now. Absolutely not at all" (*RH* 147), which leads one to believe that she had experienced the sexual fulfillment for which she and the other patients long before they die.

The second piquant romantic episode is also unpredictable and open-ended. It deals with the dismissal of the director of the sanatorium on account of his previously mentioned love affair with an anonymous young woman. This scandalous behavior reinforces the probable cause for number 37's hidden nightgown and further exacerbates the patients' unrequited love and the reader's frustration given the dearth of information about these people. Because the enigmas defy a hermeneutics of reading and attest to the experimental tenor of *Rest Home,* they contribute to a malaise and sense of apprehension that simmer beneath the surface of the novel. As if to further confound matters, the nurse who tells number 40 the "funny love story" offers a cruel reminder of reality (*RH* 167). Her anecdote about a beautiful young girl culminates in a description of the princess's mouth filling with blood as she dies of tuberculosis. The message is obvious: the fictitious "princess" could be number 40 or any other woman.

On all levels, then, love ends in indeterminacy. Oftentimes people outside the sanatorium succumb to tuberculosis, as numbers 52 and 14, respectively, recount the deaths of girlfriends and mothers. Even number 2's *happily ever after* reconciliation with his wife is not as perfect as it seems, for his silenced lover, Fifí, is still in the *real* world to which his wife and daughter will eventually return after his death. Uncertainty lingers about whether or not the bribe of an apartment and a monthly allowance will be sufficient to silence the scorned woman with the frivolous name.

In spite of the death that awaits the patients as the redheaded gardener pushes about his makeshift hearse, the heterogeneity of the narrative modes that constitute *Rest Home* also heightens the inconclusiveness of the reading process. Besides drawing attention to itself as artifice, the unyielding emphasis on written texts likewise contributes to metafictional posturing, as process takes precedence over a fixed narrative schema. This sense of a *novel-in-the-making* increases when, as number 103 is sorting through her boyfriend's letters to her, Cela surreptitiously breaks in to make public his own letter from the phthisiologist who, it will be recalled, wrote to him protesting the publication of *Rest Home.* At this point Cela again departs from the topic at hand by citing an admonition that fiction "is artifice and concoction" (*RH* 91). Cela's casual reference is no coincidence, for it brings to mind the author of *Don Quixote,* Miguel de Cervantes, whom Cela uses (in an epigraph) to soften the emotional content of *Rest Home:* "Aquí tengo el alma atravesada en la garganta, como una nuez de ballesta" (My soul is stuck, sered in my throat [*RH* 15]).[17]

Having so suspended number 103's activities, the narrator permits her to continue her epistolary pursuits, this time by way of allowing us to witness verbatim her notation concerning the letter of marriage proposal which her beloved "N." wrote her while he was a crew member of the frigate *Delfín* as it docked in Port-of-Spain, Trinidad, on 11 November. In a fashion similar to Cela's unannounced intrusion into her private fictive space, she shatters her own nostalgia by chastising herself for having taken so long to respond to the proposal, a delay that resulted in her unopened letter to him being returned soiled and crumpled a few hours before she read a newspaper notice about his death.

The true metafictional underpinnings of *Rest Home,* however, are revealed in the second half of the novel. In terms of the story, the patients have survived the summer and face an autumn that culminates in the month of November, a time that is known in Catholic tradition as the "month of the dead" (or All Souls'). Timely comments about their failing health become increasingly grotesque as they envision themselves dying, for example, like a fish who bleeds to death from the fisherman's hook (*RH* 159) or by biting their tongues to prevent choking to death (*RH* 131). Obsessive thoughts of bleeding by mouth are common, as is the realization that one's kiss is as deadly as a snake biting a child who unsuspectingly happens upon its nest (*RH* 140). Number 14 shudders at the thought of being buried in such a way that dogs might be able to dig up his cadaver, while equally misshapen is the mental image number 11 has of "the ridiculous aspects of our wedding *in articulo mortis*" (*RH* 183). However bothersome, these poetic renditions of death alert the reader to what is in store and heighten the narrative tension of waiting and wondering when each patient will die.

As their days start to be numbered, another irony intensifies the curiosity about the impending deaths. In direct inverse proportion to the information contained in the newspaper obituary notices that a few patients read about loved ones, we never know who is carted away by the gardener (at the end of each chapter in pt. 2). We see, instead, their narrative voices abruptly end in the indicated textual breaks that give way (in italicized third-person narration) to the gardener's appearance.[18] While associations are naturally inferred from the silenced narrative voice and the deceased who is in the box atop the wheelbarrow, the death could be anyone's. Our perception is further thwarted by the fact that other sick people once occupied the same rooms and, therefore, also had the same names/numbers. A case in point is the early mention that number 52 makes of number 14's death; later, in the second part, number 37 also refers to number 14's very recent death, yet we hear number 14's voice twice in both parts of the novel. A similar source of confusion arises from number 52's statement (in pt. 2) that number 37 has died, even though she is heard in the chapter that immediately follows his. Ambiguity notwithstanding, we are reminded that in the world of the (living) dead the spirit has no corporeal identity and is, therefore, aptly reminiscent of the theory of reincarnation that terrified number 37 when number 52 told her about it. Whether the numbered patients whose writings we have read are in fact those that the gardener carries off or whether the evasiveness of concrete fact is a technique that Cela uses to conjure up a sense of simultaneity is inconsequential, because where death abides chronology and tangible reality as we know them cease.

In other instances the ailing speak openly about their deaths, stating, for example, that they "see the fatal ending closer and closer now" (*RH* 181). On one occasion the extradiegetic narrator takes up number 40's words after she faints from looking in the mirror, trying to convince herself she is not old but sick and that hers is a will of bronze. This interruption is unique in that it evolves into a kaleidoscopic interplay of eleven short segments that alternate between the narrator's observations and extraneous unannounced dialogues between number 40, the storytelling nurse, and the doctor who took her diaries from her. All of them accelerate the pace of the narration and increase the impact of a fictive present that simultaneously produces the same disconcertment in the reader that number 40 feels as she weaves in and out of consciousness the larger her dosage of medication. In this context the reader is drawn forth by the extradiegetic narrator, who declares that it is up to anybody to imagine what number 40's hospital room looked like (*RH* 167). At other times the infirmed seem less worried about death than about what will happen to what they have written; for example, immediately before the faded green wheelbarrow rolls around, number 103 utters, "if I die without continuing my tale . . ." (*RH* 195). Number 11 refers to his death in theatrical terms, asserting with nineteenth-century Romantic resignation that "things happen according to what is written" (*RH* 181).[19]

On another level, however, Cela's tenacious exposé of the censorious letters that he (supposedly) received concerning his novel strike the final chord in the syncopated rhythm that these interruptions, written documents, and Cela's narrative digressions bestow upon an already fragmented narration. His friend W. L.'s question—"What impels you to publish this book?" (*RH* 201)—corroborates the work-in-progress by eliciting Cela's written response: "I intend to finish my novel" (*RH* 192). Ten pages later (and in last-stanza fashion) the epilogue resurrects the poetic genesis of *Rest Home*. Besides beginning with the same words as those of the first chapter—"now the cattle return" (*RH* 217)—it calls to mind (the theme of) life. As a way of intensifying the patients' loss of hope, as compared to when they arrived anticipating a "two-month" period of convalescence, "ya no" (no longer) is anaphorically echoed throughout the second part of the novel and the six paragraphs of the finale.[20]

The numerous commentaries on the diversity of written media that, before our eyes, have either been lost and found again or never brought to conclusion suddenly cease with the unusual third-person narration that characterizes an epilogue that succinctly rephrases what had been associated with number 52 at the beginning of the novel. In a manner reminiscent of number 40's confusion about her carefully guarded notebook pages, we too are left with a sense of confusion, questioning whether or not the people we thought had died are in fact the bodies that are taken away by the redheaded gardener. Given so much uncertainty, numerous critics believe that number 52 is the only survivor and, therefore, the principal narrator. Unlike *Pascual Duarte,* we are not told in *Rest Home* how the narrator—or the fictive Cela—came across these documents, an omission that advances our inquisitiveness and reminds us, in the long run, that all fiction is fiction.

Among the other stylistic devices that Cela uses to bring down the barriers between life and afterlife, and reality and fiction, is the play of visual fields which emanates from the many points of view that go hand in hand with their corresponding narrative voices. Number 14, for example, comments on how he "looks and looks, and looks again at" number 40, comparing her beauty to that of number 37 (*RH* 155). W. L. speaks of an old photograph that he looks at in remembering—the fictitious—Cela in his military uniform at the end of Spain's Civil War. The most adroit optical illusion concerns number 52's comments (in the first chapter of the second half of the novel) about a nurse's account of what number 37 looked like when she died. Saying that it was "espantoso" (horrifying), he, in turn, renders a bipartite view of the subject. On the most obvious of narrative levels the nurse's eye likens number 37 to "a marble statue, with her alabaster hands clasped as if in prayer" (*RH* 127), a vision that causes number 52 to imagine his dead friend a saint in heaven. On another level, however, the sanctified number 37, having gained a place in heaven, glances downward at earthly mortals, among whom are number 52 and the other patients in the sanatorium. This narrative envisioning, in turn, encourages philosophical contemplation about God and his plan for humankind as it manifests itself in the suffering in the sanatorium. Number 52 sarcastically doubts the complete happiness that, according to Catholic doctrine, is afforded number 37 now that she is reveling in the "beatific vision" (*RH* 132). In this way Cela sets the tone for what will become—in the future—an unrelenting attack on established religion.

Similar theological confusion is concentrated in the increasingly loud pleas for God's mercy which these tuberculosis patients make as their deaths become imminent. Their helplessness is intermingled with earthly concerns about finding suitable mates and achieving sexual fulfillment in this life. These preoccupations reach a strident pitch in the second part of the novel, as people like number 52 think that number 37 will not even be happy in the hereafter because she never had the chance to be united with her fiancé on earth; number 14 also bemoans never marrying or having children. These worries traverse the novel as the female patients (in particular number 40) comment that men and women do not understand each other and that, from the vantage point of their hospital confinement and progressively failing physical stamina, women would most likely never "reject" men the way they do if they were able to perceive the alienating effect it had on them both. While a more contemporary reading of this novel could deliver a pervasive male viewpoint, Cela's primary preoccupation with human beings as men and women in search of simple gratification and happiness surfaces in the remorse these dying patients feel in their solitude as the thematic binary oppositions that form the substructure of this novel rise to the most elementary of all dualities: men and women and how they get along in life.

CHAPTER 3

The Hive

Since it was first published in 1951 in Buenos Aires, *La colmena (The Hive)* has had numerous editions, some of which have as many as seven different prologues, each one a testimony to the novel's editorial history.[1] In addition to constituting a compendium of theoretical essays on fiction, they document Cela's experiences with censorship during the 1940s and 1950s in Francoist Spain. Although Cela speaks about *The Hive* in each one of them, it is the 1965 prologue that refers to the controversy that forced him to publish it in Argentina, where, due to the Peronist government that was in power, changes in his manuscript had to be made in order to satisfy the Argentine censors. In the "note to the first edition" Cela states that his novel "is nothing other than a pale reflection, a humble shadow of everyday, harsh, profound, and painful reality." He goes on to say that it aspires to being a "slice of life that is narrated step by step, without reticence or strange tragedies, without charity, exactly the way life itself transpires" (Asún Escartín 105).

Cela explains that *The Hive*'s narrative structure is so complicated that it took him five years to write. He ends the 1965 introduction with a reference to *The Hive*'s 160 characters that "swarm" about in Madrid in 1942 (Asún Escartín 106), thereby discouraging attempts to classify it as realist, idealist, naturalist, or of manners.[2] In three subsequent (separate) "notes" to other editions Cela forgoes commentary on *The Hive* and speaks, rather, of the human condition, exposing the misery, degradation, and sordidness that he perceives in life. In the introduction to *Mrs. Caldwell* ("A Few Words to Future Readers") Cela defines *The Hive* as a "novela reloj" (clock novel) which is made up of wheels and tiny pieces that work together in a finely tuned manner.[3]

While it is difficult to estimate whether this novel or *Pascual Duarte* has generated more critical attention, there is unanimous agreement among Cela scholars concerning *The Hive*'s break with narrative tradition in sporting a cinematographic narrative point of view and an open-ended series of enigmas, to which David Henn refers as "something of a literary jigsaw puzzle."[4] Again in parodic Celian imitation of biblical creation, the novel's seven chapters unfold over six days: the action of chapters 1 through 6 takes place in three days, at the end of which the narrator tells us, in the "FINAL" chapter, that "it is three or four days later" (*H* 237).[5] Had Cela given his story linear chronology, *The Hive* would unavoidably have resulted in twentieth-century naturalism. Such is not the case, however, as numerous happenings in the lives of the characters occur out of sequence: chapters 1 and 2 take place in the afternoon of the first day; chapter 3, in the afternoon/evening of the second day; chapter 4, at night on the first day; chapter 5, again in the afternoon of the second day; and chapter 6, on the morning of the second day. Since only chapters 1, 2, and FINAL follow sequentially, confusion, repetition, and simultaneity are paramount, symbolizing the teeming masses that the title of the novel obviates.

It is no surprise that, from a structural point of view, many early critics saw it as lacking in continuity. One of them, José Manuel Caballero Bonald, went so far as to create a "census" of its 296 fictitious and 50 real characters, an inventory, found at the end of some editions (since 1955), which is an indispensable guide for the uninitiated reader. Because of the techniques that Cela dared implement at a time when the Spanish novel was beginning to recover from the crippling effects of the war years, *The Hive* gave it two important building blocks: social realism (as the point of departure for testimony of life in Spain during the two decades following the Civil War) and experimentation as technique.

In light of this overwhelming number of characters, the novel opens rather prophetically as we hear Doña Rosa, the owner of the café La Delicia (The Delight), warn: "Don't let's lose our sense of proportion, I'm sick and tired of telling you it's the only thing that counts" (*H* 1). Ironically enough, that is precisely what happens (to the reader). The clearly delineated chapters notwithstanding, each one of them breaks down into anywhere from twenty-five to forty or more narrative segments. In true cinematic fashion the narrator seeks to impart socially realistic objectivity to the comings and goings of the characters who happen to pass by his (metaphorical) camera's eye, such as, for example, the man walking down the street—and reading a newspaper—to whom the narrator refers as having been "caught" *(cogemos).*[6] The apparent narrative distance is, however, deceptive, and, just as the camera has its own way of communicating what it sees, this narrator also expresses affinity for some characters and scathing loathing of others, as we shall see.

What become immediately apparent are focal points that serve as havens for these city dwellers (and for the befuddled reader), among which are the following: Doña Rosa's café; Doña Ramona Bragado's dairy on Fuencarral Street; a quiet café on San Bernardo Street; Celestino's bar Aurora (Dawn); Doña Jesusa and Celia's houses of prostitution; Roberto and Filo's apartment; Ramón's bakery; and other fictive spaces that people, such as the aging and sickly Elvira, Doña Visi and her family, and Victoria and her mother, call home. In contrast to these closed interiors are the open spaces afforded by streets and other outside sites, such as the area around the Madrid bullring. Moreover, since most of the action occurs in the afternoon, evening, and nighttime hours, references to light and darkness are constant. There is nothing haphazard either about Cela's choice of time frame; that is, at least half of the action transpires after noon because it is precisely those portions of the day which characterize Spanish social life by way of the afternoon *tertulia* (gathering, literary circle), the *merienda* (snack, tea), and the after-supper stroll. As a matter of fact, the narrator clearly distinguishes between Doña Rosa's midafternoon and early evening clientele. The monotony and alienation of these lives are shrouded by the cold of December against the backdrop of World War II in which, despite Spain's (supposed) neutrality, Doña Rosa and others sympathize with Germany.

The effects of Spain's devastation after 1939 are represented in a variety of physical ailments, from which many suffer: Doña Rosa's diarrhea, others' upset stomachs, Javierín's flatus, Roberto's false teeth, Sonsoles's bad eyesight, a young poet's fainting spell (due to hunger), Martín Marco's and Elvira's malnutrition, and so forth. The list goes on and culminates in the tuberculosis that the narrator says affects "approximately ten percent" (*H* 40) of La Delicia's customers, a statistic fleshed out in the persistent cough often heard in young and old and, specifically, Victorita's boyfriend, Paco, who is unable to work because of it. In addition, some are in need of shelter, like Martín Marco and the nameless six-year-old gypsy boy who makes his living by singing saucy flamenco tunes outside eating and business establishments and who lives under a bridge on the road to the cemetery. In order to survive or to protect loved ones, scores of young women subject themselves to degradation by oftentimes older men. Adequate warm clothing is scarce, as is evidenced in the flimsy cotton coats that do little to protect Elvira and Victorita from the harsh winds that ravage Castile during the winter months. Since medicine is at a premium, people like Victorita resort to prostitution to secure it for themselves or those they love, stimulating unprecedented black market productivity. Nowhere is the pervasiveness of desolation more reminiscent of Dámaso Alonso's 1940 poem "Insomnio" (Insomnia), in which Madrid is depicted as a city of more than one million cadavers.[7]

This is the world into which the reader enters by way of the revolving door of La Delicia, in which the first chapter takes place as the narrator's cinematic meanderings lead us from table to table, allowing us to hear and catch first glimpses of many of the people who will constitute the narrative units to which attention will be drawn. Because the characters are caught off guard and in the middle of whatever they are saying or doing, their words are of little consequence. Amid the crowd Rosa, however nasty, occupies a key position. She is loud, domineering, crass, and repulsive in appearance. Her teeth are gold capped, and her facial hair glimmers with beads of perspiration. In the advent of springtime her eyes glisten, the narrator tells us, at the sight of young girls in short-sleeve dresses. While her stare is likened to that of a mouse, her thick eyeglasses make her eyes look like those of a stuffed bird. She owns numerous apartments and, as rumor has it, keeps coffers filled with gold. By virtue of her enormous size, she bumps up carelessly against people (seated at their tables), as she yells at her waiters and musicians, spouting off insults that echo phrases from slogans of the Francoist regime. There is no doubt that she rules with a firm hand. Benevolence has no function in her place of business, and those like Martín Marco who are unable to pay for their coffee are ordered thrown out.

Little by little certain characters begin to emerge in piecemeal fashion, thereby constituting a series of nuclei of interests. Most notable among the struggling masses are Elvira, who lives alone in one room and whose supper consists of the handful of chestnuts she buys from a female street vendor; the young poet, Martín Marco, who survives thanks to his sister Filo's meager handouts and the makeshift bed that his friend Pablo Alonso allows him to occupy during specified hours; Filo and her husband, Roberto, who works as a bookkeeper for a few small businesses; Victorita and her sick fiancé, Paco; and Rosa's brother-in-law Don Roque, his wife, Doña Visi, and their three grown daughters, Julita, Visitación, and Esperanza. Surrounding these primary figures are many others who have limited, but significant, roles, acting, as critics have pointed out, as episodic, anecdotal linking devices.[8]

As poignant reminders of life in Spain in the 1940s, many young women are to be found. Among them are Purita, who waits upon the advances of Don José in the hopes that he will put her in touch with people to care for Paquito, the youngest of her five brothers (all of whom live alone); la Pirula, one of Victorita's work companions at El Porvenir (The Future) printing press who has been deemed successful for having been *discovered* by Javier, the man who provides her with an attic apartment equipped with radio, electric stove, porcelain ceiling lamp, and a bed with a moiré coverlet. Besides Rosa and the men who keep mistresses, some notable representatives of the middle class include Celestino, owner of the Aurora bar; Don Ramón, the bakery owner who loans Roberto twenty-five pesetas to buy Filo a birthday present; Mario de la Vega, who owns El Porvenir; and the physician Francisco Robles who, in addition to having eleven children, is guardian to the thirteen-year-old Merceditas, whom he bought and later gave to Doña Celia for her brothel.

As the reader meets these people in what appears to be random fashion, different situations are repeated from varying vantage points, while conversations are interrupted only to be resumed or repeated later. All the while, however, the fragmented story line subtly takes shape, as the reader is enticed into tying loose ends together to satisfy his or her curiosity and give some semblance of meaning, if not order, to the narrative. As Robert Spires, among others, so aptly puts it, the basic story of *The Hive* is almost impossible to relate because it involves over three hundred people.[9] What we actually witness is three days in the lives of primarily middle-and lower-middle-class people who meet, talk, and generally go about their business. How they will resolve their specific problems spurs the reader on, hoping to find out, for example, what will become of the chance encounter between Don Roque and his daughter Julita (with their respective paramours) in the stairway of Doña Jesusa's bordello or what will happen to the penniless Martín Marco who, in spite of his lack of appeal, keeps turning up as one of the novel's most intriguing characters.

When things seem to be getting thoroughly out of control, as the parade of more new faces continues in chapter 2, the reader is confronted with José Giménez Figueras and Julián Suárez, a homosexual couple that will constitute a cardinal point in the novel when Suárez's seventy-six-year-old mother, Doña Margot, is found murdered in her apartment (at the end of this same chapter).[10] It doesn't take long, however, to realize that any hopes of solving the murder are to remain unfulfilled, for, aside from a few comments from neighbors about how she (probably) died, nothing comes of them, and no investigation ever takes place, nor does the narrator supply any information that could resolve the intrigue (provoked so early in the novel). As if to confound further readerly detective-like practices, we are later informed that Suárez and his companion and Leoncio Maestre have been detained for questioning. These arrests, however, are not that peculiar because Suárez and his friend are, we are told, used to being picked up by the police. Don Maestre's detention, on the other hand, is more perplexing, since he is the neighbor in the dead woman's apartment building who brought the news of her demise to the others; furthermore, he reacts in a totally unexpected manner when his nerves get the better of him, and he begins frothing at the mouth. No other mention of him is made until the news of his arrest, nor are we told who found Doña Margot. Contrary to normal expectations, their names are never again mentioned, and the reader is forced to grasp at straws for possible connections, the most likely being the destitute Martín Marco who, although for no logical reason—yet for all practical purposes—easily fits the bill.[11] Cela, knowing the mind of the traditional reader, deliberately posits Martín in center stage.

Cela cleverly toys with reader curiosity when it comes to a murder. And so it goes that, when a policeman detains Martín Marco (on the street on the night of the first day), one is certain that an answer will soon be forthcoming. Since, however, such police practices were commonplace in Francoist Spain, nothing comes of the incident, probably because Martín says that he has written articles that have appeared in government newspapers. Even though this episode seems to lead to another dead end, Martín Marco is left frazzled. Instead of feeling relief at not being arrested for not having his ID with him, he experiences an anxiety that borders on panic. While it is up to the reader to decide what provokes such a reaction, nothing definite is identified as the cause of his consternation, and Martín eventually goes about his business and ends up in Doña Jesusa's brothel, where he falls asleep in Purita's arms. He resurfaces briefly on the morning of the second day, but nothing is heard of him until the FINAL chapter, in which he again becomes the center of attention, after everyone who has read the morning paper learns that he is being sought for questioning. The novel ends with Martín's family and friends frantically looking for him to hide him away for a few days until things blow over. While this is happening, he, unaware (and with newspaper in hand), visits his mother's grave and promises himself that his freeloading days are over; he vows to look for work and become a productive member of society, ironically saying out loud (about his newspaper) that "there may be just the thing in here!" (*H* 250).

Nowhere else in the novel is Martín Marco so optimistic nor so cognizant of his parasitic lifestyle, thereby underscoring the acidic quality of Cela's sense of irony and sarcasm: having gone to the cemetery to say a prayer for the thirty-fourth anniversary of his mother's death, Martín gets a newspaper from a shop clerk (who has already read it) and reads everything *except* the section in which his name appears alongside those of homeless people and anyone who had a case pending in court.[12] As Asún Escartín explains, according to the Ley de Responsabilidades Políticas (Law of Political Responsibilities), anyone who was suspected of anti-Nationalist political activities prior to 1939 was suspect and could be investigated at any moment (Asún Escartín 266–67 n. 23). Martín, having been a member of a politically active 1927 university student union called the Federación Universitaria Escolar (commonly known as the FUE), could, therefore, have been sought for this reason. Yet, since nobody knows who murdered Doña Margot nor what Martín did which caused his name to appear in the public notices section of the newspaper, no action on his part over the course of the narrative warrants our suspicion. The tendency, however normal, to associate Martín Marco with the murder is thwarted, if not ridiculed, by Cela in this masterful undermining of traditional anecdotal resolutions, reminding us of this writer's incessant goal of breaking new ground with each novel he writes.

A close reading of *The Hive* uncovers Cela's strategic narrative plotting by way of a meticulously controlled narrative of disinformation which temporarily appeases the bewildered reader, who is manipulated and teased by foreshadowing and enigmas that, although not as momentous as Doña Margot's death, foster an atmosphere of covert suspicion. Such are the following examples: a package that Paco was supposed to have left with Filo and about which Martín inquires (in chap. 2); Doña Cazuela's (Mrs. Stewpan) lover, whom we never see but who is caught in her dirty clothes hamper on the night of Doña Margot's murder; the coded message that surrounds the errand on which Alfonsito (an errand boy with tuberculosis) is sent by an unidentified man—whose car awaits outside the door of the café (on the afternoon of the second day); the physician Francisco's curious telephone conversation (in chap. 5) in which he tells someone that he will be at an undisclosed destination around nine o'clock; and the joke about the man who committed suicide because of the smell of an onion. Not the least insignificant in this web of discontinuity is the newspaper (motif), which, in addition to its key role in the FINAL chapter, is tossed about by numerous people: Doña Rosa sends Alfonsito for the newspaper; Roberto reads the newspaper as he rides the elevator to his apartment; Don Roque and José Sierra use the newspaper as excuses to ignore their nagging wives; and Martín Marco, as we know, writes for government newspapers and also carries newspaper clippings in his wallet. Because newspapers are a common source of mass information, their presence in *The Hive* intensifies Cela's virtual sabotage of tradition in Falangist Spain.

Julián Suárez's strange behavior on the evening of his mother's death is another case in point. At the beginning of a nightly ritual before going to bed, he engages in a ludicrous infantile dialogue with his mother—whom we never see. Their brief interchange abounds in sarcasm as Doña Margot tells him to cover up well and say his prayers. After permitting us to hear Suárez address her as "Mummy" (*H* 76–77) and ask for a good-night kiss, the narrator nonchalantly asserts that Suárez is fifty years old. Immediately following the nightly routine, we see Suárez arriving home one night, unlocking the door, and calling to his "Mummy!" This time, however, there is no answer, upon which we are told that the son gets nervous, is impelled into the hallway by some strange force, and, with hand on the door latch, takes a step backward and runs out calling one last time to his mother. Bewildered by the unanswered greeting and his autonomic flight response, he notices "his heart is beating very fast. He runs down the stairs, taking two steps at a time" (*H* 77), and hails a taxi that deposits him "opposite the Congress Building" on San Jerónimo Street. No explanations are offered, leaving one to speculate about whether or not he actually saw his mother's dead body or simply sensed that something was wrong.

More mystery surrounds the family of Don Roque, who, it will be recalled, accidentally bumped into his daughter at the brothel. Even though the reader is able to unravel the true nature of the intrigue, the situation merits attention and gives evidence of the theme of revenge. As a retaliatory measure for Roque's lack of sexual response to her after his chance encounter in the stairway with Julita, Lola takes down a picture of a man (Obdulio) which hangs on the wall and sends it anonymously to the daughter, who, upon receiving it, becomes frightened, the irony being that Julita's excuse to her father was that she had just had her picture taken by a photographer in that same building. Since she also told her mother about the photograph, Doña Visi automatically opens the certified envelope sent by Lola, thinking that it is her daughter's picture. She is, however, thoroughly bemused by Obdulio's portrait, only to be told by Julita that it must be a joke that somebody is playing on her. Meanwhile, Julita shows the picture to her boyfriend, Ventura, and tells him about having stumbled upon her father the previous afternoon, to which he responds that they should find another trysting place because the brothel's owner warned him to be more careful, since the father-daughter incident could cost her a good customer. In an effort to scare Don Roque into finding another meeting place, Ventura writes him an anonymous letter in which he includes the infamous picture. The accompanying typewritten letter warns that "[a] hundred eyes are watching you . . . and we know very well what way you voted in 1936" (*H* 192). While the episode is cleverly wrought in black humor, it is also reminiscent of the well-founded paranoia that was the result of the regime's obsession with (Falangist) party loyalty. Even the narrator is cognizant of the pervading mistrust, saying that "every human existence is a mystery, but the fact remains that every face is the mirror of the soul" (*H* 81), thus enhancing the foreboding that clouds everything.

Surface reality is hardly accurate as we hear, for example, the omniscient narrator say "[a] beatific smile lights up Don Pablo's face. If his breast could be opened, his heart would be found to be black and sticky like pitch" (*H* 25–26). Disclosures of this nature from the purportedly objective narrator expose an undeniable point of view concerning the lamentable state of affairs of Spanish life in the 1940s. Numerous are these utterances that leave little room for doubt about subjectivity. Given the countless people that file past the narrator, his sarcasm, irony, and caustically dry wit provoke the ambiguities that Spires sees as the novel's many "tonal and temporal paradoxes."[13] To this end Cela uses diminutives— *-ito,-ico,-illo*—to transmit intimacy and empathy or, to the contrary, scorn and belittlement. Two cases come to mind. Oftentimes Elvira, the aging prostitute, is referred to as either Elvira or "la señor*ita* Elvira" (Miss Elvira), but she is also known as "Elvir*ita,*" all forms of address underscoring the pathos of her poverty-stricken lifestyle. The diminutive is also bitingly sarcastic when, for example, the narrator describes a good-bye scene between Macario and his girlfriend, Matildita. Their conversation, together with reference to "little Matilde"—Matild*ita*—, leads us to believe that she is a starstruck teenage girl, an assumption that seems accurate until the last line of the vignette, in which we are wryly told that "Matild*ita* is thirty-nine years old" (*H* 256). Examples such as this one are everywhere in the novel. Most of the time, however, it is nearly impossible to decide whether the narrator is poking fun at or tacitly commenting on the denial that these pitiful characters use in order to be able to cope with their frustrated lives.

Woven into the fabric of the alternating short—three-to five-line—narrative segments and spontaneous dialogues are longer discursive paragraphs that stand out because of their length and the emotional charge of sympathies which are more in keeping with an editor than a reporter of events. Such bursts of sentiment envelop the most pathetic of figures: the gypsy boy, late-night streetwalkers, and couples who have no other place to be together at night than the empty lot outside the Madrid bullring. Of equally moving proportions are the closing comments of chapter 6, which lead into the beginning of the FINAL chapter, in which daybreak is described as a caterpillar that "creeps over the hearts of the men and women" in Madrid: "that tomb, that greased pole, that hive. . . . Madrid, which is like an old plant with soft, green young shoots" (*H* 236–37). It is, however, at the end of chapter 4 that the narrator's feelings transcend objectivity as he pleads the case of women who have no recourse but to live out their shattered dreams: "and several dozens of girls are hoping—what are they hoping for, O God? Why do You let them be thus deceived?—with their minds full of golden dreams" (*H* 182).

The difference between reality and illusion finds its technical counterpart in the abundance of mirrors that, curiously enough, decorate the most tasteless of interiors. Mirrors of all sorts are everywhere, from Doña Rosa's café to bedrooms and women's handbags. In the wall-lined mirrors of Rosa's café (at the end of chap. 1) some waiters watch her harshly reprimand a fellow worker; Don Ibrahín practices a pompous speech in front of his bathroom mirror (as he overhears the nextdoor neighbor ask his wife about their child's bowel movement); another café on the Gran Vía Street is also decorated with mirrors; Pirula has a mirror in her attic apartment; Julita looks at herself in a mirror before telling her mother about her new boyfriend, Ventura; and, to mention only one

UNDERSTANDING CAMILO JOSÉ CELA

more of numerous examples, an elaborate (undiscovered) system of mirrors that would deflect the sun's rays and warm artesian wells is mentioned as having been devised by someone to increase the country's crop production.

In the absence of mirrors there are other illusionary devices such as bad lighting, poor eyesight, blackouts, and store windows. Doña Celia and Marco indulge in voyeurism, while uncanny manipulation of optical fields renders further dispersion of perspective. It is as if Ventura's anonymous letter warning Julita's father about the "one hundred eyes" becomes reality—that is, when doubt arises concerning who is looking at whom. The most amusingly adroit play upon focalization recalls the infamous picture of Obdulio on the wall of Doña Celia's bordello, a scene that unfolds as a tripartite optical illusion. As one senses that the madame might be watching, Obdulio himself casts a dead stare on the room's occupants, while the mirror also reflects a ludicrous image: Roque with his scarf still wrapped around his neck and Lola in the buff sitting on the bed thoroughly disgusted because of her partner's preoccupation with his daughter (in the same love nest). The narrator also captures the rubberneck-ing (in chap. 4) of an insignificant character, Doña María Morales de Sierra, as she, ironically, spies on the policeman Julio García Morrazo, whose pacing is illuminated by lighted street lamps.

Such plays on focal perspective derive from Cela's adherence to the *esperpento* technique to subvert reality (calling to mind Rosa's plea for keep-ing perspective). So many aspects of *The Hive* lead us to the brink of people, places, and things that are *almost* but not *really* as the camera's lens would reflect them. Leoncio Maestre is *almost* run over by a trolley just as Martín Marco is *almost* hit by a girl on a bicycle and *almost* on the verge of becoming a new man. There are hints of Rosa's lesbianism and a past incestuous encoun-ter between Martín and his sister Filo, just as doctor Francisco's control of the thirteen-year-old Mercedita resembles child slavery. As Spires has pointed out, Victorita is really not that repentant about selling herself to get money for her boyfriend's medicine, which he so desperately needs.[14] Even though Pablo and Laurita are an official couple, she knows that the bon vivant will eventually replace her with another woman. Some of the tabletops in Rosa's café are the marble remains of grave markers which, turned upside down, still bear the names of the deceased. Things are deceptively not necessarily what they appear to be.

Everyone seems to be buzzing about in *The Hive,* but, as critics such as Sobejano, Ilie, and others have pointed out, it is more like watching scenes from a dream sequence because the true nature of poverty is the absence of ambition about changing and moving out of oneself. These citizens of Madrid are spiritually and emotionally bankrupt. Death, whether real or symbolic, is everywhere. Widows, widowers, orphans, and maimed survivors of the Civil War abound. The narrator knows of countless past family histories of people who have all died, leaving the survivors destitute and in search of a better life in the country's capital city. Needless to say, of course, Doña Margot's death and Martín's last visit to his mother's grave site are further examples of the reality of death. Even the obtrusive joke about the man who killed himself because of the smell of onion brings to mind, once again, the stench of the "one million cadavers" in Dámaso Alonso's poem "Insomnio." Doña Rosa has also suffered the loss, to typhus, of Santiago, a supposed marquis whose gift of the luxurious clock atop the bar is a constant—timely—reminder of his absence.

Amid the desolation one remembers Rosa's admonition, because perspective has indeed been lost, and she, as the most prominent symbol of the only recognized political party in postwar Spain, has no other recourse but to keep everyone in line, in true Francoist tradition. It is no wonder that the tables in her café are reminders of the fate that awaits people every day. Rich in themes that its critics have categorized into violence, sex, money, apathy, aggression, alienation, human misery, boredom, indecision, frustration, pessimism, death, and aimlessness, *The Hive* takes its place with other European post–World War II novels, providing ample opportunity for studies about similarities with Camus's *L'Etranger* and other works that decry social injustice and the hypocrisy of many charitable institutions.[15] Studies have also probed traces of Nietzschean philosophy and Tolstoy as well as similarities with John Dos Passos's novel *Manhattan Transfer.*[16] Despite, however, its universal appeal to (the plight of) contemporary, existential man, *The Hive* remains unequivocally Spanish. It is, therefore, a fitting testimony to the Spanish milieu in which it was conceived in which ellipsis, as Giménez-Frontín affirms, was the mainstay of writers like Cela who chose to continue writing in Spain instead of leaving the country in self-exile, as did so many of his compatriots after the Civil War.[17]

CHAPTER 4

Mrs. Caldwell Speaks to Her Son

In chapter 188 of *Mrs. Caldwell habla con su hijo,*1953 *(Mrs. Caldwell Speaks to Her Son),* the character of the same name talks about the "little bloodstain[s]" that appear every morning on her pillow. She refers to them as "portraits in blood" because they depict her dead son, Eliacim.[1] Mrs. Caldwell explains that hemming each one will permit them to remain intact (and "not ravel"); in that way her last will and testament will be carried out: that upon her death she be wrapped in "a shroud made by sewing together all the portraits of [Eliacim] which I spit out each morning" (*MC* 160). However repugnant and bizarre it may seem at first glance, Mrs. Caldwell's carefully planned handiwork is analogous to the meticulous rigor with which Cela wove together the 213 chapters of the uncommonly surrealistic fabric of this his fifth novel.

Cela began to write *Mrs. Caldwell* in 1947, finished it in 1952, and finally published it in 1953.[2] In the novel's first and often quoted prologue "Algunas palabras al que leyere," Cela says that he does not think this work conceals any hidden key that will unlock its mysteries; at the same time, however, he suggests that the future will afford him the objectivity he believes is necessary to discuss it further.[3] In preparing the definitive version of the novel for inclusion in his complete works, in 1969 Cela made good on his word and wrote (to our knowledge) the only other prologue to *Mrs. Caldwell.*[4] Recognizing that *Mrs. Caldwell* was "not understood very well when it appeared . . . [and not] even today" (*MC* 204), Cela makes a plea for its cohesiveness, saying that it is "an act of homage to order . . . [and his] avowed tribute to logical rigor" (*MC* 198).[5] The essay ends with the same unexpected candor with which Mrs. Caldwell says that she is relieved to know that the blood she spits up nightly comes from her lungs.[6] Cela's parting words also allude to blood, noting that the human heart's "mysterious and bitter crannies" shelter torrents of honey, bile, excrement, and blood, which shroud humankind's two never-ending fears: hunger and loneliness. This facile Celian aphorism gives way to stark reality: "the drowned die with all their blood inside" (*MC* 205), and even "the lunatics in the Royal Insane Asylum . . . see how the water flows . . . with a certain attention to good order" (*MC* 206).

Even though this woman has been one of Cela's favorite characters, little has been written about *Mrs. Caldwell*. While Foster sees it as an "original experiment" in light of the "new novel,"[7] Ilie defines it as a surrealistic psychological novel and the product of Cela's dialogue with Spanish poets like Luis de Góngora y Argote (1561–1627), the "Generation of 1927," and the hermetic poems of the book, *Pisando la dudosa luz del día,* which he wrote in 1935.[8] It should also be noted that *Mrs. Caldwell* germinates in *Rest Home* amid the despair of tuberculosis patients like numbers 11, 14, and 103, who envision life in terms of sailors, shipwrecks, and drowning.[9] Their deaths become the source of the dementia that eventually forces Mrs. Caldwell into London's "Royal Insane Asylum." From within the confines of *Rest Home,* then, emerges the perplexing closed space of this Englishwoman's mind, which, in turn, nurtures an incestuous love for a son who died a sailor's death in the Aegean Sea while aboard the *Furious.*[10] Moreover, it validates the obsessions that the neurotic mother commits to writing in homage to her beloved Eliacim, allowing us to penetrate a creative imagination that displays undaunting linguistic virtuosity and poetic sensibility.[11]

Like her literary predecessors Pascual Duarte and the patients in *Rest Home,* Mrs. Caldwell devotes the part of her life which we as readers know to writing. Her testimony is made manifest by Cela himself, who, he tells us in a foreword (and later reiterates in the afterword), met her in Pastrana during his travels through Spain's Alcarria region.[12] Both the news of Mrs. Caldwell's death and her letters are sent to Cela by his friend, Sir David Desverges, a "quail-castrator," an "honorary member of the Royal Geographical Society of Gwynedd," and the "testamentary executor" of the Englishwoman's will (*MC* 191).[13] At the time Cela (supposedly) made her acquaintance, Mrs. Caldwell was staying in the bedroom of the palace where the princess of Eboli died in exile (because of a scandalous love affair with Antonio Pérez, a politician and secretary to King Phillip II). Cela does not tell us how much time he and Eliacim's mother spent together, but he assures us of their fondness for each other, perhaps in part because his smile reminded her of Eliacim.

Cela's account of what his fellow traveler was doing at the time of their initial meeting defines the harbingers of her existence: the first thing we are told is that he saw her "very carefully prying up the tiles in the bedroom . . . and [wrapping them] one by one . . . in tissue paper and . . . [putting] them in" a well-ordered, big-bellied suitcase; on another occasion, after supper, she "read [Cela] the pages she was writing in memory of her beloved son." Cela further explains that among the titles that she considered giving her writings, "I Speak to My Dearly Beloved Son, Eliacim" was what she had in her notebook (*MC* 5).

As we know them, Mrs. Caldwell's pages reach us in the edited version that bears the title *Mrs. Caldwell Speaks to Her Son,* leaving us to speculate about what, if anything, the editor Cela did to prepare his own manuscript. Since he refers to the bundle of papers which Sir David sent him as *cuartillas* (sheets of paper) and not specifically *cartas* (letters) or *capítulos* (chapters), one wonders who enumerated the 213 sections of the novel and labeled them "chapters." Given her title—which Cela obviously changed to suit his own needs—one can be fairly certain, however, that Mrs. Caldwell envisioned her work as a cohesive unit. Only sporadically does she refer to what she is writing as epistolary, such as in chapter 171, in which she says she would buy a typewriter if she had some extra money so that Eliacim would be able to read her "letters" better (*MC* 143). It could also be assumed that the heading—"Letters from the Royal Insane Asylum"—which precedes the last four chapters belongs to the editor, but there is no textual evidence in support of this assumption. Contrary to the editorial comments that characterize *Pascual Duarte* and *Rest Home,* Cela's presence (as transcriber) is minimal in *Mrs. Caldwell,* thereby creating the distance of which critics of this novel speak.[14] The reader is, therefore, left with a customary Celian manuscript motif, that is replete with ambiguities.

Mrs. Caldwell unfolds as a one-sided conversation with her dead son, Eliacim, whose presence is created *in ausencia* and whose voice is heard circuitously by way of his mother's transcription.[15] What Mrs. Caldwell says to Eliacim is divided into segments, each bearing its own title and ranging in length from four lines to a couple of pages.[16] Ilie refers to them as the "prose poems" of Mrs. Caldwell's "monologue."[17] In a few instances the titles are longer than the texts, such as in chapters 23 and 103.[18] Despite Cela's previously mentioned insistence on the logic of this work, however, it is nearly impossible to discern patterns of organization amid such titles as, for example, "Trout," "Botticellian! Botticellian!" "A Hot-Water Bottle to Warm Your Feet," "The Counterfeit Coin," "Letters That Come in the Post," "Soup," and so forth. Linear chronology is virtually nonexistent as Mrs. Caldwell tells Eliacim that the city clock stopped working and that "it would be much more beautiful if part of mankind argued strongly that some Mondays are Thursdays" (*MC* 43).[19] In her ramblings Mrs. Caldwell drops the names of over seventy-five real and fictitious people, like Benjamin Disraeli, Cervantes, Homer, Mr. Quaking, and Mr. and Mrs. Fishy. She provides raucous anecdotal information about characters such as the one-legged Syrian tailor named Joshua, the unshipped sailor Eusebio W. Clownish, an accordion player who was begotten by a shark and an opium trader, and Matilda Help—

the illegitimate child of a Polish countess and a pilot in the Royal Air Force.

Everything comes to us exclusively through the filter of a narrator whose state of mind is reliably unstable, making everything she reveals suspect yet paradoxically informative, albeit indirect and piecemeal.[20] About Eliacim we know certain things, for instance: he liked and wrote poetry, and organized an occasional literary and musical soirée in honor of writer friends, causing his name to appear in local provincial newspapers; he played chess with his mother and bought her lingerie; he knew how to ski and swim and loved to go on excursions; he was about twenty years old when he died, and his birthday was 17 April. His mother suggests that his vices included drinking, gambling, and horse racing. She is also annoyed by (what appears to have been) his many girlfriends, a bone of contention about his role in her incestuous yearning for him and his conduct in general, since his mother says that he had *sabañones* (chilblains), an ailment that in Spanish literary tradition signaled the presence of venereal diseases.[21]

In an effort to instill jealousy in her son, she is surprisingly forthright about the affairs she had with the upstairs neighbor (who, unknown to Mr. Caldwell, is Eliacim's biological father), Carlo Dominici, Tom Dickinson, an Italian marquis, and so forth. Notwithstanding the sketchy details about her past life, there is solid evidence of an unstable and more than likely dysfunctional family. In remembering her father, she thinks of herself as the "daughter of the Devil" (*MC* 63). She refers to him in chapter 55 as a "corpulent presence" who, in giving her "his blessing at night, and a kiss on [the] . . . forehead . . . smelled intensely of sulphur," causing her to keep her "eyes tightly shut . . . [feeling] a little hot flush running across . . . [her] breast like a centipede gone mad" (*MC* 47).

No matter how strange her messages to Eliacim, Mrs. Caldwell nonetheless knows about world events, literature, and the classics. Given, as we shall see, the astounding surrealistic images that she imbeds in her prose writings, she is also gifted with words.[22] Even though we do not see how she acts in the *real* world (through the eyes of a third-person narrator), there is no doubt about the keen intellect she uses to capture those concrete aspects of life which, as Ilie puts it, serve as triggers to her obsessions with her ill-fated relationship with Eliacim.[23] In spite of Cela's warning against a hermeneutical reading of the novel, there is abiding curiosity about her first name, why she wrote in Spanish, and, for that matter, if her son understood the (Spanish) language she used in writing to him. In direct contrast to the formality that stems from knowing her as Mrs. Caldwell is the intimate I-thou point of departure of her chapters/letters to her primary narratee,

Eliacim, who, of course, never answers her, despite the barrage of questions she fires at him as if they were face to face.

These one-sided dialogues illustrate numerous juxtapositions: she is old and existentially alone, while the twentyish Eliacim had many friends of the opposite sex. While Eliacim traveled extensively on his training voyage (as we know from chap. 130 and the postcards he sent his mother from Gibraltar, Algiers, Naples, Alexandria, Port Said, Colombo, Singapore, Manila, and Hong Kong), yet Mrs. Caldwell only visited Spain, where, as we know, she met Cela. There is no indication of where she was from in England, even though her surname derives from "one who came from Caldwell, in Yorkshire" and has its etymological counterpart in *cold stream*.[24] The name Eliacim, on the other hand, evokes biblical affiliations; for one thing it suggests Eliakim, which in Hebrew signifies "the one who Yahweh raises up"; it also constitutes a variant of Joakim or Joacim, the king of Judah and priest of Jerusalem.[25] In the book of Isaiah (22:20–21), Eliaquim is referred to as the son of Helcias and the heir of the House of David. Even the Aegean Sea (in which Eliacim drowned) opens the door to the mythological background of *Mrs. Caldwell*.[26] Whereas these onomastic soundings are purely speculative, they nevertheless simmer beneath the surface and enrich the already diverse context that surrounds mother and son, subtly reinforcing Cela's "logic" in keeping this novel afloat in the sea of Mrs. Caldwell's disturbed mind.[27]

Mrs. Caldwell's discourse abounds in the most unexpected references to the flora and fauna of human existence and, as such, anchors it in a reality to which we are somehow able to relate.[28] This linkage with the material world thus permits her illusory meanderings to evolve and, as we shall see, eventually culminate in an exorcism of air, earth, fire, and water. Ironic, however, is the fact that her son is, of course, oblivious to his mother. Mrs. Caldwell writes with skilled control over what she says. Even though her prose is ostensibly surrealistic, she constrains her thoughts by means of traditional narrative devices that pique reader curiosity and encourage ongoing participation in the novel. In Cervantine fashion she interfaces her obsessive thoughts with brief stories about different characters. In this regard she infuses her narration with elements of the theater of the absurd by spontaneously introducing short dialogues between unknown characters (one example being the conversations between Rose and Patrick which appear in the chapter entitled "The Astronomy Student"). Similar scenes are also found in chapter 136 ("The White Rocks Beaten by the Sea"), in which fragmented verbal interchanges between an unnamed man and different women (Meg, Betsy, Nancy, Bel, Molly, Jinny, Kitty, Fan, and Maudlin) culminate in scenes of cruelty and violence. Notwithstanding their commonplace usage, these techniques reflect her disjointed, dehumanized perspective and, thus, serve to distract and mislead.

As is to be expected, Mrs. Caldwell's schismatic perception of reality permits her to frame her writings with visual motifs that constitute a thematics of violence, disintegration, and death. As early as the foreword, we are introduced to Cela's exotic friend the quail-castrator. Numerous examples of dismemberment are disseminated throughout the novel; to mention only a few, these include the ritualistic cutting of the Christmas turkey's neck; cousin Richard's neighbor who deserves to be dissected and put in the Municipal Museum; beheaded chrysanthemums and a stuffed hummingbird; men who dry flowers; and a plaster of paris replica of Eliacim's hand which his mother wishes she had. Similarly, Mrs. Caldwell also knows how to keep her reader(s) in suspense by abruptly truncating stories of provocative and emotional import, such as, for example, what happened to her on Tom Dickinson's farm, what became of the woman who adopted the little schoolboy whom Mrs. Caldwell herself wanted, how Joshua—the tailor—lost his leg, and so forth. As fiction, these stories are neither brought to conclusion, nor do they ever elucidate the particular obsession with which Mrs. Caldwell is dealing. Although they attest to Mrs. Caldwell's incoherence, they also identify her as a competent storyteller.

And so Mrs. Caldwell, in speaking to Eliacim about "la ausencia que preparo" (the absence I am preparing [183]), authors texts that from their very inception are deconstructive. Definitions are frequently negative, as she assures her son (in the chapter entitled "An Old-Time Tango") that "we are nobody . . . nobody, absolutely nobody" (*MC* 13). The tight control she has over her narration allows her to manipulate purposefully her states of mind in order to create the baffling ambiguities of the work. On one occasion (chap. 8) she even advises Eliacim that a little bit of confusion is a good thing. Her poetic credo is summed up in the words from "The Sea, a Sea, That Sea" (chap. 40): "all this is very vague, very imprecise. Perhaps what happens is that everything needs a name" (*MC* 37).[29] Since there is no true linear progression in her mind, she asks Eliacim (in chap. 3) to help her wind up a ball of yarn, to which he, of course, responds negatively. As if to retaliate, she reminds him of the *tapabocas* (muffler) she was going to make for him, one can imagine, not only to keep him warm from the cold winds of winter (according to her) but, more likely, to keep his mouth shut because what he says is too painful for. The symbolism achieves greater poignancy when she relates (in chap. 1) with glee the manner in which Eliacim one day anxiously approached her to say something that would make her laugh, only to be coldly *silenced* when she told him that her ears hurt and that she did not wish to listen to his tale.

The widening of the gaps in Mrs. Caldwell's account of her relationship with her son is directly proportional to the irony that dilutes the boundaries between fiction and reality. For this very reason one of her refrains tacitly underscores the distinction between truth and untruth. Her utterances in this regard are schizophrenic. In some instances she assures Eliacim that she is telling him the "truth and nothing but the truth" (*MC* 37), yet she also "swear[s] that . . . [she] is lying" (*MC* 33). She says that she does not "want to blame" him, declaring that "I make myself responsible for all your points of view, including the most inconsistent" (*MC* 80). Such radical posturing also takes on a lighter version as discerning comicality erupts in the listing of artifacts that Eliacim purchased as souvenirs of his training voyage: the pearl necklace is "made in Japan," the porcelain tea set that he purchased in Alexandria is "made in Germany," and the shawl and ivory box from Manila are also Japanese in origin (*MC* 107).

As Mrs. Caldwell dwells upon the confusion that characterizes everything she says about her relationship with Eliacim, the irony is more pervasive. Different circumstances provoke all kinds of admonitions from her. After speculating about what it would have been like to have had many children but to have loved only Eliacim, she says: "I don't want to insist on this point, for it would drive me crazy" (*MC* 95). A home visit from the doctor who sends her to the insane asylum causes her to wonder: "I don't know if I'm just imagining it, because at times I think they'll all end up driving me crazy" (*MC* 181). To Eliacim himself she insists: "Don't force me to explain too much what I prefer to leave vaguely veiled" (*MC* 114). In short, when confronted with so many contradictions, Cela's warning against reading in search of one particular "key" to this work takes on added significance.

Mrs. Caldwell's tottering between truth, ironic disclosures, and outright lies sets the tone for her document's self-consciousness. Somehow both she and the reader are aware that a creative process is at work: "If I had the power, Eliacim, a really strong power and not a fictitious one. . . . But I, my son, don't have any power; I, Eliacim, am nothing but a poor woman without any strength or power" (*MC* 134–35). She orchestrates every move. Sometimes she says she prefers to wait until the end to tell Eliacim something (like the scare that the mother-of-pearl snail shell gave her one night), and in other instances she flatly truncates her narration (by including, for example, allegorical stories such as the one about the boats that children alongside the riverbanks salute); on other occasions (at the end of chap. 93) she adroitly goes on to another topic. At another juncture in her discourse she makes a wry tongue-in-cheek comment about her words as textual artifice (chap. 156):

Everything we know, Eliacim, can be written on a not very large piece of blank paper. Drawing on the paper, with care to outline the strokes, the letters of the alphabet, and making the possible combinations with them, my son, one would get to put together two or three plays of Shakespeare and even of someone else. . . . The great literary works of the future, Eliacim, are asleep in blank paper, the great literary works which are still to be written. Sometimes I feel tempted to confront the blank paper, and begin to put down letters, one after another, to see what comes out. (*MC* 129)

Dichotomies of all types are the poles between which Mrs. Caldwell moves. Life confronts death, health is juxtaposed to illness, youth overshadows old age, truth is blurred by deceit, and hope is lost to despair. All these boundaries are crossed within the imaginary world that Mrs. Caldwell creates, in which her incestuous love distorts accepted versions of romantic love. Amid the confusion one Celian conflict, however, remains intact: women and men, their differences and similarities. Given this basic distinction, Mrs. Caldwell conceives of the most prosaic aspects of daily life in terms of male and female; for example, rum, soup, mining, top hats, and business are associated with men, while loneliness, tears, motherhood, and very little else have female counterparts. Rarely are men singled out according to their marital status, while women are commonly referred to as either unmarried or recently wed and young or old. Education is not seen favorably either, because it is precisely a dearth of "premarital education" (chap. 91) which contributes to the suffering that young girls have to endure in life (Adam and Eve are cited twice as the progenitors of all humankind's problems). It matters not that Mrs. Caldwell achieve fulfillment in her—real or imagined—affairs with other men. Under the best of circumstances—that is, in her dream of marrying Eliacim (chap. 204, "What a Funny Dream!")—disquieting tension persists between the sexes.[30]

The impact on the novel of these gender-based topics manifests itself in the last four chapters, that is, in the only real letters that Mrs. Caldwell wrote from the asylum to which she had been committed. Specifically, they have symbolic titles: "Air," "Earth," "Fire," and "Water," respectively. As she, literally, occupies the space provided her in the hospital, Mrs. Caldwell's existence becomes consumed with these materials, only the last of which she believes menacing. They constitute the four phases of her progressive dementia. Initially, the "strange purple-colored air" (*MC* 186) lulls her into quiet repose on her bed as she awaits Eliacim. Second, the mounds of earth that "fell from the mirror" provide her with ample space for planting "nard shoots" to remind her of dead children and form an enclosed space in which both Mrs. Caldwell and her son could, she believes, be entered in an infinite embrace (187).[31] Although she is fully aware that the fire (the third element) which consumes her room is infernal, she does not care because it caresses her body and spews forth the image of Eliacim, with hot "bent horns" (*MC* 188), crouched in a corner, his tail between his legs, and cheerily watching as she moves about in a frenzied dance of "dressing and undressing." Finally, with water coming in from all sides— ceiling, walls, floor, furniture, bed linens, and things on her dresser—she succumbs, saying that it is "something that I would like to keep away from me . . . something that I would like also to have kept away from you while there was still time" (*MC* 189).

It is no coincidence that the air, earth, fire, and water of Mrs. Caldwell's final days appear in alternating order, for they are traditionally classified as male (air and fire) and female (water and earth). By way of such an ordered finale the pivotal conflict of the novel and of Mrs. Caldwell's life struggle is brought full circle, never resolved in *real* terms yet fused together in the fictive confines of her imaginative insanity. This being the case, the quaternary plotting of the old woman's last days serves as the substructure of the novel, constituting a well-knit fabric whose visual counterpart is the blood-stained patchwork sheet she wants for a death shroud. In one way or another the artifacts, obsessions, and poetic images that constitute Mrs. Caldwell's frame of reference derive from one or more of these four life-giving elements, thereby constituting what Cirlot terms the primary coordinates of material and spiritual existence of the Western world.[32] Equally important is the symbolism of the sea and maternity in providing an appropriate site for Eliacim's final resting place. Ironically enough, he has metaphorically returned to his mother, and she, in allowing the water to engulf her at the end, finally embraces him forever. Water is, then, of utmost significance for Eliacim's death and his mother's loss: "immersion in water signifies the return to a preformal state, with its double meaning of death and dissolution, but also rebirth and new circulation, for immersion multiplies life's potential."[33]

Ilie asserts that *Mrs. Caldwell* invites a Freudian reading/interpretation.[34] It is also possible to see it as a repository of symbols, many of which are associated with the four previously mentioned elements. While these are too numerous and complex to analyze here, a few examples suffice to make the point. Besides the water that amounts to the mainstay of the story line by way of Eliacim's death by drowning, there are countless aquatic motifs.[35] These include the resort where Mrs. Caldwell, like other newlyweds, would have enjoyed spending time with her son; references to swimming classes (chap. 93), swimming pools, fountains, Uncle Albert's collection of rivers, the peculiar allegory of "River Navigation" (chap. 120), and the surrealistic "fish without [s]cales" (chap. 174) which she brings home one day for Eliacim; there are stories of drowning children, as well as theme-related titles (two versions of "Persistent Rain on the Panes" [chaps. 14 and 14 *bis*.], "Water in the Fountain" [chap. 72], and "The Broken Fountain").[36] Associated with air are flying insects and birds (pigeons), clouds, balloons, astronomy, the town's bronze bell, whose sounds float "over the mountains" (*MC* 134), and the sport of fencing (chap. 95), which lends concreteness to the air through which its athletes seem to cut to make their mark. Fire is made manifest in various ways: the strange recollection of Swedish matches (chap. 185) which she would like to have given Eliacim by the boatload, the oil lamps (that exteriorize Mrs. Caldwell's longing for times past [chap. 122]), and the fireplace (and its smoldering embers) next to which she sits to write her epistolary messages to her son.[37]

Last, it is with earth that we find the most connections, since, after all, Mrs. Caldwell, is *on earth.* For this reason growing things abound; for example, plants (tobacco, cacti, nard, the maiden-hair fern to whose tenderness Eliacim is compared), flowers, fruit (especially those produced in tropical climates), wine, and beer. Fauna includes cattle, horses (that automatically come to mind with the riding classes that Mrs. Caldwell would like to take [chap. 94]), and the often-cited stuffed deer head that hangs in her house. Earthbound motifs are common: burials, desert sands (upon which Mrs. Caldwell imagined making passionate love to her son), an hourglass, a seismograph, and Tom Dickinson's farm, where Mrs. Caldwell says she spent three days. Significant, too, is the forgotten garden that was close to Mrs. Caldwell's house (as a child), where children would often get lost.[38] Finally, there are also objects that have a connection to all four elements. Among others these include the—yet to be invented—supercompass over which Mrs. Caldwell rejoices because Eliacim will not be able to go into a shop to buy one; snow dirtied by traffic and city life; and the often-cited iceberg that gives its name to the chapter in which it is found (*MC* 178), providing an opportunity for Mrs. Caldwell to write a poem with all the semantic combinations she can make with the first line of the chapter: "sailing without compass, the iceberg flies, with you on / top, at an incredible speed" (*MC* 150).

These extensions of air, water, fire, and earth are accompanied by a constellation of chapters that relate to one or more of the five senses, among which are, for example, "Cherimoyas with Kümel" (chap. 19), "Vegetarian Cuisine" (chap. 75), "Tropical Fruits" (chap. 84), "Cooked Crayfish" (chap. 101), "Wine and Beer" (chap. 102), and "Honey" (chap. 181), not to mention the olfactorily provocative "Havana Cigars" (chap. 10). Sight motifs are everywhere and materialize into the elaborate visual imagery of Mrs. Caldwell's tireless poetic points of departure and also as subthemes that revolve around eyes, eyesight, and blindness. Mrs. Caldwell is insistent upon calling to mind her son's eyes and the way he used to look at her; she imagines them painted on the prow of the "flat river boats" of chapter 120 ("River Navigations"), and, in the third segment of the same chapter, she laments the creature (most probably a child) that she "smothered . . . against [her] lap," threw overboard without having closed its eyes, and whose glance continues to "pierce . . . [her] eyes insistently" (*MC* 97). Her fetishes include caressing her face with Eliacim's sunglasses, a practice that stopped when she lost them on a bus. In yet another demonstration of her use of understatement (which is lost in translation), a parenthetical comment to her son (about how fate separated them) is inventively ironic in its play on words, which are further displays, and subversions, of sight images: *Está **visto**, Eliacim, bien **visto** ya que todo fuerza y lucha por separarnos* (*MC* 91; emphasis added).[39] While Eliacim's use of sunglasses is undoubtedly in keeping with the social taboo of his mother's love for him as well as his ambiguous role in their relationship, it is also in line with the blindness that results from hatred and hypocrisy: "the meek, son, the resigned, the silent, keep in their hearts the intact little bags of hatred, the stored reserves of the hatred with which they dream of blinding us one day" (*MC* 59).

Music such as Viennese waltzes, whistled tunes, accordions and harps, is heard amid the tactile stimuli that spring forth from the mention of statues, soft lingerie, rocks against which the surf clashes, and crystal and china, to name but a few. As a backdrop to this plethora of earth, wind, fire, and sensory provocation is a palette of chromaticity. Reminiscent of Miró's paintings, one catches glimpses of green hats, garnet curtains, blue fur-lined slippers, black silk women's undergarments, and mother-of-pearl shells. Given that Mrs. Caldwell is a woman whose imagination is afire with sensory stimulation, it makes perfect sense that she chides her son for not having given in to his "certain inclination toward" sybaritism, for, after all: "the sybarite, Eliacim . . . [is] one who conforms to everything . . . despite what might appear to people who are not attentive to this problem" (*MC* 159).

By virtue of their titles, some segments of the novel make reference to one of the four elements either directly (as in "That Accursed Air Which Sleeps among the Houses" [chap. 145]) or indirectly ("On Foot? On Horseback? By Bicycle? By Stagecoach? By Car? On Board a Luxurious Transatlantic Steamer? On the Train? By Plane?" [chap. 56]). Other chapter headings, while fewer in number, are more to the point in terms of themes. In a manner similar to that of the quaternary foundation of the novel, the themes such as love, family, loneliness, and death which are most striking often give way to different aspects of contemporary Western life. In such chapters as "Family Life" (chap. 110) and "People Walking on the Street" (chap. 197), for example, sharp cynicism resounds concerning socially accepted norms for traditional family life: "proper names and surnames inherited from their fathers" are silly (*MC* 170), and "family life" in general is "the drug that makes families stupid" (*MC* 86). Other chapters ("The Oldest Tree in the City" [chap. 164] and "The Embers of the Hearth" [chap. 170]) address commonplaces of existentialism—namely, the passage of time, loneliness, and loss. Hypocrisy and deceit are sanctioned on numerous occasions: in the articles that Eliacim bought during his travels, the five-part chapter entitled "River Navigation" (chap. 120), "the Well-Matched Married Couple" (chap. 199), and, most important, Mrs. Caldwell's farcical marriage. Poverty is projected against hungry and homeless children and charitable raffles that cruelly spark the flames of hope. "Marriage is dirty and impure . . . [and] kills love, or at least, wounds it gravely" (*MC* 67). Conformity is criticized in "The Bread We Eat" (chap. 186), and social commentary (similar to *The Hive*) is found in chapter 197:

> The people who pass in the street, Eliacim, the sorrowful, numb people who pass in the street, my dear, with their malnutritions, their tubercular lesions, their frustrated loves, their never-fulfilled cravings, etc., walk along sowing stupidity and resignation over the evil-smelling little shops, and the calm brothels of the suburbs, a little bit with the unconfessed hope that death will catch them with their boots on, like the vagrant who made of his boot the tremulous flesh of his foot. (*MC* 170)

Given Mrs. Caldwell's alienated perception of the world, Foster's characterization of the novel in the French tradition of the 1950s is particularly astute.[40]

Because she is immersed in total isolation and deteriorating mental capacities, Mrs. Caldwell's outlook is racked with bitterness and despair. The references she makes to war remind us that in 1953—and during the five years that it took Cela to write this novel—England was still in the aftermath of World War II. It follows, then, that her discourse has been termed "surrealistic," for it runs parallel to her state of mind and being. Not only has she borne the tragedy of losing her beloved son at sea for reasons that are never disclosed, but she must also face the reality of her unrequited love. If Eliacim were as cold to her as she infers, as devastating must have been the ostracism she faced in the middle-class English society in which she lived, as evidenced in the refrain-like comment she mutters (over the last four chapters) about her "best friends" who still have not fulfilled their promise to visit her.[41] Her only reaction is a grotesque display of violent images of stepping on broken glass, plucking out eyes, poisoning, bestiality, and skulls crawling with worms. Her dreams are equally bizarre: a burning child (chap. 162) and her metamorphosis into "an eyeless pigeon" (*MC* 184) who laid "a little, round, rosy egg."[42]

Mrs. Caldwell's prose is tempestuously provocative in the face of being playfully ludicrous. It elicits a range of emotions from its readers, not the least of which are confusion, repulsion, and empathy. Depending upon the intensity of the participation in the novel, one experiences varying degrees of perplexity, frustration, anger, bewilderment, and alienation. Given these reactions, it is easy to understand why the Englishwoman, as literary creation, was an unwelcomed guest in Franco's fanatically closed Catholic society of the 1950s.

It is a well-known fact that *Mrs. Caldwell* was not well received in Spain. Just as curious are Mrs. Caldwell's two scant observations about the country she is visiting at the time that (the fictive) Cela first makes her acquaintance in Pastrana. In speaking of maternal love, she says that, "in far-off Spain, mothers bite their sons on the neck, drawing blood, to demonstrate their tenacious, unchanging love," information she received twice removed (from a Bible salesman named Mr. Burrows, who, in turn, heard it from Mrs. Perkins, a woman who poisoned her husband with nitric acid). In the next chapter, "I Love the Spanish Deck," she expresses her preference for Spanish playing cards because they are "more poetic . . . [and] an inexhaustible hatchery of suggestion . . . [where] the deepest veins of the nape of the neck perspire with a delightful and exceedingly fine perspiration . . . that only the elite are usually aware of." Mrs. Caldwell—and not Eliacim, who "never felt any great attraction for the Spanish deck" (*MC* 41)—is in awe of Spain's exotic expression of passion, the same emotion that could well have motivated Cela to bestow upon his British (anti)heroine the gift of writing/speaking in Cervantes's native language.

CHAPTER 5

San Camilo, 1936

San Camilo, 1936, Víspera, festividad y octava de San Camilo del año 1936 en Madrid (1969; San Camilo, The Eve, Feast, and Octave of St. Camillus of the Year 1936 in Madrid), or, as it is more commonly known, *San Camilo, 1936,* is the first novel in which Cela confronts the topic of the Spanish Civil War. Because of the experimentation with novelistic technique which differentiates it from his previous longer works of prose fiction, it marks a significant juncture in his career as a novelist.[1] In a book written in 1991 by a fellow Spaniard and journalist in homage to Cela for having been awarded the Nobel Prize for literature, Luis Blanco Vila declares that Cela changed forever after writing *San Camilo, 1936.*[2] While Cela's earlier novels, specifically *Pascual Duarte* and *The Hive,* continue to generate scholarly debate, *San Camilo, 1936* (particularly right after it was published in 1969) engendered an emotionally charged polemic about the author's political stand with regard to the Civil War and the licentious milieu that frames the novel.[3] In an effort to grasp the difficulties of the mildly schizophrenic (technical) format of the novel, critics have labeled it everything from historical and testimonial to mythical and structural.[4] Cela has said on numerous occasions that *San Camilo, 1936* is a novel immersed *in* the Civil War rather than one written *about* it. In 1976 he told Edmond Vandercammen that he had conceived of his work as "a fresco" of the anguish and insanity of a group of men who knew nothing about what was happening on 18 July 1936, when the war officially began.[5] His former secretary, Juan Benito Argüelles, recalls the genesis of this novel, saying that it was the only time that he had seen Cela compose a novel on the typewriter,[6] adding further that he asked Argüelles to move into a different office because he (Cela) was not able to write at the thought of somebody looking at him.

Reminiscent of *The Hive*'s teeming masses, *San Camilo, 1936* abounds in three hundred pages of historically real and fictitious characters who mill about Madrid in the days immediately preceding and following 18 July, the day on which, ironically, St. Camillus of Lelis is venerated in the Catholic Church as the patron saint of hospitals.[7] As has been observed by many critics, the bizarre use of punctuation marks enhances the challenge that Cela always poses for the reader. The *párrafos-río* (river-paragraphs) of which Maryse Bertrand de Muñoz speaks are as common as the sentences that go on for pages with only commas to indicate brief, transitional pauses.[8] On a technical level the *esperpento* is a primary point of departure for the stream of consciousness of the anonymous, twenty-something-year-old narrator who refers to the "droll and grotesque air" of incidents that take place around him (*SC* 140).[9]

Proceeding along a primary axis circumscribed by a tensely unstable, political undercurrent, the story deals with what happens to the characters—including the unnamed narrator—whom we get to know during three days that culminate on 18 July 1936. Cela's stance in *San Camilo, 1936* is purposefully nonhistorical and piercingly sarcastic.[10] The narrator, exasperated by history's "heartless cunning" (*SC* 273), declares on numerous occasions that it is useless to keep an accurate account of people, places, and dates; he says that "historical figures must be seen from a distance" (*SC* 108), an assertion more befitting the 1969 Cela than the 1936 anonymous narrator.[11] The narrative discourse is, therefore, an ebb and flow of second-person monologue and third-person narration.[12] The novel opens with a relatively objective observation that almost immediately turns upon itself in direct address, assuming the dialogic coordinates along which it develops:

A man sees himself in the mirror and even feels comfortable addressing himself in a familiar way, the mirror has no frame, it neither begins nor ends, or yes, it does have a splendid frame gilded with patience and with gold leaf but the quality of its pane is not good . . . maybe what's happening is that it reflects the astonished face of a dead man still masked with the mask of the fear of death, it's probable that you are dead and don't know it, the dead are also unaware of being dead, they don't know anything at all. A man examines his conscience and nothing becomes any clearer, no, you are not Napoleon Bonaparte, neither are you King Cyril of England [.] (*SC* 3)

As the primary structuring motif for the novel, the mirror is the symbolic thematic counterpart of thirty years of reflection, something the narrator calls a "recapitulation" (*recapitular* [to recapitulate, take stock of]). Being one of the significant common threads of the novel, the looking glass is strategically positioned at the beginning of five of the novel's ten chapters. As if to provide the reader with an immediate mirror-like representation of the "realities" of the story, Cela included his photograph opposite the title page of the first edition of the novel, labeling it "Camilo José Cela in 1936."[13] For this reason many critics have described *San Camilo, 1936* as an autobiographical catharsis of Cela's part in the Civil War and the postwar period during which the Francoist regime was positioning itself as the sole arbiter of Spanish life (and politics) for the next three decades. Such obvious parallels aside, Cela made a point of disassociating the narrator from real life by including among the narrator's buddies a character named Camilo José Cela, who was an unpublished poet.[14]

Cela's 1969 novel about his country's Civil War has the same structural underpinnings as *El carro de heno o el inventor de la guillotina* (The Haywain or the Inventor of the Guillotine), a play written in 1968 by Cela.[15] *San Camilo, 1936* is a triptych with an epilogue that doubles as a monologue by the narrator's favorite uncle Jerónimo (Jerome/Hieronymus), a Krause intellectual reminiscent of Andrés Hurtado's uncle Iturrioz in Baroja's novel, *El árbol de la ciencia,* 1911 (The Tree of Knowledge).[16] Parts 1 and 3 are each divided into four chapters and, respectively, portray the day before and the octave following the outbreak of the war. Entitled "St. Camillus' Day," the second part of the novel is undivided and stands at the core of the historic events.[17] Each part of the novel begins with an epigraph that highlights the bellicose nature of Spanish history, none more poignant, however, than the dedication itself: "To the conscripts of 1937, all of whom lost something: their life, their freedom, their dreams, their hopes, their decency. And not to the adventurers from abroad, Fascists and Marxists, who had their fill of killing Spaniards like rabbits and whom no one had invited to take part in our funeral."[18] Each segment and all of the subdivided chapters resonate with refrains (such as *no la mates* [don't kill her] and *huele a gato muerto* [it smells of dead cat]) and motifs such as, for example, radio transmissions and references to the Montaña Barracks, which, as we shall see, encapsulate the development of the story as well as the tone and theme of the novel.

Thus organized, the narration originates in a young Spaniard who is searchingly looking into a mirror, the object that (in accord with Herzberger's assessment of its seminal importance) progressively metamorphoses from flat to parallelepiped to ovoid/spherical to a bloody jellyfish. More significant are the narrator's own doubts concerning whether or not it ever really existed, speculating further on the applicability of Max Planck's "theory of wave mechanics" to mirrors that are normally found in whorehouses (*SC* 278). Given the narrator's negative self-appraisal, his first-person discourse results in a cerebral disclosure that reflects a parallel distortion of reality. At one point—and on the day of the outbreak of the war—he admits that perspective has been lost and sarcastically states that the day will probably be remembered as a *[s]ancamilada* (*SC* 141), given history's propensity for affixing the-*ada* suffix in an effort to trivialize it.

The narrator's obsessive and desperate self-searching matches in large measure the undercurrent of refrains that constitute the novel's rhythmic cadence—hence, the impetus for his journey of self-understanding and forgiveness.[19] He defines himself as the assassin who he could become and the men who he is not: Napoléon, King Cyril of England, Buffalo Bill, St. Paul, and the "Cid." Despite his psychological alienation from the rest of humanity, he recognizes that he is every Spaniard, a realization that allows him to incorporate into his own schizophrenic narrative odyssey the other story line: decontextualized people, places, and things; sentence and conversation fragments; opinions and social commentary; and someone else's sketchy third-person observations about what is occurring in Madrid in July 1936. With few exceptions he suppresses most anecdotal fillers. The familiar sense of simultaneity which Cela controlled so well in *The Hive* accelerates so much here that it forces total abandonment of narrative control, as what the narrator is saying ends with the suppression of punctuation marks and in the middle of a word: "you are not Napoleon Bonaparte but neither are you King Cyril of England cut off your right hand before it is too late the destiny of tools is very bitter very bitter very bi" (*SC* 167).[20]

We learn that this self-conscious narrator has numerous preoccupations: girlfriends and prostitutes, decisions about school and future life plans, and, of course, the increasing political tensions in Madrid. References point also to Cela's life in prewar Spain: his girlfriend Toisha (aka Tránsito), his acquaintance with Pedro Salinas, questions about life and self-worth, and an avid interest in writing. At the onset of his self-scrutiny in the mirror the narrator does not see the Celian motif of the "star on his forehead" which would have distinguished him from everyone else: "you are fodder for the catechism class, fodder for the brothel, you are cannon fodder, you are the unknown soldier, the man on whose forehead no little star shines, men who are meat for the gallows are usually more self-assured" (*SC* 4). He knows, nonetheless, that he is "being allowed to live . . . and . . . to sum things up, above all to sum things up" (*SC* 5), an awareness that legitimizes his compulsion to provide written testimony of his perception of what is going on around him.[21] He tells himself he is only obliged to write about what he knows (rather than invent confusing stories [*SC* 20]). On the other hand, he realizes that a risk of writing from memory could result in turning things into novels, something he refuses to do. At first he insists that he is only "writing to God" about the events taking place on earth (*SC* 18); however, once the civil disturbances turn into war, he bitterly reproaches himself for naively having thought that God cared about the human condition when, in (his) reality, he is certain that the opposite is true.

Taking its cue from the growing political unrest in Madrid, his poetics of writing solidifies as he faces himself in the mirror: his duty is to "spit words out of [his] . . . mouth, strip [himself] . . . of words, wash [himself] . . . of words" (*SC* 68). Gazing at the skinny, tubercular figure that is reflected back at him in the mirror, he admonishes himself not to "[miss] a single one of [his] . . . last moments, take precise note of every detail, make use of an efficient notarial prose," so that he can learn "algebra" in order to express his agony and to "form a sporting idea of death" (*SC* 175).[22] In (slightly) more objective contexts he makes generic comments on novels themselves, all of which are applicable to *San Camilo, 1936.* As if to defend the scatological and what many critics term censurable aspects of his novel, Cela's narrator says that "it doesn't seem as though anybody sleeps during a revolution, that doesn't make sense but that's the way it is, in a novel nobody pisses or shits either and everybody thinks it's perfectly natural and asks no questions" (*SC* 189). Referring to the bloody assault on the Montaña Barracks, the narrator speaks of the "moving little novel" that each dead person carries close to his heart (*SC* 206). And, in so doing, he equates the novel with war and death. When coupled with comments about how confused he gets with people's names and the phrases he uses to transcribe the disjointed conversations, speeches, and pronouncements that are heard all over Madrid, it becomes apparent that his *writerly obligations* are motivated by those exterior events that strike the dissonant chord that impels him to continue his own inward journey. The more violent the situation becomes on a national level, the more he incorporates details of people's depraved behavior, commenting that "this crowded and endless parade is not easy to understand" (*SC* 256).

The momentum that is proportional to the growing tensions in the novel is also suggestive of the previously mentioned structural similarity with Cela's play *El carro de heno,* which is dedicated to Hieronymus Bosch and whose title imitates the Dutch painter's triptych of a hay-bearing cart (moving from earth to hell). Similar maneuvering occurs at all levels of *San Camilo, 1936.* The first part of the novel moves to the beat of the events that surround the deaths of the two prominent figures whose assassinations exacerbated the events leading to 18 July 1936.[23] Specifically, the deaths of the young Republican lieutenant of the Assault Guard, José Castillo, and the right-wing Calvo Sotelo, deputy of the Alfonsist monarchist party Renovación Española, occurred respectively on 12 and 13 July 1936. Added to the high-profile list of murders is also the foul-smelling prostitute Magdalena, whose death completes the tripartite funeral processions that usher in the second part of the novel and the outbreak of the war.

Moving in and out of his self-conscious monologue, the narrator embellishes it with incidents and names of people whose primary Saturday night activities find them in their favorite houses of prostitution. So numerous are these characters that the capital of the country is perceived as a single hyperbolic house of ill repute. Further denigration follows, as mention is made of all the individuals who have met violent deaths (throughout the first segment of the novel): prostitutes like la Chelo (who killed herself by drinking bleach), drunkards, the drowned Asterín, and Juanita Rico Hernández (a friend of Engracia, a young Republican militant who appears later in the novel). The depths of repulsion are sounded by reference to fetuses found in the toilets of the Pleyel movie theater. Everything proceeds like a resounding funeral dirge as the officiating narrator proclaims a metropolitan "ubi sunt?": "the city is like a dog, it turns around and around before getting to sleep, and also like a hare that sleeps with its eyes open to see whether it's got to run away, sometimes you think cities can run away and obliterate themselves, where's the city?" (*SC* 59). Because Madrid is awash with death, pesky flies swarm about, most commonly turning up drowning in the cups of coffee which metonymically represent "almost all of Spain [which] is sitting in the café and waiting" (*SC* 70).

Printed messages bombard the reader and city dweller alike. There are advertisements of products for the prevention and treatment of balding and Ladillol to get rid of crabs. One prostitute, Aixa la Mora, has "Vivre libre ou morir" (Live free or die [*SC* 51]) tattooed around her naval, while references to traditional historical note taking are dismissed as unreliable and insignificant.[24] Unmistakable, too, are other forms of dispatch such as the biting social commentaries that relentlessly assault the first portion of the narrative text. Sometimes the result of the narrator's direct observations, the harangues are more closely associated with conversations that characters have in various circumstances throughout the novel. Among the most memorable are the following: Don Cesáreo and Román Navarro's opinions about "this business of tearing poor helpless girls from the arms and the protection of selfless holy women like the Sisters of Charity" (*SC* 30); the Luna clinic's two different rates (according to economic status) for services rendered; Engracia's foolhardy dream "of a Spain of strong and chubby children, of a Spain without illiterates or unemployed workers or exploiters" (*SC* 37); the place where Paca and Fidel live, near the cemetery and Abroñigal creek, where "dour rats trot shyly and rapidly always escaping from something, and the mice . . . look at the scene of their domestic adventures with their lively little eyes" (*SC* 95); Tudescos Street as a place where "they stab a whore to death . . . at least twenty times . . . there are plenty of whores and besides crimes of passion don't count or don't count for much" (*SC* 61); and Virgilio and Roque Zamora's pitiful nightly routine:

"[Virgilio] brings a little container of stew or some other dish to eat late at night, he heats it a little on an alcohol burner and enjoys his meal, Roque Zamora knows that when he arrives in the morning a container with a little sauce and half a roll will be waiting for him on the shelf over the basin in the men's room" (*SC* 188).

As if in step with the funeral entourage of the first part of the novel, characters emerge in bipartite fashion and in syncopation with death's three-beat movement. Things fit into twos and threes as names become more recognizable in pairs: the brothers Olegario and Cándido; the two *tísicas* (consumptives) Juani y Lupita; Soledad's two daughters, Solita and Conchita (both of whom have been impregnated by Rogelio); María Victoria's brothers, Felipe and Alberto; Leopoldo's two cousins who became priests; and so forth. Most obvious, of course, are the married and otherwise amorously involved couples: the pregnant Virtudes and husband Victoriano; Don Roque and Teresa; Sánchez Somoza and his unfaithful wife, Clarita; the homosexual Matiítas and the prostitute Aixa la Mora; Joaquín and his wife-turned-prostitute, Margot; Don León and Matilde; the news reporter Jesualdo and Enriqueta; the student-activist Engracia and boyfriend Agustín; the narrator and Toisha; and the list goes on. Nicknames and aliases highlight the dualities, the narrator's reflection in the mirror, and, of course, the Camilo José Cela of the photograph (of the first edition of the novel) and the character of the same name, who is a friend of the narrator.

Initial consternation with decontextualized names and truncated conversations gives way to a degree of familiarity which in turn creates, as in *The Hive,* a suspenseful curiosity concerning these people, complicating the narrative movement of sporadic yet tightly controlled dissemination of information about these people and the murders of Calvo Sotelo and Colonel Castillo. On the one hand, the reader is curious about the political front as growing tensions surround the rumors of a military uprising.[25] There is also natural inquisitiveness about when Virtudes will give birth, what role Engracia will play in the military uprising, where the right-wing Don Roque will take refuge in Republican Madrid once the revolution begins and he has to flee Doña Teresa's boardinghouse precisely when they announce their engagement, and so forth. Other, more picaresque couples occupy our attention, yet their peculiar situations are never resolved because information about them is never provided: Clarita and her lover, Raúl Taboada (who were given baths of scalding chocolate by her husband when he found them together); and Margot and the two children she abandoned to her husband, Joaquín, in making her decision to become a prostitute and stay in Madrid. A further source of tension is the narrator's self-absorption. Forming a cohesive unit, these levels of interest follow the three principal directions of the discourse—that is, pure fiction, history, and narration—leading the reader through an otherwise impenetrable, hallucinatory labyrinth.

And so, as the two political figures are laid to rest with accompanying rituals and rhetoric, the prostitute Magdalena goes unnoticed to her final resting place, a common grave where she will commune with other undesirables while Madrid goes about its business, ignorant of the impact the military revolt will have on the lives of its citizens. Joining in this slow-motion dance of death, which is played against the tide of people who find it difficult to sleep that Saturday night, is the punctilious appearance of the ragpickers, milkmen, bakers, tramway employees, hosemen, road sweepers, *churro* sellers, and chirping of early-morning birds who signal the dawn of the infamous Sunday morning that explodes in the second part of the novel.

Even though the narrator's watch has stopped working and Antonio Arévalo tries to shoot down the ball of the ministry clock (at the end of the first chapter of pt. 3), constant attention is paid (in the second part) to clock time as people awake to the sound of radio transmissions about the news of the military uprising in Morocco. Numerous dual perspectives color the manner in which events are retold, such as those afforded by the eyewitness Miguel Mercader and the narrator concerning the incidents surrounding Colonel Castillo's assassination; in addition, we hear a chorus of interrupted, disjointed conversations between two (or more) people in their favorite bars, casinos, restaurants, and so forth. This gives way to the events of 18 July as they blend into a symphonic simultaneity of radio announcements and fragmentary rhetoric-laden discourses, serving, in Camayd Freixas's words, as a veritable "heteroglossia" of linguistic sign systems and perspectives.[26] These speechlike pronouncements become audible focal points of the places in which people routinely congregate: whorehouses, movie theaters, bars, boardinghouses, military barracks, private houses, and the mortuary. Fragments of military tactical strategies are associated with the names of key figures, such as Casares Quiroga (the prime minister of the Republican Left) and leading generals such as Franco, Queipo de Llano, and Fanjul. Even the masses are heard shouting "weaPONS, weaPONS, weaPONS . . . !" as news of the uprising reaches the mainland (*SC* 150).

Individual deaths continue to counterbalance the more than one million Spaniards who died in the Civil War. Juanita Rico Hernández's seemingly unimportant murder and the narrator's mention of King Cyril's demise close the first part of the novel only to have the following segment commence with the reminder of a 14 April car wreck that resulted in the death of Doña Matilde, Don León's wife and the mother of Dámaso Rioja, one of the narrator's good friends.[27] Death beckons life as Virtudes's pregnancy becomes a source of concern, given the escalating street chaos that she and her husband survey from their balcony before retiring on that Sunday night.

Virtudes's expected child also possesses a threefold significance: in heightening the reader's curiosity about what will happen to her, it holds a symbolic show of hope—the birth of a child—amid so much destruction. It also helps to accelerate the technical advance of the action and exacerbates the latent grotesqueness of civil wars. By the time the third segment of the novel begins, Victoriano is confused for the enemy and shot in the back as he runs to get help for his wife (chap. 1). Virtudes gives birth by herself and is discovered by the neighbor Doña Jesusa who is sent to find Virtudes's mother, the madame named Sacramento (chap. 2); her stillborn baby girl is wrapped in the pages of the magazine *Blanco y negro* (White and Black) and given over by her grandmother to the flames of the kitchen stove (chap. 3); finally, the new mother dies herself of puerperal fever, while Doña Sacramento frantically runs from one pharmacy to another in search of "corrosive sublimate . . . and permanganate" (*SC* 233), simply to be referred, ironically, to a house of prostitution, where such supplies might be found.

Virtudes is not, however, the only private citizen to undergo an ordeal. Alongside her are the thousands of others who are caught in Madrid at the time of the uprising. Among these are the soldiers in the Montaña Barracks, many of whom are the friends of the narrator. As they die in the assault, his own sense of cowardice and abnegation grows. Engracia dies defending the Republican cause, Andrés and his girlfriend are shot dead, and the narrator's friend Guillermo Zabalegui's cadaver is identified and claimed by his strong-willed aunt Mimí.

There remains the unsung victim Matiítas, the homosexual whose death is attended only by the reader and the navel-embossed prostitute Aixa la Mora. For all of Matiítas's insipidity, his death is perhaps the most chilling: in utter desperation in his attic apartment and with the Tangerine prostitute present, he positioned a newly acquired rifle in such way as to kill himself with one muffled, anal shot.[28] His body was discovered days later because of the odor of putrification which is pulsatingly repeated throughout chapter 4: "There must be a dead cat in the attic, it stinks to high heaven, how about you going up to the attic? yes ma'am, there must be a dead cat, it smells dead, and I didn't even notice it!" (*SC* 254). In typical Celian parlance, although we never see anybody discover the fly-infested cadaver, we are told in bitter tongue-in-cheek fashion that the only other witnesses to Matiìas's death were the pictures (of professional boxers and his mother in her wedding dress) which hung on the wall of his dingy cubicle.

Nowhere in the novel is the tragedy of civil war brought home so convincingly as in the pathos of Matiítas's insignificance as an agent of fictive and social change. Here is a man who dreams of not being homosexual, who regularly reads to his blind uncle, and who suffers emotional and physical abuse at the hands of partners such as Don Fausto. When the uprising begins on the streets of Madrid and arms are finally distributed by the Republican government to the people, Matiítas finds himself suddenly in possession of a weapon with which he does not know what to do yet something that will confer him with masculinity. By virtue of his need for sexual fulfillment, he is no different from the "upstanding" citizens who are familiar faces in the thriving brothels of the nation's capital. Matiítas is a totally alienated everyman who falls victim to the machinations of this particular moment in history. He is the anonymous Spaniard who gets caught in the crossfire and who does not know enough to escape like the narrator (who gets away by withdrawing inside himself) and the others who flee Madrid for Valencia. The poignant method of his self-destruction literally expelled his inner self for the entire world to see: "Matiítas is lying on his bed naked and dying . . . the bullet came out his belly, the blood is pouring out his belly and his ass and a sad drop of viscous semen is hanging from his penis" (*SC* 224). On a more sublime level he epitomizes Madrid, as comment is made that "in the attics of Madrid there must be many dead cats, dozens, hundreds of dead cats" (*SC* 276).

The narrator, on the other hand, interiorizes his outer self through a sophisticated means of self-destruction which, however, never leads to total annihilation. And therein lies the desperation that obsessively haunts him as he experiences the changes, symbolic breakage, and subsequent metamorphosis of his particular instrument of torture, the mirror. While Matiítas's weapon obviously leads to his death, the narrator's mirror "tool" *(herramienta)* becomes a vehicle for creativity, as he listens to his uncle Jerome tell him, at the end of the novel, that their present time is not the apocalyptic end of the world at which time "the sun, instead of rising from the horizon, will rise from the bitter mirrors of wakes, from mirrors tired of portraying the trembling funeral candles of useless disconsolateness" (*SC* 290).[29] His words provide the nephew with an imprimatur for his poetics of writing, which, however annoyingly fragmented, remains nevertheless a mimetic, albeit distorted, representation of life.

For all practical purposes the sermonesque epilogue of *San Camilo, 1936* is out of character in the novel. It is also bothersome in terms of what some critics have pointed to as the "make love not war" lesson that Jerome preaches to his nephew. On the other hand, it purposefully caps off the tridimensional superstructure of the novel. By anchoring itself in the "three . . . battered theological virtues" of faith, hope, and charity to which the narrator tries to cling in his last encounter in the mirror (*SC* 279), Jerome's "sermon" amounts to (as José Homero summarily puts it) a paraphrased version of "but the greatest of these is charity,"[30] as the nephew is advised to go out, meet Basilia—the daughter of Cecilia, his uncle's paramour—and "love . . . like athletic puppies" (*SC* 287).

oficio de tinieblas 5

The critics who have studied the novel *oficio de tinieblas 5,* 1973 (service of darkness 5)[1] disagree about its literary merit and the identity of the second-person *tú* (you) narrative voice. All seem, however, to be in agreement concerning two things: its use of sexual license as a metaphor for freedom from societal oppression and its significance as a symbol of the crisis of twentieth-century life which has now become, many years since *oficio* was published, commonplace in discussions about the end of the millenium. Despite its recognizably Celian attributes, *oficio* is unlike anything else Cela has written, a fact that supports his disclaimer that, "naturally, this is not a novel but rather the purge of my heart" (*odt* 7).

oficio is composed of 1,194 segments called *mónadas* (monads), an intentional borrowing from Leibniz to refer to the simplest, indivisible units of living things. When used by Cela, the monads resemble stanzas of poetry which either alternate with other monads, are grouped together thematically, or serve (e.g., like m. 6) as framing devices for ensuing monads. Except for occasional commas and numerous semicolons and the three ellipsis points with which it begins, the novel is devoid of punctuation marks. It is written entirely in lower-case letters and is divided numerically (arabic numerals), some monads as short as one line and others extending for three pages. At times they represent sequential blocks of quasi-anecdotal nuclei, but in general they are annoyingly incoherent.

Written between 1971 and 1973, *oficio* is the narrative counterpart of Cela's two previously mentioned surrealistic dramatic works, which clearly lay the groundwork for what Darío Villanueva judged to be one of Cela's most hermetic works. In those plays everything centers around public executions as a way of demonstrating the public's insatiable thirst for blood. This, in turn, creates emotionally charged scenarios that permit the incorporation of quasiclassical choruses that, in themselves, manifest society's complicity in twentieth-century human depersonalization, a theme that surfaces with unparalleled vengeance in the novel.[2] From this decisive turning point in his writing spring forth related themes that occupy a place of seminal importance in *oficio*—namely, history as fiction, man's inhumanity to man, and the legacy of Adam and Eve. The literary corollary that accentuates the morbidity of his disillusionment is, of course, the death of literature and the duplicitousness of words as mere verbal icons, realizing that "truth does not nest in words it agonizes in words and dies with them better yet truth does not live anywhere not even in silence" (m. 902).

The full title of *oficio* consists of sixteen lines of bold-faced text which read as follow:

office of darkness 5 or thesis novel written in order to be sung by a chorus of sick people as the adornment of the liturgy with which is celebrated the triumph of the blessed and the circumstances of the bliss as follows: the torture of saint theodora the martyrdom of saint venantius the exile of saint macarius the solitude of saint hugh whose passing took place beneath a shower of abject smiles of gratitude and is commemorated on the first day of april[.] (*odt* 5)

It is followed by two epigraphs and a bibliographical listing of works written in Spanish which also bear the title *oficio de tinieblas*.[3] In an article Cela wrote and published in December of 1973 in *Papeles de Son Armadans* he speaks exclusively about *oficio*. Recognizing full well that there most likely exist other works that have escaped his inventory, he states that the number 5 of the title represents an alogical ordinal number that is "paradoxically abstract, fluctuating and indeterminate."[4] He cites Bosch, Picasso, and Goya's influence and explains his novel's threefold "service" in the following terms: an outlet for the "pus" that has been produced by disillusionment and pain; vindication of literature (by means of the *antiliteratura* [antiliterature] which this novel represents); and unbridled freedom of expression. Thus conceived, *oficio* crosses the threshold of logical thought into "the frontier in which thought almost is not thought any longer" (m. 433).

Taking its cue from the long version of the title, the narrative discourse models the chorus of sick people by way of the myriad of voices that accompanies the parade of bizarre countless fictional entities that group together many archetypal characters, among whom the most prominent are: the immediate family members of the anonymous *tú,* commedia dell'arte characters, the executioner, ulpiano the stone cutter, the war hero ivón hormisdas, benjamín the tax collector, the baron with conjunctivitis and an orange-colored mold, a harelip boy, the clown (with peacock feather used to tickle others into sensual arousal), the blind Danish tourists who visit Italian museums, and the clergyman-bullfighter-guerrilla warrior, to name only a few. In keeping with the (feigned) liturgical austerity of the (sub)title, the dominant organizing principle of the narration is the *letanía* (litany) which emanates not only from the spontaneous conversations that these characters carry on with one another but also from the narrator's labyrinthine monologue and those pathos-charged contexts in which he interfaces his words with the Latin intertext of canonical litanies such as, for example, "ora pro nobis ora pro nobis" (pray for us).[5]

Cela's fellow journalist Luis Blanco Vila believes that the death of Cela's younger brother Ricardo was foremost in the author's mind at the time of the writing of *oficio,* an assertion borne out in monad 902, in which the narrator speaks of having painfully to accept the reality caused by "your brother who dies in silence" (*odt* 158). The first of April is the other important date that serves as a point of departure for surrealistic chanting of wave after wave of disjointed poetic verbal images, for it marks the day on which Francisco Franco proclaimed the end of the Spanish Civil War and the beginning of his thirty-six-year dictatorship. It is also said that, in writing this novel, Cela enclosed himself in total darkness for hours on end as a means of fostering a creative process that simulates the nether realms of human experience, not at all unlike the three decades of darkness which characterized Spanish life and letters during Franco's regime.[6] Surrealism is, then, a logical place of refuge (in *oficio*) for a narrator who begins by saying that "it is comfortable to be defeated at twenty-five years old" (*odt* 9) and ends his monologue 1,193 monads later by taking his life, reminiscent of how much "more comfortable it would have been to have been defeated at 0h 0' 0'" (m. 1194).

Almost as if to assuage the guilt left behind in *San Camilo,* the *tú* narrator in *oficio* walks the same self-deprecating path. By enclosing himself in his own subconscious *office of darkness,* he confronts the repulsive bloated image of himself in the mirror, sits in front of the "black wall of his coffin" (m. 1104), and makes the only choice available to him: to choose the way he wants to die. Because of his despair, his choice separates him in time and space from tangible reality and allows him to bond with his true self. Thus overcome with obsessive guilt and recrimination, he keeps company with the madness, frustration, and insanity of his psychological, creative, and real darkness and subsequently produces his own record of *reality.* This testimony reverberates in the voices of countless real people (the Roman emperor Trajan, Malcolm X [m. 20], James Meredith [m. 205], and Gypsy Rose Lee); officials who supposedly enable society to function (the executioner, the tax collector, hoards of unnamed *funcionarios* [office workers], seminarians, tourists, professors, students, and so forth); and, finally, classical and mythological entities of Celian coinage. Included also in this hallucinatory world is an extensive inventory of names referring to Satan and references to flora and fauna which signal the bestiality that abounds in the Boschian backdrop of this novel. Metamorphoses, too, are commonplace; it is noted, for example, that Colombina goes from being a woman dressed in rags of gold to Pierrot, a Prussian colonel, a gypsy, a woman with a lift in her right foot (and later in her left foot), and so forth. Similar mutations also have thematic repercussions as, for example, love is defined in a variety of heterosexual, homosexual, and bestial terms. In line with this blatant iconoclasm is a merciless challenge to middle-class values. Even more poignant is the lesson to be learned about *history as farce* when ivón hormisdas is proclaimed a war hero in the Barbary battle only later to have his deeds rewritten as the hero of countless other wars.[7]

Despite the intentional chaotic, nonsensical display of surrealistic associations, disassociations, mutations, fusions, and annihilation, there is a decided order and logic, however peculiar, which emerges in self-referential monads (nos. 50, 101, 203, 407, and 815), other cross-references (mm. 786 to 792), and fourteen obituary notices that begin in monad 794 with the woman with a lift in her shoe and end with the narrator's own death notice.[8] Given the absence of anecdotes that would hold together all these disparate elements, the plotting of characters, places, and events amounts, as Burunat says, to a "prose poem" that at best yields a systematic constellation of poetic associations from which to draw numerous interpretative possibilities.[9] Other ordering principles include some of the following: the clown-with-peacock-feather's "dodecalogue of the laws of Venus" (m. 803)—or treatise on the nature of sexual intercourse—and its corollary (m. 1,145); the litany that ulpiano the stone cutter writes in commemoration of ivón hormisdas's death (m. 885); and the listing of holy martyrs which the clever Welshman composes as micro-litany (monad 1091). As a timely reminder that none of this is supposed to make sense, the highly self-conscious narrator says that "we are attending the multiple breakage of a routine that is simultaneously produced in one-hundred different fronts and [that] it is preferable that the *great catastrophe* catch us stark naked like your cousin's girlfriend who when naked resembles a mutilated seagull" (m. 449; emphasis added). On another occasion it is advised that "of the contemplation of everything that has been said no effort should be made to obtain general consequences" (m. 853). To be used as a rule of thumb with which to gauge the reading of this litany, we are given a "grammar of copulation" (m. 1164) which really translates into "love one another because you are to die shortly" (m. 1163). Additionally, Apollinaire-like calligraphs are found, such as in monads 1042 and 1039 *bis* and 1156.

Regardless of the obstacles of this deliberate and frustrating elusiveness, the reader is indeed summoned to partake in the madness thanks to the use of the second-person form of address which serves as the sole onomastic designator for the *(tú)* narrator. Given the option in Spanish of addressing another formally or informally as either *usted* or *tú,* respectively, the latter is more intimate and speaks directly to the heart. Even though the schooled reader recognizes the familiar usage as consistent with stream of consciousness, the enticement to define oneself as *tú* is incisive, oftentimes blurring the distinction between the narrator's self-dialogue and one he could sustain with the reader. Moreover, the polyphonic nature of the discourse is greatly augmented by the mandate that this be considered a "thesis novel written to be sung by a chorus of sick people," a directive that ensconces another channel for dialogue among the voices in the choir, the narrator's own *tú,* and the reader.

Be that as it may, the confrontation with *tú* locks out all objectivity. Whether envisioned as the addressee of the proposed chorale or simply as a polarity of the narrator's split consciousness, the axis around which everything centers is intermittently objectified by a first-person *yo* (I) which adds still another perspective to his inner voyage toward death. At first, because of the absence of traditional narrative markers between narration and dialogue, it is uncertain whether or not the *yo* is simply the manifestation of the unassuming dialogue that takes place between his cousin and his cousin's girlfriend, as is the case in monads 366 through 375. The *yo* reappears in monads 989, 994, and 997, in which its hold over him strengthens as it purports to possess knowledge about him which no one else knows, concerning "your system that today does not yet break the religious and extremely hard magic shell of upstanding principles but which will in one or two hundred years most likely be habitual" (m. 994). Going on to chide him into consulting authoritative dictionaries to verify what the *yo* is telling him (m. 1017), it validates its very authority. In short, despite his undeniable yet amorphous self-recognition, the *tú* cannot escape his tragic existence.

His thought processes echo queries similar to those of the narrator of *San Camilo, 1936* regarding whether or not he is dead or alive (m. 3), in an attempt to find solace in not having been responsible for the fates of the four saints named in the complete title of the novel: "you did not participate in the torture . . . the martyrdom . . . the exile . . . the solitude . . . you were a clumsy spectator and that is your grave sin" (mm. 16–21). He is reminded that he will have to pay with blood for his error and that there is neither a "glorious end" (m. 26), nor are there any "advantages" awaiting him (m. 27). He hesitates about facing himself honestly and lacks resignation to meet his fate—death—despite the courage, boredom, and absurdity that characterize his life. Numerous other pieces of residual, fragmented biographical information enhance his connection to *San Camilo, 1936:* a Filipino girlfriend who died of tuberculosis (m. 960), a burgeoning adolescent curiosity about prostitutes and customary incursions into their neighborhoods (m. 645), a collection of favorite memorabilia (m. 594), and a perception of God's indifference (m. 80). Above all, though, this *tú* is totally alone, having recently buried his brother (m. 902), father (m. 734), and cousin (m. 1085)—none of whom are listed in the obituaries.

Although we are never granted access to anything beyond this profile of him, we have a growing sense that we are in effect learning more about him. A good example of this is found in monad 332 (which most critics signal as important), in which he confesses that "you always played with the cards face up and you lost you always fought with an open heart and you lost you never doubted the words you heard and you lost now it is late to turn back and even to make an examination of conscience." Allusion to Cela's military service is made in terms of "floating on top of cadavers you saved yourself from the shipwreck and after your picture came out in enlightened magazines" (m. 596). In spite of his efforts, he/*tú* is: "unable to get away from the feeling that for years you have been wasting your time fooling everybody around you . . . and it shows in the glow of the look in your blinking and in the almost unseen sweat that moistens your forehead that you are far from telling the truth from thinking the truth" (*odt* 799).

In an equally convincing, albeit fragmentary, way we gather enough information to know that this *tú* narrator is a writer who not only hears the inner "voice that suggests you tell" (m. 308) and you "take all the time you need" in doing it (m. 186) but which also offers sustained self-commentary concerning his choice of words. Impressive also is his understanding of a poetics of the absurd from which his creative writing springs: "the absurd does not lead to cruelty but rather to mercy those people with dirty and romantic imaginations think it's the opposite but those egotistical and timid people are wrong" (m. 591). As his suicide draws near, the narrator composes a long monad about his writing in existential alienation: "(solitude solitude) you can't sleep you work too much you work without stop writing down words one after another pedestrians ask you why and you don't have an answer (solitude solitude) those who understand life are writers" (m. 1149). On the one hand we see the need for control ("do not allow your word to flee freely and copy down the customs of the convent's silent mummies" [m. 462]), yet little by little he relinquishes his grasp of reality as "the typewriter is rebelling" against him (m. 1170). Moreover, he is on guard to uphold faithfully one of the primary tenets of encoding which characterizes his writing—namely, never to call anybody "by their name" (m. 106).

Of all the names that dot the novel's 1,194 monads the cardinal rule about nomenclature is dutifully observed when it comes to the narrator's family members. At the very moment that reference is made to his father comes the warning not to "pronounce his name" (m. 42), an admonition that in effect *becomes* his name, for every time he speaks of his father it is in terms of "your father do not pronounce his name." Only once is the rule broken (m. 458), when the name Claudio (Claudius [m. 458]) slips out as both his and his father's name. In defiance of the regal implications of the name, however, the monad describes his father's iconoclasm and liberal thinking, both of which caused him to be buried in a "civil cemetery behind the atheist's grave" (m. 58). The family member most often mentioned, his anonymous male cousin, assumes philistine proportions, as his identifying tag represents a fusion of the words *tu primo* (your cousin) into *tuprimo* (m. 76), because "your cousin does not have a name it is not the ironduke the dukedelabruyère dukedelarochefoucauld rosaluxemburg the blindduchess nor safo dressed as a lancers' capitan from before the war of 1914" (m. 70). Generic, too, are the references to his mother (*tu madre* [your mother]), grandmother (*tu abuelita* [your grandma]), and grandfather (*tu abuelito* [your grandpa]).

As one critic puts it, the non-Iberian flavor of *oficio* extends itself unmistakably to the narrator's relatives,[10] and, as family ties become more of a dominant motif in the increasingly nonsensical discourse that involves an ever-growing number of metamorphosed fictional characters, his family is a grotesque hodgepodge of mutants who, nevertheless, have a foothold in reality. Among his *father do not pronounce his name*'s quirks is having tape-recorded the chirping of dead birds and the "insane song" of his wife's dead lovers (m. 838). His mother, in turn, was unfaithful to her lovers—who are metamorphosed versions of the "interior minister of bunga" (m. 308, 502, and 907, respectively)—by having relations with her husband/*his father do not pronounce his name*. Upon receiving the news of his grandfather's death as a war hero while heroically "defending position 1-and-2-and-3" in Africa (m. 704), his grandmother's brightly polished amethyst suggests her communion with the underworld; she is, at the same time, the owner of a sought-after kaleidoscope through which all of her lovers want to look. She also has the reputation of being a voyeur of sorts, for she stands behind the partition in *hiscousin*'s bedroom, from where she watches him and his girlfriend, turns up the volume on the tape recording of the dead birds, and raucously applauds the couple's actions.

[H]iscousin, however, is the most noteworthy relative, for upon him is bestowed the lengthiest commentary. The peculiarity of his other relatives pales in comparison with *hiscousin*, as he is deliberately brought into focus with great care. He is first seen in a big bedroom, in which reference to his bed, otherwise known as the *cama de las frustraciones* (bed of frustration [m. 73]), emerges as another important motif in the novel. Hanging on his wall are lithographs of Goya's *Maja desnuda* (Nude Maiden) and a picture of Our Lady of Sorrows. Attention is also drawn to the "somewhat crooked and a little bit fondled" image of the Virgin Mary which is among his possessions (m. 74). In the corner of his room stands a sink filled with cherry liqueur, which he and his girlfriend drink through plastic (feeding) tubing. *[H]iscousin*, impervious to his girlfriend's constant crying, from time to time beats her and his mother. He is an intellectual who, besides having a keen interest in Egyptology, recites verses (Schiller) and writes fables. In keeping with the looking glass motif of the grandmother's kaleidoscope, *hiscousin* also looks at himself in a mirror of polished metal (m. 158), often masturbates in view of a smaller mirror, and even confesses his sins in front of a Portuguese mirror.

As further evidence of *hiscousin*'s importance, we learn of his past existence in Cesarea of Capadocia, where he was the personal valet of Trajan, with whom he fell into disgrace on 3 July. We are told that *hiscousin* suffers greatly and oftentimes wishes to escape. He too is a saint—*san tuprimo* (saint yourcousin)—whose feast day is, ironically enough, 1 April, the day of his supposed martyrdom. The betrayal that led to his sainthood is confirmed by the Spanish saying "cría cuervos y te sacarán los ojos" (a dog bites the hand that feeds it), evoked by the crow *(cuervo)* which nests with him in his "bed of frustrations" (m. 883). While on the one hand there is little evidence to suggest anything particularly Spanish about this relative, the sign of an upside-down question mark that is imprinted on his forehead is telling (m. 903), itself indicative of the perplexing nature of the relationship that exists between the narrator and *hiscousin*. Even more bizarre is the raid on his house one night when he, in the company of his girlfriend, was dreaming of "non-Caucasian fetuses" (m. 124). *[H]iscousin*'s peculiarities aside, reference to the ire provoked in the narrator when he thinks about *hiscousin* attests, nevertheless, to their symbiotic relationship, which seems to revolve primarily around the unspecified nature of the wedge thrust between them by *hiscousin*'s girlfriend.

Whatever cohesiveness exists in the narrator's endless register of names is due to the personal nature of his family ties (however odd they may be). Considering the fascination his (generic) family members have with the tape recording of the dead birds, his genealogy assumes the archetypal proportions of

Adam and Eve's progeny: "adam and eve used to use a serpent that was nourished by birds so that it would whistle to them the song of dead birds" (m. 120). As if to reiterate the significance of his ancestry, the narrator later states that "satan gave our mother eve a pair of horns from his occupation and eve as a token of her love gave them as a gift to adam *your father do not pronounce his name* used to get a kick out of this theory *your father do not pronounce his name* was not superstitious" (m. 1082). Cela's bold meshing together of creativity and biblical truth explains the metamorphoses of his family's love interests, for they too provide a paradigm for a *creation* grounded in the surrealism of the narrator's logic.

Given the fodder that Adam and Eve fed the serpent, the dead birds' chant is Cela's version of the manner in which the *forbidden fruit* lured humankind into a victimized existence of life as funeral procession, much the same as the logic of the obituary notices of *oficio.* The saints listed in the title—and strategically called to mind throughout the narrative discourse—change places with the numerous characters that seemingly come and go at random. Instead of resounding with festive joy, the liturgy of their passing into sainthood echoes their torture, exile, and martyrdom, thereby positing literary creation between the opposing poles of life and death and joy and sadness. For this reason the metered litany-like cadence that cements the substructure of the novel is a mock version of the biblical Sermon on the Mount in which the beatitudes are proffered as a consolation to all the suffering peoples of the world, for bliss in the hereafter is to be their reward.

In *oficio,* however, such promise bodes a morbidly scatological existence, and, for that very reason, those who have been charged with singing the monads constitute "a choir of sick people." In the narrator's own *office/service of darkness* the *bienaventurados* (blessed/sainted) are really the cursed, for theirs is the kingdom of insanity and death; their inheritance is the world of civil strife (in Spain, Bosnia and Herzegovina, and Palestine), holocausts, Vietnam, prejudice and discrimination, and political assassination, of which the narrator is painfully aware as he directs his thoughts, past the one-thousandth monad toward their apocalyptical end.[11] What gives substance to Adam and Eve's inferred "origin of the species" is the novel's blueprint of reference points that chart humankind's progress. Mentioned periodically throughout the novel, the following coordinates guide the persecution that is implicit in the hagiographic nomenclature that frames the novel: the Roman emperors (Claudius and Trajan) and Lake Tiberius (as metaphor for Christ's Sermon on the Mount as well as the cruelties of the ruler after whom the body of water is named).

This is the world that the narrator has inherited, through which he has to navigate with only "the map of tenderness [on which] are pointed out all . . . [types of] geographical accidents: the lake of indifference the river of inclinations the sea of danger the pathway of gratitude the country of sweet letters the city of beautiful verses" (m. 601). To assist him further in his journey is the steady stream of advice he gives himself; this, in turn, amounts to a virtual compendium of aphorisms that are rooted in the overriding admonition "no, say no to everything" (m. 151) and "no and a thousand times no, I shall not tire of repeating it . . . do not accept any pact whatsoever . . . do not go over to the side of the angels if you do not wish to be marked with the stigma of a traitor" (m. 427). Adrift in this sea of negativity is the mandate to "get into the habit of loving too much in order to love enough" (m. 601). Instead of reading and believing "the fallacious histories that are retold in illustrious historical accounts" (m. 1020), he is reminded that what he needs to do the first thing every morning is to use as metaphor a neighboring five-story house as a mirror of "the mystery of the universe" (m. 1020).[12] Only in this way will he find the peace that comes from acceptance of his aloneness and mortality (m. 1021). Therein lies the amalgam of life, in the *service* of living and breaking the boundaries that enclose the darkness of all "the solitary people the vicious people the virtuous solitary people" (m. 1097).

In a fashion reminiscent of a poem (by Juan Ramón Jiménez) about poetic inspiration derived from the ever-present yet invisible birds' song, the obstreperous narrative voice of *oficio* seems also mindful of the legacy that was passed on to him by *his father do not pronounce his name*'s outrageous tape recording of the song of the dead birds.

CHAPTER 7

Mazurka for Two Dead Men

In 1984 Cela was awarded the prestigious Premio Nacional for Literature for *Mazurca para dos muertos (Mazurka for Two Dead Men),* which he wrote and published the preceding year. By 1990 it had sold over 235,000 copies and had been acclaimed as a masterpiece that represented the culmination of his career. As we are reminded by Janet Pérez (an astute and vigilant critic of Cela's work over the years), this novel closes the ten-year hiatus of "novelistic silence" which followed the publication of *oficio.*[1] Given Cela's forty-year tenure as a novelist (since *Pascual Duarte* in 1942), it is no surprise that *Mazurka* is a repository for many of the thematic, structural, lexical, and ethical threads that constitute the narrative fabric of Cela's prose fiction. Yet, given Cela's proclivity for avoiding a servile imitation of his own style, this novel is, as should be expected, different in many respects. Here the reader intuits from the outset that it will deal with family rivalries.[2] Because of a thirst for vengeance which results from the murder of Baldomero "Afouto" Gamuzo by Fabián "Moucho" Minguela Carroupo, the warring factions are divided along the lines of the Carroupo family of outsiders and the native Galicians who make up numerous kindred units: the Guxindes, Moranes, Casandulfes, and Gamuzos, among others.[3] Having suffered the radicalized stream-of-consciousness technique of *oficio,* one is immediately struck by *Mazurka*'s return, albeit an absence of chapter divisions, to traditional narrative commonplaces such as the use of textual markers—paragraphs and dialogues—and standardized punctuation. In a fashion reminiscent of an earlier Cela, paratextual documentation is again present in the form of the three additional texts that frame the novel: an introductory (and not altogether accurate) map of Galicia, a "Forensic Report" that is included as the "Sole Appendix," and a Galician-Castilian vocabulary used in the novel.[4]

Instead of taking place in the interior of Spain, the action develops deep in Galicia, Spain's northwestern-most region and a part of the country which is reputed for its Celtic origins, superstitions, legends, and storytelling rituals.[5] Besides Cela and Franco, Valle-Inclán, whose work continues to be of seminal importance to Cela, was born there.[6] Despite critical consensus that, by the 1970s, overwhelmingly dismissed Cela's importance as a novelist in Spain, his master craftsmanship reappears in *Mazurka* as demonstrated in the perfectly controlled fictive logic of the narratological dimensions of the work. Continued use of the litany-based structural underpinnings that Cela so boldly exploited in *oficio* make *Mazurka,* as one of its narrators explains, "a never-ending story . . . an endless sequence of deaths moved by inertia" (*MTDM* 300). Noteworthy are parallels with Latin-American novelists such as Gabriel García Márquez *(One Hundred Years of Solitude)* and Juan Rulfo *(Pedro Páramo)* who transcend chronological and spatial boundaries in defining reality in terms of the spiritual and creative dimensions of the human psyche and experience. There are so many widows and so much death in *Mazurka,* by way of war, freak accidents, suicides, murders, and illness, that death assumes as great a tangible reality as the starkness of life in Cela's rural Galicia. In the words of Miss Ramona's father, Don Brégimo Faramiñás, "when life dies, death is born and begins to live" (*MTDM* 212), or, as one of the narrators explains, "life trots along at the side of death, apparently that's God's law" (*MTDM* 253). Numerous fictive spaces either are located in or involve the mention of places such as the Santa Rosiña de Xericó cemetery (*MTDM* 135), the *cruceiros* that mark the places where people died, and various coffin factories such as El Reposo (The Repose).[7]

Adega is, then, not exaggerating when she tells don Camilo at the outset of their conversation that "there are only dead men around here" (*MTDM* 16), among whom are Afouto and Moucho, whose deaths facilitate one of the principal encoding devices as the novel develops rhythmically along the lines of the mazurka, a musical composition of Polish origin which confers a dissonance to what would be an otherwise commonplace title. More specifically, the mazurka "Ma petite Marianne" (My Little Maryanne) is one of the many tunes in the repertoire of Adega's blind brother, Gaudencio Beira, who lives at La Parrocha's house of prostitution and earns his keep by serenading the clientele with his accordion.[8] However popular "Ma petite Marianne," though, it is a "forbidden mazurka, well, not quite forbidden but the closest thing to it" (*MTDM* 283), which Gaudencio is adamant about playing only on two specific occasions: the days that Afouto and Moucho are murdered. As such, the song assumes as much importance as the sacred rite of Catholic burial, the "sung Mass" (*MTDM* 100). Furthermore, in being dedicated to Afouto's memory, it is part of local lore and serves as the "mazurka of mourning" par excellence (*MTDM* 202).

In addition to its exotic and decorative function, the mazurka blends in perfectly with various levels of subtext that constitute the secrecy and prohibition that, in the midst of a civil war, make for the suspense that builds up as the novel progresses. Only three individuals are privy to this music: the already mentioned blind man, a raven that has learned to whistle a few bars of it, and, as we shall see, a privileged character named Robín Lebozán. Because of their unique qualities (Gaudencio cannot see, the raven cannot speak, Robín does not go to fight in his country's civil war), each one of them stands out as a *bearer of the secret* and a vehicle for accessing the (fictive) truth concerning the murders of Afouto and Moucho. Inasmuch as "the accordion is a sensitive instrument that suffers when something goes against the grain" (*MTDM* 100), the mazurka, not being a part of Galicia's musical tradition of bagpipes nor of Spain's legendary Moorish stringed instruments, is a fitting reminder of the Carroupo family of outsiders—called *zapateiros* (cobblers [*MTDM* 63]) by the locals—who moved into the area and killed a native son, Afouto.[9]

Simply put, *Mazurka* is about what don Camilo finds out concerning what happened to his family in Galicia during his years of absence from his homeland. Since his relatives are the primary source of information, the narrative discourse is deeply rooted in Galicia's oral/aural tradition, and, as such, it evolves from the people with whom he chats in numerous old haunts, such as Ramona's two-hundred-year-old house, which itself is the site of "great mystery and nobility, as well as many's the tale of passion, illness, and calamity" (*MTDM* 69). Strung together by a protean, extradiegetic narrator whose voice is intertwined with those of others, the dialogic segments that surface as a result of the oral point of departure manifest themselves in the rhythmic, strategically plotted, yet spontaneously decontextualized, conversations/dialogues that serve as guideposts for the entire discourse. Heard everywhere are advisory responses such as, for example, the answer that is given to the question about "the nine signs of the bastard" (*MTDM* 4) which distinguish the nine Carroupo brothers: "Be patient. You'll find out soon enough" (*MTDM* 5).[10] These interchanges, usually occurring only between two people, are never introduced in terms of identifying the conversationalists. With few exceptions they are very short, oftentimes ending in such a way as to give the impression that one of the speakers has assumed the role of the narrator, who advances a narration that frequently provides a follow-up diegesis for the theme of the previously truncated conversation. Other significant and more subtle, muted dialogues and conversation markers are also embedded in the fabric of otherwise—and apparently—purely narrative segments.[11] Once activated by the reading process, they make for a symphonic panoply of narrative voices befitting an atmosphere in which mythic time subtly corrodes pretenses of historical chronology. In its place is a narrative present that is well outside the past time of the recollected events yet endlessly fused to it in decidedly spiral, if not essentially circular, progression.[12]

76

To be certain Cela's inclusion of an epigraph from Edgar Allan Poe's poem "Ulalume" is itself a warning about veracity and narrative omniscience: "our thoughts they were palsied and sere, / Our memories were treacherous and sere" (*MTDM* i). By framing the actions of the Guxinde and Carroupo family within the context of the Spanish Civil War, Cela's disdain for historical rendering is unmistakable, as he successfully debunks that period of Spanish history of its mythic proportions, subordinating it, as we shall see, to the development of the animosity between the Guxinde-Carroupo enemies, permitting in that way the narrative unfolding to occur along already established lines.[13] That is why someone—probably the Casandulfe Raimundo—at the beginning says that "we are right in the thick of things . . . [and] the beginning is right in the thick of things, and nobody knows what the end has in store" (*MTDM* 35), only to be contradicted toward the end of the novel in equally convincing terms: "fate has ordered their lives because all that has been settled even before we came into this world" (*MTDM* 275).[14] Since people speak from memory and readily admit that "the truth of the matter is . . . all very faraway" (*MTDM* 230), multiple points of view gradually replace the early premise of "this [being a] true story" (*MTDM* 9), thus adding a subtext of doubt, error, and contradiction to the manifold layers of narration.

While the reader's natural curiosity to identify the different narrators with the members of the Guxinde and Morán families leads him in and out of what Masoliver Ródenas calls narrative "traps,"[15] the voice with which the novel opens juxtaposes the immediate present of Galicia's gentle and unceasing rainfall with the past by relating Lázaro Codesal's death in the battle of Melilla (Morocco). Although unknown at that point in the novel, Codesal's deconstructed presence—by way of his absence—provides one of the key symbolic refrains that allows the narrative present to transcend its twentieth-century place in history and evoke centuries of Arab domination of the country.[16] Not only does Cela vindicate the Moors' importance in Spain, as Masoliver Ródenas asserts, but he also substantiates the mythic dimensions of his novel by claiming that Lázaro's death caused that "the line of the mountains was blotted out by the Moors, so that they could tell the Christians: thus far come the fig trees and no further."[17] The symbolic destruction of the mountain's visible barrier is replaced by an invisible line that, while inherently divisive, legitimizes the existence of two different worlds in terms of their respectful coexistence, as symbolized in the fig trees. In one comical, short interchange someone asks another if they have heard the news about the Moors having crossed the Strait of Gibraltar—referring, of course, to the eighth-century Moorish invasion of Spain as well as to the arrival of Franco's Moorish troops on the mainland at the beginning of the Civil War—only to be told that it is old news (*MTDM* 140). The theme resurfaces in the novel in another conversation in which two people share their opinions about the Moors; one party affirms that, although they were not treated well by the foreigners, "they seem no worse than the Christians" (*MTDM* 217), a view that conveys cynical Celian tongue-in-cheek sarcasm.[18] The Moors are also present by virtue of the belief that holds legendary their place: "Below the River Miño, to the south that is, midway between Orense and Castrelo, between the Rábeda valley and the Ribeiro . . . There are still plenty of Moors living in Galicia, it's just that you can't see them because they're dead and bewitched and wander below the earth" (*MTDM* 125–26).

Acting as virtual link between fiction and (historical) reality, Lázaro Codesal is said to have died at age twenty-three at the hands of a Moor while the Galician soldier was in effect "at the Tizzi-Azza post in Morocco" (*MTDM* 1), not, however, engaged in combat but simply resting under a fig tree and unobtrusively masturbating as he looked at a photograph of Adega.[19] By association in death his presence is made known by Adega's constant reference to him as "mi difunto"; he is also tangibly felt in the person of Moncho Preguizas, a fellow comrade in Melilla.[20] Himself having had a leg amputated while serving in north Africa, Moncho brought the tale of his friend's death back to Galicia, where it gained legendary proportions amid family, friends, and acquaintances. Moreover, by virtue of his relationship with Adega, Lázaro's death is simultaneously linked with the two men immortalized by the mazurka, as an authoritative narrative voice warns that "Adega isn't the only one who knows these stories" (*MTDM* 12). In this way the tone is set for the three hundred pages in which other important voices fade in and out depending on what they know and remember about the incidents related to the two infamous murders around which the novel takes shape. The more people say what they remember, the greater the infamy. Moucho Carroupo not only kills Afouto but "maybe another ten or twelve to boot" (*MTDM* 200), consequently sharpening the suspense and preparing his fate.

What is talked about, then, is really the same thing over and over again, and usually stems from what different people remember about other individuals and events. As in any typical long-overdue reunion of people who have not seen one another for many years, their accounts take the shape of family gossip, people's particular physical attributes and personality traits, what they did with their lives, and how the Civil War subsequently affected them.[21] Almost everybody is remembered as having had some sort of moral or physical problem. Hardly anybody escapes without some visible defect, perhaps the most outstanding being Marcos Albite, who "is missing both legs and . . . lives in an orange-painted crate with four wheels [and whose] . . . bow bears a five-pointed green star with his initials . . . outlined in gold thumbtacks" (*MTDM* 36). There are numerous *parvos* (half-wits) as well as other characters who suffer from mental retardation and dysfunctional behaviors, such as Pepiño Xurelo (Plastered Pepiño), who likes to fondle children and, as a result, agreed to be castrated in order to get out of jail for his crimes; plentiful, too, are the women, like Rosa Roucón, who are given to alcoholic drink. While Ramona's relationship with her nurse, Rosicler, hints of lesbianism, many married men frequent La Parrocha's house of prostitution. Priests have mistresses and abuse the childlike mentality of Catuxa Bainte, "the half-wit . . . [who] runs about Esbarrado hill in her birthday suit" (*MTDM* 4), and Benicia, Adega's sensuous daughter, who is "a heater and a pleasure machine rolled into one . . . like an obedient sow" (*MTDM* 25). Bearing the brunt of the mercilessness with which Cela ridicules hypocrisy among the clergy is Father Merexildo Agrexán Fenteira. In addition to having fathered "the half-wit from Bidueiros" who was hung by the local people "as a sort of trial run," the priest "looks as though he has a pine tree beneath his cassock" (*MTDM* 13) and has a head that swarms with so many flies that people can see him coming from great distances.[22] Those who marry often have families of as many as fifteen children, whereas others either leave Galicia, like don Camilo, or never marry, such as Ramona (otherwise called Miss Ramona, Moncha, and Mona) and the writer-intellectual, Robín Lebozán Castro de Cela.

The gamut of people who make up these families is conducive to the plethora of points of view which emerge regarding names, events, and places that form both the background and the primary axis of the story.[23] As personal histories are called to mind, short anecdotes also become part of the narration, such as, for example, the legends about Basilio Ribadelo and Mariquiña (from the hamlet of Toxediño), whom the Moors rewarded in gold for different services rendered, pending, however, strict secrecy concerning the source of their newfound wealth. A colorful distant relative is "the Saintly Fernández" (*MTDM* 79), who lived centuries before in Galicia (and who is playfully remindful of Cela's relative by the same name). Some recall him as nearly having achieved sainthood, yet others outwardly disagree about the written accounts that exist concerning him. In an attempt to verify his true identity, different types of references are made: an entry—that had been signed by Camilo de Cela (in the prestigious Spanish *Espasa* encyclopedia); the fact that the narrator's "great-grandfather" was a compiler of the same encyclopedia; ten to fourteen letters from Diderot and Alembert attesting to the controversial holy man's lineage; and, last, the sanction by Father Santisteban, S.J., "a real saint" (*MTDM* 79), who advised

79

aunts Jesusa and Emilita (because the letters were found in their old family homestead) to burn them on account of their heretical nature. In keeping throughout the novel with a commonly expressed concern for genealogical authentication, Adega herself, in an early conversation with don Camilo, says that "the papers . . . showing where the family of the dead man that killed my old man . . . hailed from" were stolen by "the clerk of Court in Carballiño" (*MTDM* 96). Many other examples demonstrate the disparity that exists between the written text and oral tradition, such as what happened to don Camilo's grandfather when he went to Brazil after killing Xan Amieiros.[24] It is also not uncommon to hear the conversants correcting and accusing one another of having made things up:

> Folks think that us Guxindes and Moranes are the same but we're not, folks get confused about this business of relationships, we are all descended from Adam and Eve (but not Ponferrada women, Aunt Emilita says, Ponferrada women are descended from the apes, thank you very much), not all Guxindes are Moranes but all us Moranes are Guxindes, it's as clear as mud but there you are. (*MTDM* 104)

Perhaps one of the most disturbing complexities deals with the names of characters and the manner in which they appear at times in catalogue-like fashion; for example, as the nine Gamuzo brothers are presented explicitly according to their birth order, the Carroupo men are simultaneously identified in terms of the nine previously mentioned "signs of the bastard," a narrative tactic that deliberately aims at confusing *facts* of the narration. Besides this numerical intertwining of opposing factions, the Gamuzo "martyr" Afouto was renown for the shining star that he had in the middle of his forehead, while the Carroupos, too, have a distinguishing "pigskin pockmark" on their foreheads (*MTDM* 18). People are sometimes remembered by their nicknames on one occasion, by first and/or one or two family surnames at other times, or by a combination of the same in other instances. A case in point involves Afouto's assassin, Fabián "Moucho" Minguela Carroupo, who is easily confused with "Moncho" Preguizas, one of Adega's former suitors, who is obviously on the side of the Gamuzo family. And, of course, there is the previously mentioned gifted raven, whose name is also Moncho. Moreover, misinformation is common, such as, for example, Roque, the third Gamuzo brother who, "although he isn't a priest . . . is known as the Cleric of Comesaña" (*MTDM* 8).

Almost as if in total defiance of simplistic interpretations regarding supposed autobiographical parts of the novel, Cela undauntingly includes at least four characters who are named Camilo: Camilo the gunner, don Camilo, Camilo the nephew, and the older don Camilo Polavieja, a general who fought in Mindanao, Philippines (*MTDM* 114).[25] Furthermore, there are other applications of the name Camilo Cela: Camilo de Cela is cited as having authored *La hacienda de nuestros abuelos;* reference is made to the village of Cela do Camparrón (*MTDM* 31); and Marcos Albite repeats over and over again the name Camilo as he whittles the gift of a small wooden statue of St. Camilo for don Camilo (the saint's namesake). Such clever disclosures are more ironic in light of the identifying tag "de Cela" (of Cela) which, as a grammatical indicator of possession, is attached to places and names like Robín Lebozán's, allowing Cela literally to claim subtle authorship/possession of the same and, at the same time, to disparage historical accountability. Characterization is also achieved simply by means of commonly translatable names such as, Moncho Requeixo Casbolado (Lazybones), Perello (Demon), Concha da Cona (Concha the Clam), Afouto (Lionheart), Cabuxa Tola (Crazy Goat), and many others. Cela audaciously invents a saint—St. Carallán (*MTDM* 9)—who, as "patron of the male sexual organs," is invoked by the people.[26] As the *stories* are heard again and again from slightly different points of view, the things that did not make a great deal of sense at first gain greater clarity as the tension mounts concerning avenging Afouto's death.

Foremost among the knowledgeable people with whom don Camilo speaks are the Casandulfe Raimundo, Robín Lebozán, Adega, and Ramona, all related by blood. As is often the case with Cela, there is a dichotomy between men and women which is outwardly visible in the legendary mandrake plant of the Santa Rosiña de Xericó cemetery. Men are celebrated for their physical attributes (hyperbolic genitalia, prowess, and defiance in the face of danger), and women have the responsibility for *telling the tale* and avenging their dead. From a (probable) female narrator Robín Lebozán learns:

> That's the law of the land, Robín, and some wretch or other—you know who I mean—is trying to go against it but you cannot go about wantonly killing in these mountains . . . mark my words! . . . In our families, Robín, both law and custom are respected, but even if all the men were to die then there's still Loliña Moscoso and Adega Beira to avenge their dead, and both of them are decent, courageous women. And if they, too, were to die, then there's me[.] (*MTDM* 210)

It is, then, to the matriarch Adega that don Camilo first turns for information. Given, however, the close association of Adega's *difunto* (deceased man) with Afouto's murderer and the fact that the vengeance is propelled primarily along matriarchal lines, insistence upon referring to the assassin as the "dead man that killed my old man" (*MTDM* 96) permits all narration to overcome the time constraints of the personal *stories* of the widows and to establish the suspense by which the yet-to-be-achieved (though already surmised) future is strategically recounted. In this way momentum builds as intrigue becomes the primary encoding device for a text that is astonishingly self-referential. In the words of another narrator, "for the time being the dead man is not yet dead though die he will, there's no rush" (*MTDM* 295).

As the background information concerning the Spanish Civil War is filtered through the comings and goings as well as the enlistment in the army of the Guxinde, Morán, Gamuzo, and Casandulfe men, the real buildup begins once the war is over. In other words what matters most to the characters is Fabián Minguela's death, rather, and not the senseless, incomprehensible Civil War. The very fact that Robín Lebozán refuses to enlist in the army precisely when "Franco is appointed *Generalísimo* of the Army, Air Force, and Navy" is telling indeed (*MTDM* 197). Besides subtly subverting the supposed grandeur that surrounds the chief of wartime operations, it forces us to pay closer attention to Lebozán: he is an intellectual and a pacifist of sorts who is good-looking and from a privileged family. These details, in turn, underscore his increased importance as one of the primary keepers of a text that could easily constitute the raw material of *Mazurka* itself.[27] To be certain, the Civil War appears at first glance to have played a significant role in the lives of the family members, for they tell their stories with points of reference which oscillate between before (*antes*) and after (*después*) the war, emphasizing always changed customs and families; some identify themselves "as Nationalists" (*MTDM* 244), while others resist political pigeonholing.[28] Family anecdotes, such as the rift between don Cleto and his sister Emilita, constitute incisive microcosms of what is going on in the larger context outside of Galicia and underscore the fact that most people had no idea about the significance of the war:

> Uncle Cleto was delivering speeches: Citizens of Galicia, the new dawn of salvation and Spanish independence has broken! "I never knew that your Uncle Cleto was so patriotic."
> "No, he wasn't. It just depended on how the mood took him." (*MTDM* 184)

Upon a closer examination of the facts and as more attention is paid to Robín's unusual literary interests, the true focal point emerges: the day that Afouto's death is finally avenged. Moreover, of greater significance (toward the end of the novel) is the clarification about the two important dates on which Gaudencio played the mazurka: "Rauco from the inn explained to Fauto Belinchón González, the Civil Guard, that Gaudencio only played the mazurka *Ma Petite Marianne* twice: on the Feast of St. Joaquín in 1936 and the Feast of St. Andrew in 1939. 'I hear tell that it was on the Feast of St. Martin in 1936 and St. Hilario in 1940.' 'Then you heard wrong . . . '" (*MTDM* 296).[29] While the pointedly public correction suggests a spiral closure, it also undermines once and for all the reliability of omniscient narrative authority. It must be remembered that originally someone insisted that the truth "will, in due course, figure in this *true story*" (*MTDM* 8–9; emphasis added), an affirmation that categorically cites 1936 and 1940 (*MTDM* 4).

Various narrators remember loved ones who died in some of the important battles of the war (Teruel, Santander, Madrid, and the Ebro and Jarama Rivers), but the "war myth" itself is sabotaged by the fact that, despite the "list of lads wholly exempted from military service" (*MTDM* 208), far more deaths are attributed to freak accidents than anything else.[30] Great care is taken to scatter various bits of biographical information about Cela's controversial participation in the war (and subsequent medical discharge) by means of the way in which Raimundo and the gunner Camilo's war-related injuries were treated in a Logroño hospital, where they coincidentally ran into each other.[31] It is no coincidence that the concerted effort to avenge Afouto's death begins after the two of them return home upon their discharge from the army. Until that time the story is recounted in vague, almost archetypal, generalities: "Nobody heeds the prudent onward march of the world spinning and turning as the drizzle falls with neither beginning nor end: a man denounces another man and later when he is found dead in the gutter or in the ditches of the cemetery there are few qualms of conscience: a woman closes her eyes and . . . nobody cares: a child falls down the stairs and is killed, all in the twinkling of an eye" (*MTDM* 99). As a matter of record, the precise information concerning Afouto's death is withheld until Franco's proclamation as *Generalisímo* of the Nationalist troops. Only then do we learn how Afouto was captured and subsequently murdered: lying in wait for Afouto and Cidrán Segade, Fabián Minguela sent ten of his men to capture them. Cidrán turned himself in only after Fabián's crowd set fire to his house; witnessing the burning were Ramona (who wouldn't let Raimundo and Robín Lebozán go to their assistance), Adega (who was knocked unconscious and tied to a tree), and, of course, Afouto himself, who killed one of the enemies and only turned himself over to the others after they had seized his wife, Loliña Moscoso, and their five children.

From this point on the narrative consciousness is more noticeable by way of comments like "do you realize that my big moment has come? And about time, too!" (*MTDM* 199) and "from this moment onwards nobody shall call him by his real name ever again" (*MTDM* 206). Numerous references are made to a manuscript that Robín spends his nights working on at Ramona's house. On one occasion in particular, a simple line of dialogue (with Ramona) turns into a lengthy soliloquy about the confusion wrought from time and memory:

> Indeed, there's no doubt I've earned myself a cup of coffee. Some things are very far away and others close at hand. Memory churns up the order of events and names of people, memory doesn't give a damn, the truth of the matter is it's all very faraway. At that time Benicia was only a little girl and Adega—recently widowed—still a fine figure of a woman, Mona was always very elegant, stories jostle inside your head though in our family there was never a plausible account, this is no scrutiny of conscience even though it may appear so[.] (*MTDM* 229–30)

Without a doubt the significance of Poe's "palsied and sere" thoughts, as quoted in the epigraph, lends added authority to Robín's words, for he, too, had quoted Poe on another occasion, when he sat in a rocking chair and read "all the above aloud" (*MTDM* 143). Besides the raven Moncho, who learned to whistle a few lines of "Ma petite Marianne," Robín is the only character who actually hears echoes of the famous mazurka at times other than Gaudencio's accordion rendition at the officially sanctioned times. In finding a seashell (behind his books) which his deceased mother had given him years before, Robín is able to hold it to his ear and hear "the skirl of Blind Gaudencio's mazurka" (*MTDM* 283). This power asserts his privileged access to the true significance of the mazurka. By way of association with the manuscript topic, periodic comments are offered concerning the self-correction that is made by whoever is in charge of the text (e.g., writing "arp without an aitch" [*MTDM* 232]). This, in turn, suggests that *Mazurka* is a product of Robín's pen and that it has been brought to light by a more objective extradiegetic narrator.

Knowing better than to permit such a facile categorization of *Mazurka,* Cela creates other options concerning authorship of the novel, as, for example, don Camilo also takes notes and keeps lists of items to bring for his cousins: "I must make a note to ask my cousins in Corunna for more cheroots to give to Marcos Albite. I have to repay him for his carved St. Camilo" (*MTDM* 58). Other characters also keep written records, such as don Jesús Manzanedo, who is "extremely meticulous . . . and . . . keeps a note of the deaths in a little book"

(*MTDM* 160), only to have a narrator say later on that everything don Jesús wrote in his notebook was a lie (*MTDM* 143). There are also literate women, such as Adega and Ramona, who had favorite authors like Gustavo Adolfo Bécquer and Rosalía de Castro and who kept written accounts of things.[32] Be that as it may, Robín Lebozán's association with the manuscript is heightened by the fact that he is the one who, "on All Souls' Day 1939 [when] the Second World War had already begun . . . upon the Feast of St. Charles" (*MTDM* 270), summoned to Ramona's house the twenty-two "blood related" men who take part in planning Moucho's death. Don Camilo and "Camilo the gunner" in attendance (*MTDM* 271), it is, ironically enough, the former's silent glance in Tanis Perello's direction which seals Afouto's fate by initiating the action that will culminate in the family's revenge, for it will be Tanis and his well-trained canines who resolve the long-standing feud.

Since there is no specific indication in the first part of the novel about how the vengeance will be accomplished, the suspense mounts systematically from the moment that the men file quietly out of Ramona's house. From time to time until the deed is carried out, characters question "When will we hear the skyrocket?" (*MTDM* 295), that having been indicated as the signal that would alert the families to the long-awaited execution. In hindsight it is easy to appreciate the syncopated rhythm of these questions and the emphasis that is placed on the hunting dogs that Tanis breeds. Indeed, two of them do the actual killing, a deed that is reflected in the forensic report concerning the victim's manner of death: "in the absence of human intervention and in the absence of signs of a struggle or human aggression, the cause of death, from a medico-legal point of view, may be said to be accidental" (*MTDM* 312). Additionally, movement is sustained throughout the novel by the refrain-like references to "the song that grates in the axle of the ox-cart" (68), which subtly propels the musical subtext of the novel.[33]

Initially, however, Tanis's male and female dogs (Kaiser and Sultan and Moor, Blossom, Pearl, Witch, and Butterfly) seem mere details of the rurality of the setting, one in which many of the characters own named pets famous for their extraordinary accomplishments.[34] Significant among these is Ramona's menagerie, which includes two swans (Rómulo y Remo), a Russian greyhound (Zarevich), a cat (King), Rocambole the parrot, and a macaw (Rabecho); there is also Manueliño Remeseiro Domínguez's previously named raven, Moncho, who learned to whistle the "Marseillaise" (as well as bars of "Ma petite Marianne"); uncle Cleto's dog, Véspora; and the exotic bird "shaped like a peony rose with fur instead of feathers, bright green fur, which the natives called the Little Jesus Cured," which Moncho Requeixo discovered "in the Cáticas archipelago" (*MTDM* 35). Characters, such as Cabuxa Tola and Policarpo, are animal and bird trainers, while still others, like Policarpo la Bagañeira, who lost three fingers to a horse's bite, have had peculiar encounters with different types of animals. Exotic, rural fauna also resides in the area. Worthy of commentary are the fearsome Zacumeira wolf and the werewolf Manuel Blanco Romasanta, who was saved by a Chinese doctor only to die of sadness from being locked up. The frogs that live in the Antela lagoon are remarkable because they share a common home with a legendary submerged city called Antioch, whose dead ring church bells on "St. John's night."[35] The lagoon is also part of the local lore, due in large measure to an apocalyptical prophesy written in 1595 by a Benedictine monk named Arnaldo Wion, who predicted the return of Christ at the end of the millennium, when the succession of popes would end and the waters of the Antela would dry up, leaving a legacy of chaos, hunger, and death.[36]

The one time, however, that the constant Galician rain actually stops is on the day that radios, amid great confusion in the Rauco tavern, blare the news of the outbreak of the Civil War.[37] Compared at different intervals in the novel to a litany, mercy, and God himself, the rains and drizzle that provide the "infinite patience" (*MTDM* 1) which shrouds the atmosphere of *Mazurka* are also the source of water for the mysterious Antela lagoon and "the Bouzas do Gago spring where both the wolf and the odd stray she-goat drink" (*MTDM* 303). Moreover, the same water protects Tanis Gamuzo and his two dogs, Sultan and Moor, as they lie in wait for Fabián Minguela to appear in the das Lamiñas mountains, where, stopping to take his own lethal drink of water from the das Bouzas spring, he fulfills his destiny:

> it rains upon the living, upon the dead, and upon those who are about to die . . . it rains as always through the whole of life and the whole of death, it rains as in war and in peacetime, it's great to see the rain falling without an end in sight, the rain lashes down like before the sun was invented, it rains monotonously but also compassionately, it rains without the heavens wearying of raining and raining. (*MTDM* 303)[38]

CHAPTER 8

Cristo versus Arizona

Following the lead of the clan rivalry in *Mazurka, Cristo versus Arizona,* 1988 (Christ versus Arizona),[1] unfolds in Tombstone (Arizona) around 1881 at the time of the infamous shoot-out at the O.K. Corral between the Earp and Clanton families. The event, as cast against the backdrop of the Mexican Revolution and the American expansion westward after the Civil War in the United States, is transmitted to us by a sincere and naive, albeit wholly unreliable, first-person narrator named Wendell. His graphic language is a timely reminder of the harshness of life west of the Mississippi River in the burgeoning pioneer, mining, and cow towns of the second half of the nineteenth century. The lack of punctuation (other than abundant commas) underscores his rudimentary education and the dialogic flavor of a discourse that spans 238 pages of what has been carefully laid out to give the impression of an unsophisticated stream of consciousness. So purposefully rough is the texture of the narration that it is easy to imagine Wendell surrounded by dance hall girls, loud music, and raucous cowboys as he sits at a table in the Irishman Oso Hormiguero's (Anteater's) saloon and converses about the past with numerous old cronies and barmaids. Blanco Vila's assertion that *Cristo* poses great difficulties for Spaniards because of the unfamiliar territory that it covers is borne out in the fact that very little has been written about this 1988 novel. In addition, the same critic points to Cela's tight-lipped attitude about the significance of the work, leaving readers with the same unorthodox aridity as the Arizona territory that is brazenly evoked in the stark, provocatively enigmatic title of the novel.[2] In Celian terms Tombstone's infamous Allen Street is found in every city of the world and, thus, provides him with a metaphor that is similar in scope to his "office of darkness." In this case his office is that "desert" that is located precisely where streets end and "the writer finds a bundle of papers . . . [that he] publishes, sometimes with his name and others with that of a weak enemy"—hence, for Cela, the cradle of literature.[3]

In place of the prologues that characterize Cela's early novels, a simple autobiographical statement introduces *Cristo,* saying that he went back to Arizona "a few months before putting the finishing touches on the novel" in 1987, in order to "refresh his memory" (*CVA* 5). It took him a little over a year to write, and it displays some of the same undaunting linguistic patterns as *La catira* (1955), a novel that also takes place outside of Spain—in the interior of Venezuela—and imitates the regional dialects, register, and syntax of that South American country. In *Cristo,* however, the linguistic codes that spring forth from the title surpass Castilian usage by way of English, Latin, and Mexican terminology. The direct results of the linguistic amalgamation are immediately apparent in the first line of the novel—in Spanish—and suggest not only Spain's polemicized presence in America but also the hybridized cultures that flourished thereafter in the New World and, in this case, in the southwestern part of the United States: "My name is Wendell Espana, Wendell Liverpool Espana, maybe it isn't *Espana but Span or Aspen,* I never found out for sure, I have never seen it written, Wendell Liverpool Span or Aspen, span means distance, [a] while, and aspen means trembling poplar, some say I tremble" (*CVA* 5; emphasis added).

What follows Wendell's declaration prepares the way for the narrative phraseology that structures the diegesis, namely, self-referential corrections concerning the manuscript that Wendell is in the process of composing and abrupt, decontextualized conversation fragments in which he explicitly states— and with purposeful regularity at the onset of his tale—that he is telling it "according to how they told it to me" (*CVA* 5), thereby muffling his own voice with numerous others in an intricate web of narrative layers that reduplicate themselves and reflect Wendell's lack of sophistication as a narrator. Wendell includes everything in his "true" account: stories that people tell him about others in Tombstone and the places surrounding it, accounts of the fate of Pancho Villa and other legendary figures of the Mexican Revolution, Mexican *corridos* (popular ballads) sung by women, conversations between people, works of prose fiction such as novels by Doug Rochester and D. H. Lawrence, concoctions of snake oil which—according to sworn, written testimony—supposedly cured people he knew, and, most significantly, well-metered fragments of a *letanía* (litany) to the Virgin Mary which, as we shall see, are encoding devices that he (as narrator) and others use within the same narration. In addition to regional symbols (the Mexican *zopilote* [buzzard], the saguaro cactus, rattlesnakes, and coyotes), a number of primary subtexts emerge as dominant throughout the novel: the Earp-Clanton saga, the Mexican Revolution, the fate of *forasteros* (foreigners)—specifically African Americans and Chinese—in the Wild West, the plight of the Native American at the hands of the *blancos* (white men), and, of course, Wendell's own life and family by way of his father, mother, and brothers and friends such as Gerard Ospino and Adoro Frog Allamoore.[4] Whereas Wendell openly says that "in this chronicle many friends have helped . . . [him]

with their encouragement as well as their stories," he is forthright about including "some lies as decoration" (*CVA* 124), none of which bothers him in the least: "these things never are clear because people turn things around on purpose, mix everything up to the point of not realizing it, perhaps they do well because history is treacherous and vengeful like the sand that the wind shifts about so as to confuse lovers and border guards" (*CVA* 197).

So much "he said, she said" leads to a syncopation of truth versus untruth, particularly in light of Cela's propensity for imbedding spontaneously unexplained conversations into his narrators' texts. In commenting on numerous occasions about, for example, the questionable veracity of the Earp-Clanton legend, Wendell indirectly alludes to one of the most obvious messages that he wishes his chronicle to convey—that is, that "words are always treacherous and end up betraying the person who pronounces them" (*CVA* 85). Unmistakably, yet with equal subtlety, Cela lodges the theatricality of life against what is perceived to be real and thus undermines any semblance of veracity and verisimilitude concerning what Wendell *Espana or Span or Aspen* narrates.[5] This narratorial license is exercised most frequently in the recounting of emotionally charged events, such as the O.K. Corral incident and, more specifically, the numberless hangings that characterize Wild West law and order.[6] None, however, provokes more bitterness than Tony Clints, a black man who realizes that his execution will be the one time in his life in which everybody will be paying him attention; for that reason he pathetically asks permission to wear a flower in his buttonhole on the day of his scheduled hanging. Using terminology such as *scenes, protagonists, main characters,* and *puppets* (*CVA* 127), Wendell infuses his narration with a stagelike quality that converts both narrator and reader into spectators rather than mere passive readers.[7] He also pretty much excludes himself from the "action," except at those strategically placed narrative junctures in which he recounts in refrain-like fashion the ever-changing "seven maneuverings" that he and Gerard Ospino would undertake for fun on Saturday nights.

Since one gets the distinct impression toward the end of the novel that Wendell is a very old man at the time of the completion of his "chronicle" (*CVA* 111), it makes sense that what he is telling is not so much a product of his own recollection as that of the many people to whom he, like don Camilo in *Mazurka,* had to turn to find out about things that happened at the turn of the twentieth century. He has no qualms about saying that somebody has told him something he does not recall: "I do not remember anymore . . . everyday I become more forgetful, I do not know if I said it once it seems to me that . . ." (*CVA* 219). He is oftentimes overheard pondering the philosophical premise that memory is life, which, once forgotten, is the same thing as death. And so, while he never explains why or for whom he has taken the pains to put all of these collected memories on paper, he realizes that some interested person "will probably correct his spelling mistakes" (*CVA* 55). Likewise, he is aware of a "reader of this chronicle" (*CVA* 111), yet he paradoxically states at the end of his manuscript that he does not want it to be published until the very "last man and the last woman" (to whom reference has been made in his chronicle) have died because "writing can do a lot of damage to people and more than one was crushed by the law through its fault, behind the gallows there is always a written paper" (*CVA* 224). As a matter of fact, for Wendell written words have such a deleterious effect that they make "happiness flee" (232), "many men [—having—] brought about their downfall by talking" (*CVA* 30). From such a pronounced and sustained dialectic between truth and its opposite, and Wendell's distrust of the written medium, results a document that is a legacy of contradictory testimony about a time in the history of the Western world which, given the stature of the United States in global affairs in the greater part of the twentieth century, achieved undreamed-of proportions by the time Wendell reached old age in the 1980s.[8]

On "the perhaps mistaken date" of 20 September 1917, when he was "twenty or twenty-two years old" (*CVA* 7), Wendell met and paid for the favors of "Matilda . . . Mariana . . . Sheila (or as some called her) . . . Cissie" (*CVA* 54) in one of the houses of prostitution which he and Gerard Ospino frequented on Saturday nights.[9] Recognizing the mark that Wendell's father had branded on his hind end when he was five years old—to commemorate the dawn of the new century—the prostitute told him that he was her son and therewith became his primary fount of information, telling him what others had told her. Even though their family reunion of sorts is, like Mrs. Caldwell's love for her son, ignominiously shrouded in the social and moral taboo of their incestuous relationship, far greater is the pathos of Wendell's own self-discovery, not having known previously "who [he] . . . was, from where [he] . . . came, or who were [his] mother and father" (*CVA* 7), until the fortuitous anagnorisis. In unique Celian tongue-in-cheek fashion Wendell literally comes alive as a result of his mother's words.[10] By listening to Matilda, he learns that his father's name was "Cecil Espana . . . Cecil *Lamb*bert Espana" (*CVA* 11; emphasis added), a man who performed the ritual branding on all of his sons, Wendell being the first-born, who only got the mark at five years old so that, being older, he would never forget the burning sensation of the incident. In discovering that he had eleven brothers (the only ones he knows are Mike San Pedro [aka Bill Hiena] and Pato Macario), Wendell is also told other things: that shortly after the branding ceremony he was sent to the Hospitium of St. Bartholomew, that his maternal grandfather was hung in Pitiquito, and that his mother, at ten years of age, was sexually molested by Búfalo Chamberino on the day she made her First Holy Communion. Of his adult life scant information is made available beyond his escapades with Gerard Ospino, his closest friend, who was left sterile because of having been bitten in his missionary days in Port Tiritianne by a green turtle. We know that Wendell lost three of his fingers while at work in a sawmill and that he speaks of a woman named Clarice as if she could have been his wife, while offering no clarification in this regard in spite of intending to "be clearer about it later" (*CVA* 153).[11]

Emphasizing that "in those days it was customary not to know one's parents" (*CVA* 16), Wendell continues to learn more about his family—that is, that his father was skilled as a carpenter, bricklayer, and mechanic and that his mother's three brothers (Don [Jessie], Ted [Nancy], and Bob [Pansy]) were homosexuals, two of whom died in the "European war" and in prison (*CVA* 11), while Nancy worked for another homosexual, Abraham Lincoln Loreauville (otherwise known as Parsley), a wealthy black man who lived in New Iberia, Louisiana. The information provided him by his mother was of little consequence to him in comparison to the one thing he remembers which serves throughout his narration as a metonymic reminder of his father: he was the owner of an alligator named Jefferson who spoke English and Spanish, recited poetry, and neighed like a horse (*CVA* 5), feats that used to be publicly refuted—in similar refrain-like fashion—by Zuro Millor, "the bloody half-breed" who, besides having the peculiar habit of sleeping with an inflatable doll named Jacqueline, ended up murdered by Cecil Espana for his constant "lies" about the gifted pet alligator. In terms of parentage Wendell and Pascual Duarte also have some things in common, Wendell being a hybridized, implicitly mild-mannered rogue whose naïveté affords him the poetic license needed to transmit (by way of his document) the brutality that characterizes this chronicle of death, depravation, and squalor in the Arizona territory of the 1880s.

In keeping with the novel's previously mentioned polylingual point of departure, Wendell experiences three name changes, which collectively point to the linguistic diversification that defines the multiculturalism of the southwestern United States. Before finding out about his parents, he says that people knew him as "Wendell Liverpool Lochiel" (*CVA* 75) then later as "Wendell Liverpool Espana . . . or . . . Span or Aspen" (*CVA* 5). He speculates further about the confusion of having been called "*Craig Tiger Brewer . . . or Craig Tiger Teresa* after I found out" (*CVA* 205), only to dismiss the peculiarly Americanized name with another assertion about his authorship of the manuscript he is preparing. Wendell's dismissal of the strange and ludic, non-Hispanic name indirectly legitimizes his use of Spanish as his native language, resorting only occasionally to English words and phrases. On a more subtle level, however, the transformation of his surnames represents his ties with Mexico, Spain, and the English-speaking world.

In vacillating between Span or Aspen, Wendell provides a polysemic and derogatory interpretation of his ethnicity which can be both the phonetic mimicry of an anglicized pronunciation of "a Spaniard" as well as the etymological variant of his Spanish ancestry. Although Spanish is obviously his mother tongue, Wendell often uses it ironically to denounce Spanish practices that he deems harmful. Among these sanctions is a subtle reminder that one such Don Diego Matamoros (don Bill Killmoors) is also known in Tombstone as "the apostle *Santiago* who baptizes with boiling chocolate those who do not have pure blood" (*CVA* 31), an incidental fact that sharply rebukes Spain's inquisitorial mentality as manifested in the fanaticism with which it persecuted the infidels in the name of St. James (Santiago), the patron saint of the country.[12] Being that Lochiel is a small town in the southernmost part of Arizona on the border with Mexico, while Liverpool represents England and, therefore, the British presence in America, the use of the word *Span* acquires additional significance in illustrating the relationships that exist between the countries: English presence in the United States, Spanish presence in Mexico, and Mexican presence in the Southwest. Literally speaking, then, one of Wendell's names is cleverly accurate, for it symbolically *spans* two, if not three, continents.

Apropos is Wendell's explanation of his choice of words, saying that "he does like Spaniards" (*CVA* 7). This implies that he either has direct knowledge of how they speak and write or, more symbolically, that he is reclaiming his Spanish heritage (whatever it may be) while at the same time asserting his awareness of linguistic differences between the Spanish language as it is spoken on both sides of the Atlantic. In the Tombstone of his younger days, where the three skulls—named faith, hope, and charity (*CVA* 219)—which Anteater kept in a cage in the latrine in his bar illustrate the macabre tenor of life there, Wendell is fully aware of the harshness of his chronicle, saying that "one has to commit the brutal act in . . . [one's] own language and with the same tongue as that with which one curses and blesses" (*CVA* 30). Although the only information that we are provided about his childhood and education deals with his years in St. Bartholomew, it is evident that he not only learned to read and write in Spanish but that he is able to use English, however sparingly, and in a manner that is not uncommon to life in bilingual/bicultural situations in which code switching is commonplace. He knows the names of such people as Big Minnie, Irish Mag,

Copperhead, Gold Dollar, Pumice Stone, and Lady Gay as well as those of houses of prostitution such as the Establishment. He is also aware that Chief Sitting Bull's real name is Tatanka Yotanka. From time to time he spouts phrases like "necking and petting" (*CVA* 99) and "looking for run down houses, also 1 or 2 family lots, will pay cash" (*CVA* 212). He is knowledgeable about places outside of Arizona and makes reference to Florence, South Carolina, the place of origin of a character named Betty, whose family owned a lucrative funeral home there. Open, of course, to speculation is whether or not his limited use of English is merely a product of what would have to be an excellent memory, particularly given his advanced age, and an ability to transpose the "foreign tongue" onto paper. What is, however, uncanny is his transcription of the two contextualized uses of Latin which are circumscribed in his text, those being the litany to the Virgin Mary and Zach Dusteen's knowledge of Latin.[13]

Whereas Cela's scorn for hypocrisy among priests is unabashedly portrayed in the caricatures of such clergymen as those in *Mazurka, Cristo's* treatment of religion is more elusive in that it is directed at the extended arm of the Catholic Church which was responsible for the evangelization that supposedly motivated the Spaniards in their colonization of the New World; in other words, preachers and missionaries are the target of Cela's carping. An ideal case in point is the rogue-turned-zealot Zach Dusteen, a widower, father of five sickly boys, and paramour of the well-known prostitute Irma the blonde (*CVA* 69). Dusteen's newfound Christianity serves him well in providing him with a life mission that allows him to travel from place to place toting Bibles and preaching repentance, a profession about which Wendell editorializes in true Celian fashion:

> prayers are plays on words, God does not listen to them because he laughs at inventiveness and even at the meaning of the words, also at the value of the parables and their very gentle moral lessons without feeling, with intention but without meaning, God has another, much harder and truthful voice and he does not allow himself to be confused no matter how much they tell him about showy, eloquent mysterious tragedies, Zach Dusteen knows how to tell falsehoods half-closing his eyes and breathing heavily, he is also able to lie. . . . Zach Dusteen knows the Bible by heart but makes mistakes in certain places, nobody is ever perfect[.] (*CVA* 207)

Other religious men and women match Dusteen's zealousness and deflect further Cela's disdain for the church. Specifically, these include the "lay men [and women]" like Timothy, and Father Octavio Lagares and Sister Clementina, who cruelly abused the children that lived in the St. Bartholomew home. Father Douglas Roscommon, on the other hand, is not among the abusive priests, yet he too is caricatured by way of the mumps that prevented him from growing into true manhood. And there is also Reverend Jimmy Scottsdale—a missionary of sorts—who, upon his arrival at the Tanee Reservation, infected all the Native Americans there with a sexually transmitted disease that caused them great embarrassment and consternation. Quite appropriate, then, is the anonymous commentary that "the God of Christians is not as tough as Christians [themselves]" (*CVA* 199).

The linguistic counterpart of Dusteen's Latin is, of course, the aforementioned litany. With the exception of the first time that it is recited—in transliteration of the Greek, *kyrie eleison* (Lord, have mercy [*CVA* 11])—all subsequent recitations follow a bilingual format and are oftentimes contextualized in episodes of exaggerated obscenity, almost as if to ward off the scandalousness of the same: "the litany of Our Lady is the breast-plate that preserves us from sin, I say *mater castissima* and you say *ora pro nobis*" (*CVA* 101).[14] Within the complicated dialogic framework of Wendell's chronicle—everybody he talks to who gives him their recollection of a particular story or event—it is virtually impossible to pinpoint whether others voice the intercessions to the Virgin Mary which appear regularly or whether Wendell himself is simply repeating something that would most likely have been drummed into him during his pupilage at St. Bartholomew. On the one hand, he establishes a clear relationship between a woman named Cyndy and the litany:

> all the names written down in her Mass book, written down in code, with the litany it is easy to keep track and also to remember the names of the young gentlemen, Cyndy does not begin the alphabet with *a* like everybody else but rather with *h* and after that everything else follows, the litanies are sixty-one and each one of them corresponds to a man with whom she has gone to bed at least three times . . . now she is going on the second round of the litany . . . Cyndy amuses herself sometimes reviewing her litany and recalling memories and pleasures . . . (*CVA* 174)[15]

Again, close to the end of the novel Wendell refers to "the key to the litany in Cyndy's Mass book" as being "difficult but one has to know it and she does not tell it to anybody" (*CVA* 223), thereby hinting at the possibility of viewing the litany intertext as another encoding device. However enticing the hermeneutics of decoding the "litany according to Cyndy," it must also be remembered that the first voice to echo the *kyrie eleison* litany sounds in context very much like that of the narrator himself as he very well could simply be repeating what his own mother is saying to him, given that she is his primary source of information and, for all practical purposes, the framer of the diegeses that constitute his discourse. She tells him that:

> now that I see that . . . it [the reality of our scandalous relationship] does not matter to you, I can tell you many things, some are very funny and others not so much, deaths do not always have to take place in the gallows or in the electric chair, they can also come about by gunshots or beatings or in the hospital or in one-hundred different ways . . . neither are all stories about death, there are some about contraband, about ghosts, about love, Tombstone was a very hot town[.] (*CVA* 9)

On yet another level Wendell defines the litany as a means of keeping track of the people who have died, given that "life is separated from death by a very delicate thread" (*CVA* 46). In near-circular fashion the final part of his manuscript extols the ritualistic, liturgical tone of the preceding discourse by means of the *Agnus Dei* supplication with which the novel ends:

> the pages that remain behind are mine I wrote them in my own handwriting little by little keeping all the rules of grammar . . . now I am running out of litanies and I should put an end to my chronicle . . . the written word can do a lot of harm to people, now I am running out of litanies and I feel as if my head were aching . . . the litany of Our Lady is the armor-plating that preserves us from sin I am already out of *ora pro nobis* litanies and now come the three that invoke the lamb of God which is the animal that symbolizes meekness I say *Agnus Dei* . . . you say *parce nobis domine* I repeat *Agnus Deis qui tollis peccata mundi* and you say *exaudi nos domine* I repeat again *Agnus Deis qui tollis peccata mundi* and you say *miserere nobis,* the only thing left for me is to ask God that the dead forgive me. (*CVA* 238)

In similar fashion the Catholic Mass begins with the *kyrie eleison* as a petition for God's (and Christ's) mercy and concludes almost immediately after the *Agnus Dei,* the "Lamb of God" invocation, which precedes the distribution of Holy Communion. While the primary purpose of this Catholic rite emphasizes the exchange of Christ's death for the redemption of humankind, Wendell's manuscript is symbolically offered up too, not, however, to plead so much for God's forgiveness as much as that of "the dead" whom he hopes will forgive him (*CVA* 238).

Alongside the thematic religiosity of the litany, Zach Dusteen, and others like him who are in the Arizona territory for the purpose of proselytizing is the sustained quasipolemical discussion that ensues from the title of the novel—that is, an explanation of Christ's activities in Arizona, almost as if he too were a fictive character to be included with the others who appear in the novel. Cela's admonition that his use of the word *versus* is in keeping with its Latin roots (meaning "going toward") substantiates the notion that *Cristo* is a rallying point for differing perspectives on the Christianization of the New World / Arizona in light of the rhetorical question that inaugurates this subtext of the novel. Someone states first that "Christ does not wear spurs but commands death" (*CVA* 22), while another, perhaps the same person, asks "if you know if it is true that they brought legal action against Christ in Arizona" (*CVA* 32). These statements provide the groundwork for the two sides of the discussion, the stronger emphasizing over and over again that "Christ is much harder than Arizona" (*CVA* 52), that "it is Christ who wants to bring legal action against Arizona" (*CVA* 137), that "Christ goes towards Arizona . . . Christ does not go against anybody" (*CVA* 177), and that "Christ is God" (233). While it could be argued that Dusteen might be the one who is defending Christ, there is no textual documentation to prove it. What stands out, however, is (as *Pilar Rotella's article* implies) a decidedly strong difference of opinion which pits one side against the other, hence the antagonism that, despite Cela's etymologically purist use of the term *versus,* issues forth from the title of the novel.

In stark contrast to the gentleness of the Lamb of God are the threateningly legalistic and rugged associations of Christ "wearing spurs" and being "harder" than Arizona itself, an anthropomorphic view of the Son of God from the perspective of those very inhabitants of the Arizona territory who represent, by extension, the Sodom and Gomorrah that is Tombstone (*CVA* 211).

Except for the tenderness with which *la china María* (Chinese Mary) is depicted toward the end of the novel, "bad intentions know no borders and grow like the worms in dead people" (*CVA* 99), replacing compassion, itself being nowhere to be found in Tombstone. Because of the mistreatment in St. Bartholomew which he witnessed as a child, Wendell repeats one of the more moving ethical statements of the novel: "nobody should live without being loved a little, even though it is almost next to nothing" (*CVA* 91). The one act of "charity" which is performed by the former nun Ana Abanda is portrayed with such pitiless sarcasm that it cannot be taken seriously as a work of mercy but, rather, as an ironic reminder of Erskine Carlow's physical imperfection.[16] The same is true of any other action that reflects the slightest glimmer of kindness. False bravado supersedes tenderness. Fear is all around, as Wendell dreads being "sent to hell" (*CVA* 147) and fears that the pus that oozes forth from the mark branded on his rear end is a punishment from God for his incestuous relations.

The cemetery at Boothill (sometimes called la Colina de la Bota [in Spanish]) which Wendell mentions from time to time constitutes a monument to Tombstone's inhabitants, most of whom would never have been heard had it not been for Wendell Liverpool Espana, who is, in reality, their spokesman. By serving as their mouthpiece, the narrative segments of the novel acquire, similar to *Mazurka,* a dual, if not multiple, dialogic counterpoint that fosters in the reader the impression that, in addition to numerous narrators, there are just as many fictive narratees: those to whom Wendell is directing his discourse as well as he himself as the receiver of stories that are being told him by people like his mother, Abbie Adams, Joe Bignon, Sandy Hartford, and others. Not without notice is the presence of an oftentimes unnamed *usted* ([formal] you) or Gerard Ospino's suggestion about how Wendell should arrange the manuscript: "you should put order in what you are explaining so that people do not get confused, the best thing is to tell according to the dead people" (*CVA* 79), something, responds Wendell, is easier said than done. He is also reminded— perhaps by Gerard?—that "it is not necessary to talk about this as if it all had occurred already, one may also tell it as if it were just still happening" (*CVA* 44). At another point in the discourse an anonymous voice breaks in and says that "I too believe that from here on in it might be convenient to say the litanies two by two" (*CVA* 114), giving strong evidence of a coparticipatory viewpoint regarding the manuscript. In effect, these and other related textually self-referential suggestions are tantamount to an acknowledgment that an orderly record of the people, places, and things is bound to end up riddled with doubt and sealed with customary Celian confusion.[17] For this reason Wendell's off-the-cuff references to specific dates are as nonchalant as his account of peoples' names, aliases, and nicknames. A far cry from the meticulousness of a historian, Wendell's complacency with his own surname(s) extends itself to those that are included in his memoirs because, according to his way of thinking, it is perfectly natural for people to call "themselves whatever they wish" (*CVA* 40), given that "almost everybody changes names at some time" anyway.

In his writerly naïveté Wendell is honest in giving credit where credit is due. For example, he says that his knowledge of the happenings at the O.K. Corral comes directly from Black Jane's daughter, the mulatta Jane Kolb, who "would relate it with real gusto . . . like children's stories" (*CVA* 163). Another source of information is sheriff Sam W. Lindo, whose veracity Wendell believes could very well have been "copied from a calendar" (*CVA* 69). On other occasions he states that what follows is a conversation that took place between different individuals. Now and again he transcribes the written testimony of people, like Mamie Emmy, who have experienced a cure from elixirs, while in other situations he allows us to overhear people like Vicky Farley and Paul as they "confess" their sins to Father Roscommon, who prescribes for their penance a combination of whiskey and holy water "to combat their inner fevers" (*CVA* 33). Wendell also uses other people's words as if they were his own, pausing briefly to include the kinds of self-referential comments that permit his readers to understand the nature of his undertaking: "this really ought not go here but I write it so that I do not forget it" (*CVA* 109).

Among the hundreds of characters that Wendell recalls are Sam W. Lindo, Zuro Millor, the Konskie twins, Vicky Farley (half-man and half-woman), Ana Abanda, Taco Mendes, Eddie Peugeot (the "whitest" man ever seen), Jimmy Scottsdale, Octavio Lagares, Corinne McAlister (the prostitute who let the deranged Andy Canelo do whatever he wanted in her presence), Cam Coyote (the snake hunter), Jesusito Huevón (the animal castrator), and Balbino the Indian quack (doctor). Each of them fits perfectly in the hyperspace that is the Tombstone of Wendell's recollection, a place inscribed in a scatologically hallucinatory panorama of human beings in all of their imperfection.[18] Francisco Paco Nogales and Taco Mendes have glass eyes; Adelino Biendicho has one ear and Anteater one testicle; Zach Dusteen's sons, Jim, Nick, Alex Joe, and Zach, have bad eyesight, halitosis, inflammation of the testicles, and stutter or are retarded; and the list goes on. Even the dead cannot rest in peace, as many cadavers, like those of Agripino Twin and Teodulfo Zapata, are mutilated by ravaging fish or other human beings (in revenge for past grievances). Prostitutes and their clientele subject themselves to indecencies beyond description. Individuals such as Sam W. Lindo, for example, suffer from milder physical decay but are equally as repugnant because of their "black gums and teeth" (*CVA* 6).[19]

Those who have not been marred outwardly have, nevertheless, been visited with other types of deprivation, the most common being poverty, hunger, and abandonment (by parents, husbands, wives, or other companions). "Because [they] . . . had to eat" (*CVA* 21), women turn to prostitution, an activity that amounts to nothing more than a means of securing a livelihood.[20] Countless orphans and deranged children and adults suffer, while those not of European descent are among the most maligned, such as, for example, the previously mentioned Native Americans of the Tanee reservation and those who died in 1917 on "Augustus Jonatás' derailed train"; scores of black men and women such as Tony Clints, Vicky Farley, and Euphemia Escabosa; and Chinese laborers such as Wong Chi Hung and Wu, who lived and worked in villifying, subhuman situations.

In these infernal surroundings daily life is conducive to similarly radicalized pleasures and forms of entertainment. There is no middle ground for people to find contentment, as the specter of countless hanged men, "blue and green and gold-colored flies" (*CVA* 220), and *la negra Patricia* (black Patricia) slitting children's throats pulsate like a heartbeat. Favorite pastimes include defecating on people's doorsteps, drinking whiskey through their noses, smearing their anuses with honey to attract the ants so as to produce a tingling sensation, watching the snake named Dorothy (kept in a large glass jar in Anteater's bar) eat live mice, urinating on ant holes, watching flies agonize in liquids because their wings had been plucked, and decapitating chickens to use their heads for decorative purposes.[21] Among the more "dignified" forms of enjoyment are a scant few—namely, the Mexican ballads—*corridos*—which are not always so mild-mannered. When reading is mentioned, it is limited to publications such as the *Tombstone Epitaph, La Voz de Nogales* (Nogales Voice), and *El Diario de Sarasota* (Sarasota Daily). Bob Oasis, a cowboy from Doug Rochester's novels *Bob Oasis the Lovesick Cowboy* and *Full Moon over the Río Grande* (*CVA* 34), is a kind of hero, but the act of writing is symbolically ridiculed by the theft of two typewriters: one that belonged to Rochester which was taken by the Indian Cornelio Laguna for use as a tourist attraction, the other by another Native American named Rodrigo Aires, who stole the typewriter that supposedly adorned D. H. Lawrence's grave.

Besieged by so much degeneracy, one wonders how Wendell rose to the heights of writing this socially conscious manuscript, an accomplishment that remains unexplained in his text. Wendell's document gives eyewitness testimony to the same protracted ills that ushered in the twentieth century as it is about, at the end of his lifetime, to channel the course of the next millenium. Poverty, hunger, alienation, discrimination, racism, exploitation, and spiritual deprivation are, by now, a legacy that Wendell *Espana or Span or Aspen* painfully hands over to the next generation that will be engaged in the same struggle as the one that is painfully familiar to his brother Bill Hiena: "life is nothing more than winners and losers and . . . the desert with its snakes is better than lice-infested jail" (*CVA* 90).[22] Fully aware of what his chronicle entails in terms of what he is reticent about having published, Wendell proclaims that "here nobody is against anybody, Jews, Hispanics, Indians, Blacks, here we push and shove that is for certain but we all fit, we fit clumsily but we all fit for the time being nobody has fallen off the earth" (*CVA* 224–25).

In deathbed fashion Wendell's plea is all-inclusive in imploring that "we examine our conscience and confess our sins in front of" a heart-shaped stone found in the desert and covered with sins (*CVA* 230). As meaningful as the proverbial "life that flashes before ones eyes before dying" is Wendell's ten-step confession, which professes more about him than anything else in the novel. Particularly moving is his childlike perception of death, which comes down to meeting God face to face: "standing up and without bearing arms with one's hat in hand with a lot of humility, in front of God Our Lord it is useless to walk like a macho and breaking and ordering about because he is able to melt us down with just a glance, Christ is God and one cannot get in with anything but mercy" (*CVA* 233). In what appears for all practical purposes to be Wendell's total acceptance of the end of his life, death is as tender as the Lamb of God, upon whom he calls for mercy.

CHAPTER 9

El asesinato del perdedor

In one of the first reviews written of *El asesinato del perdedor,* 1994 (The Murder of the Loser), Miguel García-Posada defines Cela's novel as a surrealistic version of Francisco de Quevedo's biting "black humor" which culminates in the dizzying phantasmagoria of a narrative discourse that is both a "hallucinatory carnival" and a "universal *esperpento.* "[1] Having come full circle in *El asesinato,* Cela has converted his long-forgotten Pascual Duarte into one of the principal schizophrenic narrative voices of the novel, Cela's first major work of prose fiction since winning the Nobel Prize in 1989. The Galician Nobel laureate holds little back here in freely expressing a long-awaited self-vindication that is most apparent in the second part of his 1993 autobiography, in which he does not disguise the thoughts that still plague him concerning those detractors who did everything within their power to condemn him for *Pascual Duarte* and *The Hive* (*M* 340–48).

The first of two novels published in 1994, *El asesinato* is a crucible for Cela's narrative fiction to date.[2] First off, it utilizes the seminal Pascual Duarte criminal-turned-writer motif as an alluring structuring principle for the narrative discourse; it also makes reference to *Madera de boj* (Boxwood) the novel that Cela has been promising to complete since 1989. Finally, it cushions its nuclear plot with apocalyptical realities of the twentieth century: the AIDS epidemic, the civil war in Bosnia, the complexities of the New World Order, the crisis of credibility and efficacy of many judicial systems, and the media's viciousness in foraging human tragedy.[3] *El asesinato* is a Pandora's box of narrative devices (multiple narrators, points of view, and narratees) which expand beyond readerly tolerance the traditional boundaries between literary genres.

In bold defiance of narrative conventions the novel utilizes theatrical mime and poetic associations that demonstrate Cela's impeccable command of Spanish and his propensity for scatology. By subverting the supposedly objective historical rendering of "reality," Cela exposes the fate and victimization of the main character, Mateo Ruecas Domínguez, who, in turn, serves as a poignant metaphor for humankind's place in a Western society that grows more unwieldy as the close of the twentieth century approaches. As a means of heightening the futility of finding out the true nature of Mateo Ruecas's "crime," a textured, self-conscious narration is woven together by means of references to letters, manuscripts, people's confessions, different oral and written accounts of "what really happened" to Mateo, public speeches and related demagoguery, female authors, and at least forty-one allusions to what would have been better titles for "este libro" (this book).[4] As in *Mazurka,* the reader knows from the beginning that Mateo was unable to cope with the ordeal and killed himself.

Inversely proportional to the novel's curiously brief epigraph—"Fac ita"—are references to the *errors* that invoke the wrath of the gods, mistakes that constitute the symbolic point of departure for the recounting of what happened to Mateo Ruecas "in one of these years" (*AP* 233) on the fateful day that he publicly displayed his affection for his girlfriend, Soledad Navares, in the nameless bar in a small Galician town (known only as "N.") at the very time that the young judge don Cosme happened to enter the same establishment. From the beginning of the Ruecas story we are told that everything people know and say about the incident "is probably a lie," an opinion that is fundamental to all elaboration on the matter: the young judge's word against that of "the witnesses" supposedly in the bar at the time of the event (*AP* 26). Because of his lack of worldly sophistication, the twenty-year-old Mateo was ill prepared to protest his arrest and what followed it: eight days of incarceration, during which he was raped, sodomized, and otherwise abused; and the trial, in which he was sentenced to five months in jail, fined 30,000 *pesetas,* and disqualified from securing any publicly funded teaching position for seven years (itself a pointed commentary on the educational system). Soledad Navares, being only sixteen years old, was also unable to proffer much of a defense and received a similar reduced sentence.

Unaccustomed to the fear-turned-paranoia and degradation to which he had been subjected in jail and incapable of believing the words that he read every time he looked at the written notification stating that, because of their clean, past record, neither he nor Soledad would have to go to jail, Mateo hung himself on 7 February from the lintel of the stable of his family's home. His suicide provoked so much unrest among the townspeople that his friends, in retribution for his death, deposited fecal matter on Don Cosme's door at the Fonda la Milagrosa (Miraculous Inn [*AP* 47]), where he lived since coming to town as a reputedly inexperienced judge.[5] The events that befall Mateo also warrant the attention of Esteban Ojeda, a narrator who, identifying himself as Pascual Duarte and a friend of the Ruecas family, wrote down his testimony about what happened to Mateo. So great is the injustice perceived to have been perpetrated that the novel ends with the inclusion of a "Letter of Warning" written to don Sebastián Cardeñosa López (clergyman from La Coruña) by Juana Olmedo. As a concerned citizen who was a part of the "Mateo Ruecas Coordination" effort that had collected 400,000 *pesetas* for the purpose of bringing legal action against the judges of N.N. and B.B. for their part in Mateo's death, Juana pleads the case for reform of "article 431 of the Penal Code" (*AP* 237), which refers to what constitutes "public scandal."

El asesinato is fraught with social commentary and unabashed criticism. Its outwardly antagonistic sarcasm targets the enclaves of power in industrialized societies, and it is purposefully blasphemous with regards to language and content. It defies the smooth transmission of facts about Mateo Ruecas and sports an iconoclasm that questions the heroism of individuals, like Joan of Arc, whom history and society have deified. It is characterized by a halting narration that is intentionally interrupted with spontaneous, anonymous dialogues between characters either from narrative segments immediately preceding or who become the focal points of the subsequent narration. Given Cela's proclivity for obliterating factual objectivity regarding the Ruecas case, chronology is not of the essence. Other couples, real and otherwise, form part of a fictive framework that deliberately mixes people of the twentieth century with historical, legendary, literary, and invented characters from other epochs, bolstering, therefore, one of the frequently heard refrains of the novel: "these elementary and cheaply sold crimes usually become diluted into the vague strata of the social, national, local conscience finally and when all is said and done, end up becoming a part of folklore, popular dime-store romances, poems sung by blind people, street theater and ballads" (*AP* 205).

The dilemma between fact and error regarding Mateo Ruecas transcends its own limits and exacerbates the nature of fiction versus reality. Hearsay abounds as narrative comments make no attempt to conceal the fact that what is being told is based largely upon what "they say" (*dicen*). For that reason a narrative voice resignedly accepts the notion that "nobody should try to wrap words up in the opposing thinking" (*ML* 55), in spite of the fact that Cela does precisely the same thing in *El asesinato*. In addition, then, to pitting one "truth" against another in multiple inane fictive circumstances, occurrences of little consequence to Mateo Ruecas are proliferated, once again beyond readerly tolerance. On the other hand, incidents of a more immediate nature (which would traditionally occupy narratorial as well as readerly attention) are intentionally inconclusive; among these are the axe murder of the eight members of the Aguacatala family and Adrián Ortega's death by knifing. Because nobody cares about them, these murders go practically unattended in comparison to interest in what Mateo Ruecas was *said* to have done. Ironically, the scene of Mateo's crime is one of two things: either it is so unimportant that neither the bar nor the town has a name, or, to the contrary, its intended anonymity is generically suggestive that the same thing can occur anywhere.[6]

An array of "stories" about different couples which fill the obvious gaps surrounding the Ruecas case deflect attention away from and at the same time symbolize the universal injustice that was wrought upon Mateo and Soledad. The proliferation of paramours ranges from the generic to the most wildly idiosyncratic: the blind countess and the bandit; Pamela Pleshette and the bishop of Restricted Beach (Florida); Doña Waldetruda and her elderly, wheelchair-ridden lover, Don Zaqueo; Doña Paula and Valerio II; and Claudina and Estefanía Yellowbilled's nameless boyfriend; to name only the most flamboyant, oddly matched twosomes (homosexuals not excluded). And the parade of circus-like characters continues until the end of the novel, as more famous characters are added to the list: Hugh of Champagne, Count Ramón Berenguer, and (supposedly famous) clergymen. Notable among these are distinguished men whom the narrator has unscrupulously dubbed members of a "club" of homosexuals which includes high-ranking (fictitious) church and government officials, such as Pope Urban CLIII, Cardinal Sergio Bustelo Guillarey, and others.[7] Included among these degenerates are also men whose sexual appetite is so insatiable that Cela uses it to defile further the pomp and circumstance of aristocracy and at the same time underscore the commonality of basic human needs. A case in point is the rape of Felícula de Valois by Acursio Acursio's fellow members of the religious order of Templars.

Despite challenges to the traditional fulfillment of narrative expectations, the reader's point of view is acknowledged in some of *El asesinato*'s unidentified conversations. For example, someone chides another individual (who has to be one of the narrators) for not having "put this last paragraph in Latin" (*AP* 88), only to be told that it had not been done that way "so that the reader would not encounter difficulties." Another voice says he or she is "beginning to be bored by all these Western stories" (*AP* 220), as if to read the mind of the reader concerning the unrelenting barrage of amorous vignettes strung together to form a narrative discourse of 238 pages.

Against a constellation of so many disparate couples, their accompanying stories, and what they say to one another, Mateo Ruecas is, as in "real" life, a mere speck of humanity whose life and death went virtually unnoticed, except to a handful of people. As a means of emphasizing a society and (Catholic) church's unhealthy obsession with sex and the hypocrisy surrounding it, Cela includes scores of prostitutes, both named and anonymous, to whom the narrator(s) and other characters constantly refer and who usually end up either in the gallows or some other public forum that constitutes a cheap form of entertainment for onlookers, such as Doña Waldetruda, who go to great lengths to arrive on time for the execution of these "criminals."[8] Such is the case, for example, with a "docile Moorish prostitute" whose hanging is uproariously applauded by spectators (*AP* 125). The same fate awaits a "Portuguese prostitute" and numerous other women (*AP* 11). On another occasion a "little grandmother" *(abuelita)* takes her last breath to the sound of "the guffaws of everyone present" (*AP* 147), while a narrator refers to the breathtaking spectacle of an older woman's "naked cadaver" (*AP* 146).

Providing additional "entertainment" during these executions is the refrain-like appearance of the familiar "choral mass of beggars" who, like their counterparts in *oficio,* perform in public places only to be ridiculed, maligned, and mistreated by onlookers. Besides surreptitiously meriting Cela's compassion, these individuals constitute an important part of the theatrical subtext of the Mateo-Soledad story line. As such, it exacerbates the dehumanization of Mateo Ruecas, the farcical nature of the legal proceedings brought against him and his girlfriend, and, most significantly, the confusing separation between fact and fiction. Not surprising, then, is the inclusion of Punch-and-Judy show puppets that move about in *El asesinato* in as matter-of-fact a way as the "real" characters. Moreover, the fusion of theater and nontheater—that is, the narration of the facts about the Ruecas case—produces a generic narrative mutation that brings to light the public's thirst for violence, crime, and retribution, which, in turn, taps into the theater of the absurd which Cela cultivated in his plays. From this come the Chaplinesque vignettes that constitute numerous pockets of fictive activity, in which it is not uncommon to witness, for example, Marta Señeri being driven around by her boyfriend on the handlebars of his bicycle or, Juan Grujidora and his cousin Baltasara as they, too, ride their bikes from the "greenhouse to the morgue and back" (*AP* 206). Within this context Ierónima Illiescu tells Adán Platja ("commentator of Sexto Aurelio Propercio's *Elegies"* [*AP* 171]) that, if he likes the study of folklore, psychology, and history, then he will most likely end up "writing puppet theater" (*AP* 172), an avocation akin to Cela's ingenious plotting of the events of this novel. As a "cast member" of *El asesinato,* then, Mateo Ruecas not only gets lost in the shuffle of so much insanity; he also falls prey to its schizophrenic narration, converting its fairly uncomplicated dilemma into a maze of purported "factual" information.

The rudimentary nature of Mateo Ruecas's story notwithstanding, it is dispersed at various intervals over the course of the novel by a complex network of narrative voices that, although at times clearly identified, as in the case of

Esteban Ojeda, on other occasions emanate from what resembles a schizophrenic narrator whose voice could easily be that of any number of characters dwelling deep inside his persona. The resulting plurality of viewpoints concerning what happened to Ruecas obliterates narrative objectivity, particularly given the dialogic point of departure which is a signature trait of Celian prose fiction and one that, more than anywhere else, activates the entire narrative discourse. Such is the function (in part), for example, of an unidentified *señora* (madame) who responds to what appears to be a question asked of her by an unnamed narrator: "tell the incident as you wish" (*AP* 29).

Although there is little room for doubt concerning Esteban Ojeda's primary role in the authorship of the segments that deal with the Ruecas account, *El asesinato* begins in a way that is reminiscent of *San Camilo*: a third-person narrator is focused on Michael Percival the Stooped-over, as he, "one Ash Wednesday many years ago, at least two-hundred" (*AP* 7), looks at himself in a mirror and tells his reflected image that he could very easily kill him with a knife he has used many times in the past to accomplish daring as well as sentimental deeds (like carving hearts with sweethearts' initials in the bark of trees). This rather typical focalization of an apparent paragon of strength and the author of notable exploits, however, immediately turns upon its own seeming objectivity. By attaching itself, within the same paragraph, to Percival's first-person digression, it leads into a formally designated (rather than a stream-of-consciousness) conversation between Percival and his mirrored self. Viewed structurally, the abrupt move from one level of narration to another sets the tone for the narrative discourse while also thematically laying the foundation for a string of narrative and dialogic segments that, no matter how disjointed and absurd, revolve around the fixed coordinates of hatred, violence, injustice, repression, scatology, and death, to wit Michael is described as speaking:

> with a certain studied serenity and in a low voice. —With this knife I could kill you easily but I am not going to do it, I only want to warn you about it. Listen to me carefully. Do not make little of your enemy, try to infect him with some humiliating illness . . . [not necessarily] AIDS or leprosy or nostalgia . . . show yourself sorrowful at the funeral, wailing loudly, you know, tears and weeping and sweating, also drool and foaming and pus, pimples of pus, that is more difficult. —Yes. May I go to the bathroom? —Yes, but don't be long or get distracted along the way. (*AP* 7)

With nothing more than a passing remark that "all will be clarified in due time" (*AP* 7), the next narrative segment introduces Pamela Pleshette and her paramour, the bishop of Restricted Beach, one of the many illicitly united couples that, other than their questionable relationships, have nothing in common. In spite of the fact that we learn nothing significant about Ms. Pleshette, hers is the first voice to offer an alternative for the title of the novel, saying that: "This book should be called according to how its confused female author has decided, either *Penultimate Floodgate or Mateo Ruecas's Impossible Love,* or else *Penultimate Floodgate and Notification of the Murder of the Loser Mateo Ruecas* (the editor is moved by other desires)." She goes on to suggest other titles, assuring that "towards the end or a little before this premise will be repeated for the solace of the dying" (*AP* 8), leaving the reader to ponder whether or not she is the aforementioned author. When, however, her promise is indeed fulfilled at the end of the novel, nothing is resolved because someone (who could very easily be identified as Don Sebastián rather than Ms. Pleshette) repeats the same title suggested by her, saying that he or she knows "only too well that this book should have been given the title that its *confused female author* decided" (232; emphasis added). Yet another extraneous character, Tomás Cerulleda, is brought in as a means of speaking out concerning a controversy that is an important refrain in terms of accelerating the plot development and underscoring Cela's bitter cynicism for certain Western power structures: "—It is very dangerous for judges to be young and gullible, a judge ought to be serene, old, and skeptical since justice does not have as its mission to fix the world but rather to avoid its further deterioration, that is enough" (*AP* 8).

Despite the incoherent chain of components that set the narrative discourse in motion, Pamela Pleshette's and Tomás Cerulleda's words are prompted by the same familiar dialogic underpinnings that characterize Michael Percival's narration-turned-dialogue and, therefore, subsequently reinforce the narrative-conversational format of the novel. In Pamela's case (and with her head rested upon Estefanía Yellowbilled's boyfriend's shoulder) she speaks as if to herself about her husband's suicide, the topic that prompts her comments about the aforementioned titles. Similarly, Cerulleda directs his discourse to "his cohort of silent drinking buddies" (*AP* 8), none of whom responds to his long diatribe about Don Cosme's incompetence as a judge.

Confronted thus with blatant incoherence, the reader is further perplexed by a third-person narrative commentary, in the next paragraph, which confirms the existence of yet another narrator, who resorts to a brief, first-person observation about "the executioner" who, although not actually responsible for killing Mateo (because the latter hung himself), is an equally significant Celian figure in the Ruecas story: "The narrator goes back to the thread of his discourse, Pamela Pleshette had already finished. He arrived late, *I* do not know who, nobody knows who nor what, but he arrived late" (*AP* 9; emphasis added). The blueprint, then, for *El asesinato* is made up of seemingly faceless individuals who strike up conversations that are vehicles for introducing the major themes of the plot, all of which culminate in the overriding (Celian) preoccupation with death. From here stems the related refrain that characterizes the senselessness of Mateo's death: "—Have they taken away the dead man? Nobody answered and the doctor raised his voice a little bit more, not a lot. —I say, have they taken away the dead man? The dead man, in a barely audible voice, said to him: —No; I am still here, maybe I will not go until Monday because the undertakers went swimming in the river" (*AP* 12). Time and again the same question is asked in different ways and most often without a satisfactory reply: "—Why do you prefer death to life? —It's the opposite: why do I disguise the death of death and life with rags and interrupted pleading sighs? —You should know! —No; I do not know. I ask [others] or I ask myself, it's all the same. There shouldn't be too much confusion in this. —It's inevitable" (*AP* 49).[9]

Just when there seems to be neither rhyme nor reason to the stream of anonymous conversational vignettes and endless opinions about what the title of the novel might better have been, the first-person narrator who was faintly audible earlier in the novel surfaces and assumes more control over the Ruecas story, clearly identifying himself as the friend of Mateo's father, Lucas Ruecas (*AP* 18). In giving his testimony about Mateo Ruecas and Soledad Navares, this narrator identifies himself in a number of ways that lead us to believe he speaks from firsthand experience. Significant, too, is the fact that his "spiritual director, who is also a lawyer" is "the judge of N." to whom Mateo made the statement that ended up indicting him (*AP* 60). Furthermore, the heretofore nameless narrator is also a death row prisoner who, like so many prostitutes in the novel, is awaiting public execution. Out of the blue he responds to the previously mentioned anonymous *señora,* in reply to a letter she wrote him requesting a couple of invitations to "the execution" (*AP* 27), in which he says that he is "the main character, the hero of the party." Although he tells her he has not yet asked for them, he is certain there will be no problem in getting the "tickets" for her, since "society is very condescending when it comes to leading actors." In addition to knowing many of the facts about the case, how Mateo was treated in jail and by the judge, and the specific dates on which events occurred, the prisoner-narrator is conscientious about the written account he is keeping, being careful to cite references, such as his transcription of the sentence that was handed down to Mateo: "what appears between quotations is copied from the sentence" (*AP* 84).

Having somewhat gained our confidence, he identifies himself as Esteban Ojeda, who, it turns out, is a metamorphosed Pascual Duarte:

My name is Esteban Ojeda and I was famous some years ago, when I wrote some pages that began in this way: I, sir, am not vicious although I have plenty of reason to be, etc. Now I say that it is unspeakable and antisocial, that is to say, dreadful that judges do not mature amidst bundles of papers, case records, and red-tape . . . Don Cosme, the judge who killed Mateo Ruecas, has yet to mature, the Holy Spirit protects him in every thing and helped him to pass his examinations but he didn't give him enough time for maturity[.] (*AP* 101)

Ojeda's declaration does much more than tarnish his erstwhile credibility concerning what seemed to be a plausible narrative account of the confusion surrounding Ruecas. If Esteban believes that *he* is Pascual (or Mateo for that matter), how then is his delusional account to be trusted? Furthermore, he is undermined by the extradiegetic narrator, who again offers third-person observations about Ojeda, describing him in such a way as to confuse him with Michael Percival by way of a narration that dovetails, like Percival's, into a similar first-person digression: "Esteban Ojeda likes to write in the first person, it is always easier. It's as if I were Mateo Ruecas, I close my eyes and I feel like Mateo Ruecas, the loser about whom is spoken in this *true account.* My girlfriend's name is Soledad" (*AP* 116; emphasis added).

As if to exploit thoroughly our doubt concerning what is ironically the lengthiest and most complete account of the Ruecas incident, the Esteban-Pascual-Mateo prisoner-narrator sums up by positing fact with fiction: the soccer match that Mateo, Soledad, and their friends were watching in the bar on the fateful day ended in a score of "Spain 3, Northern Ireland 1, *chances are that everything that has been written down here is a lie and that nothing happened there"* (*AP* 117; emphasis added). While he resembles Pascual Duarte in his preference for staying in his cell to write (rather than taking advantage of permission to go outdoors), he, on the other hand, subtly parodies his own written word: "almost all the [names] that appear in these pages are false" (*AP* 167). The intentional misinformation is, however, prompted not so much by him as by his "spiritual advisor," who does not want him to write down real names, much less that of the judge identified as "Don Cosme [who] . . . does not know his own name, Don Constancio, Don Claudio, Don Alfredo, Don Ladislao, Don Efrén, Don Abel Ernesto, Don Cosme, you decide" (*AP* 219). In short, no better an indictment of the entire legal system is provided than Esteban's confusion.

109

Provoking more chagrin about the already schizophrenic narration are the "facts" that verify the tripartite reality in which Ojeda lives. In the Ruecas realm he knows the specific details of Mateo's suicide and where the men's toilet is located in the bar where Mateo committed his "crime"; furthermore, he is familiar with Mateo's parents and friends, and he knows Mateo's nickname, El Pinche (The Scullion), as well as those of his friends and the fact that they were "young men that belonged to the draft [call-up] number 82" (*AP* 19).[10] As Pascual Duarte, Ojeda knows verbatim the first lines of Pascual's memoirs. In his own world Ojeda, sentenced to die for crimes that are never revealed, is well aware that everything amounts to what other narrative voices also believe to be "the plot for a *sainete*" (one-act farce [*AP* 9]). Even Juana Olmedo's purportedly objective letter is sealed with complicity, as she, too, judges to "be a *sainete*" all of Don Cosme's personal declarations regarding the case, as they were printed in various newspapers (*AP* 237).

Superseding all possible narrative voices, whether Esteban Ojeda's or not, is that of the anonymous narrator. In the introduction to Juana's "Letter of Warning" he identifies himself as having "drafted the previous narration" so that others might avoid "these bitter, irreversible situations" in the future while also warning against the harm that history can have on future events (*AP* 234). The welcomed admission of authorship is, however, as suspect as all other narrative pronouncements, precisely because of the numerous allusions to other possible sources of authenticity regarding the facts of the case, many of which define him more as an editor-transcriber than a bona fide third-person narrator. Along the same lines and in what are most likely his own narrative comments, he speaks candidly of information from multiple sources: other notebooks (*AP* 50); the "confusing" transcription that is noted in different texts (*AP* 221); the "editor's . . . wishes" that precluded the title Pamela Pleshette had originally suggested for the book (*AP* 232); the "paper" found in Mateo Ruecas's pants pocket after his death; and "this (—unidentified—) paper" containing opinions about the contriteness of Mateo's attitude before dying (*AP* 95).

Before this narrator ever refers specifically to Esteban Ojeda, he intentionally undermines his own identity by dropping bits and pieces of autobiographical information about when he was a child in Iria Flavia (Cela's birthplace), his aunt Katy, and the period of time during which he boarded at the Jesuit school of Mevagissey (*AP* 87). In light of the two first-person narrations one wonders whether or not the childhood sketches pertain to him or to Ojeda. Additionally, he registers more confusion when he speaks with one of his many fictive conversation partners about the "official version" of yet another suggested title for the novel (*AP* 30). Since these comments, however, really deal with a hypothetical title, the dubiousness of the already unreliable Mateo-Soledad story is doubly magnified. Similar plausibility is replicated when "Las dudas de la soledad" (The Doubts of Loneliness) is cited as another title for the novel, this time with an explicit reference to its "malicious author, miss Mary Tavistock" (*ML* 91).

In a dialogic interlude someone asks whether or not he or she *(usted)* would have preferred writing editorials in an important newspaper (*AP* 194); since the question characteristically follows a narrative segment, it is assumed to be addressed to the narrator because of all the attention that he or she has given the Ruecas case. Besides knowing to mete out in litany-like fashion theoretical titles for the novel, the transcriber-narrator is well versed in other disciplines, as evidenced in his sarcastic reference to Don Cosme and Diderot: "Don Cosme was always ignorant of Diderot's objective of strangulating the last king with the last priest's intestines" (*AP* 87). He is conversant about writers, such as Shakespeare, Gustavo Adolfo Bécquer, Cervantes, and Luis de León, as well as philosophers and historians, such as Seneca, Archimedes, and Plutarch. However fictitious they are, he also knows about such texts as *The Observer of New Orleans* which are often either in outright error or of questionable content, like Mr. Ted Carew's articles in the *"New Ciri Post"* concerning the "elegance" of prostitutes who work in brothels (*AP* 157).[11] In questioning whether Claudina and Estefanía Yellowbilled are sisters or sisters-in-law, he says that the "chronicles" are mixed up. He even has the nerve to dispute the authenticity of the Dead Sea Scrolls (Los Papiros del Mar Muerto) while at the same time parodying his own narration:

I am almost certain that it has already been said that Nicolás Mengabril, who played the bugle, learned in Africa, very well, had deflowered Martirio:

    a) with his finger,
    b) upon leaving catechism class,
    c) in the doorway of Ms. Ródena's house.
(AP 100)[12]

As a further pièce de resistance concerning the questionable nature of the narration, he comments on other acts of violence which also go relatively unnoticed—that is, the beheading of Prisciliano in *la Porta Nigra de Tréveris* and an injury sustained by Bishop Sisnando somewhere in Galicia. These two news items are flanked by another question-and-answer conversation in which someone asks him if he has read Sisemón Mayhew's book *El muermo o la decadencia de las iniciativas* (The Boredom or the Decline of Initiatives), whose thesis deals with the author's "theory of the disguise of situations, feelings, and sub-

111

missions or the syncope of the SSS." Shortly after the sardonic allusion to what amounts to a published version about concealment (the disguises about which Mayhew wrote), the narrator includes a brief interchange between himself and a hamlet dweller, in which the former asks for a smoke, only to be told no, because "that has already become a part of history" (*AP* 163).[13] The decontextualized incident alludes to Cela's earlier, carefree days when his "penchant" for walking trips through Spain yielded a vagabond persona that was transformed into the narrator of numerous, popular travel books.[14] In weaving this into the fabric of this absurdist novel, Cela blurs the temporal boundaries that distinguish one fictive space from another, thereby unreservedly embracing the obscurity that surrounds the Mateo Ruecas story. In doing this, he injects it with a nostalgia that Michael Percival equates with death (in his deliberations about what lethal disease is advisable to use to gain control over one's enemy: "AIDS, leprosy or nostalgia").

The strange, disjointed circumstances concerning the numerous characters which provide a context for the Ruecas story reveal the uncertainty and incoherence that are so vital to the development of *El asesinato*.[15] For example, about the *abuelita* (little grandmother) named doña Dulce Nombre Gaudarela y Mondim de Basto and her three grandsons, Cam, Sem, and Jafet, we are told that her communicative skills leave a lot to be desired, since "she said three or four words that nobody understood" (*AP* 147). Another character asks what Gómez's cleanliness has to do with an Indian soldier's public hanging, to which he is told that it has "[a]bsolutely nothing" to do with it (*AP* 90).[16] Lorenzo the Scrupulous, upon being interrogated by Pope Urban CLIII, says that he "understands nothing nor admits to anything" (*AP* 222), while Virginia Chatrian (a eunuch in the court of the Czar of Russia) divulged untruths to the whole world purposefully to confuse everyone (*AP* 229). And so grows the list of outlandish characters who eclipse the relevant "truths" of the case, circumscribing it with the same linguistic expressions of violence, ludicrousness, and scatology which recall Cela's theater.

In *El asesinato* Cela's flights of linguistic virtuosity are a simulacrum of the verbiage of legal proceedings. Herein also lie frequent, superfluous references to Latin and plentiful self-conscious narrative asides about how to write/spell certain words: *aves con zeta* (birds [spelled] with *z* [*AP* 60]), *fritanga* or *fritura* (fried dishes/foods [*AP* 91]), *azafrán* or *cachumba* (saffron [*AP* 207]), and so forth. In keeping with a linguistic consciousness that is both self-referential and thematically linked with considerations about the Ruecas case, somebody says to the narrator that he or she "should measure with much more care the language that he or she uses" (*AP* 146). Furthermore, it is advised that the use of adjectives does not lend itself to objectivity: "in reality nobody should ever use adjectives" (*AP* 139). It is not surprising, then, that characters such as Felícula de Valois and one of the men that sexually abused her also engage in sophisticated verbal exchanges that evince the richness of Cela's lexicon while deliberately advancing the linguistic muddle of the novel.

As words cloud the real issues, we are diverted farther and farther from the story line—that is, Mateo Ruecas's arrest and subsequent death. For this reason, then, it is impossible to know for sure that the accused was in effect as belligerent as reported when he told Don Cosme that he, as Soledad's boyfriend, could and would do whatever he wished with her, that being none of the judge's business. Other versions of the "case" are equally suspect: whether or not Mateo really did "confuse Don Cosme with a tourist or a businessman" and, therefore, became careless in publicly showing his affection for Soledad (*AP* 44), something—one would assume from Juana Olmedo's letter—which every Spaniard should have known was against the law (because of sec. 431 of the Spanish Penal Code [*AP* 237]). For that matter there are so many accounts about Mateo and Soledad's indiscretions that nobody knows for sure exactly what they did. At one point the narrator goes so far as to say that he is transcribing *the* conversation that Don Cosme had with Mateo in the bar (only to transform it into a dialogue between the blind countess and the bandit who blinded her). Also questionable—although very probable given all the evidence to the contrary in *El asesinato*—is Don Cosme's having misinformed Mateo that he needed neither lawyer nor witnesses to testify for him because all that would "do nothing more than complicate matters and put the magistrates in a bad mood" (*AP* 201).

If Esteban Ojeda is in fact telling the truth about having copied word for word the sentence that was handed down to Mateo on "Holy Innocents' Day" (the Spanish equivalent of April Fool's Day), how are we to assume that he was made privy to it (was it because of his close friendship with the Ruecas family?) and that it was indeed a bona fide legal document: "the proven facts constitute an infraction of public scandal 'because they offend standards of decency constituting an undesirable spectacle of suggestively obscene attitudes, that are reserved for . . . more private circumstances . . .'" (*AP* 84). Also unresolved is the situation in which he saw the carefully folded suicide note that, if taken at face value, provides a written expression of the pathos of Mateo "the loser" in his final appeal to Don Cosme:

do not blame anybody for my death I kill myself because I do not wish to go on living well I don't know if I wish to or not neither am I able to go on living surely I am not able to go on living I believe that it would have been better not to have been born nor lived or to have died when I was little or at least before going to jail my life has not been a long one but lately I suffered a lot since I went to jail I suffered a lot and since I got out of jail I have a guilty conscience day and night sometimes I can't sleep I ask God's pardon . . . and my parents Lucas and Sagrario . . . and my girlfriend Solita . . . and my friends . . . and I ask your forgiveness Don Cosme you who wanted to straighten me out[.] (*AP* 94)

In light of such diametrically opposed viewpoints the dichotomy between "winners" and "losers" not only relates directly to the story but further intensifies the thematic impact of a novel that is a pitiless diatribe against the abuse of power at all levels, as evidenced in the figure of Abraham el Lelilí, a weak-kneed potentate. Parallel to each other are the refrains of how Mateo Ruecas was never the same after he got out of jail (because of the successive barbaric rapes he endured there) and Don Cosme's obsession with his own guilt and avowed lack of responsibility for the prisoner's fate: "eight days in jail cannot brand anybody" (*AP* 79). What is narrative pathos for Mateo Ruecas amounts to the contemptuous conversion of the judge into a ludicrous puppet whose declarations of innocence as well as competence had to be published in newspapers to appease people's hatred of him. In a sense both characters, Mateo and Don Cosme, are actors in a late twentieth-century commedia dell'arte of government-backed politicians who, in turn, "act the part, fake the setting, and do not break the deck" (*AP* 228), as they wave to those who, having died of hunger, file past them on the way to their graves (*AP* 59).

Regardless of the tangential nature of the part Juana Olmedo had in the events surrounding the death of Mateo Ruecas, her closing commentary regarding what seem to her to be "grotesque/exaggerated [*esperpénticas*] situations" serves as another quasiobjective affirmation of the atrocity that was begotten of simple, human emotion (*AP* 237). In *El asesinato* Cela goes way beyond chiding Spain for its ingrained obsession with the sinfulness of sex and uses Mateo and Soledad's courtship as a metaphor for the dehumanization of society, ever reminding us of those behaviors and attitudes that have, in one way or another, turned the Western world (that is portrayed in *El asesinato*) into the farce that it is. Mateo's feelings for his girlfriend led him to embrace her in public; and his fear, in turn, was transformed into paranoia because of the abuse he suffered at the hands of an inadequate penal system. On a broader scale Don Cosme's incompetence has more far-reaching implications, for it is his very insecurity which provokes the human tragedies that have been a scourge on humankind: the Spanish Inquisition, the civil wars in Bosnia and Herzegovina and Spain, and the extermination of the Jews during World War II, to name only a few that are cited in *El asesinato*.[17] When all is said and done, Cela resorts to an idea that is as basic as doña Rosa's opening statement in *The Hive,* in which "in reality everything boils down to perspective" (*AP* 185), a premise that holds universal appeal: "we should view everything with our own eyes because all outside interpretations are false, every single one of them" (*AP* 175).

CHAPTER 10

La cruz de San Andrés

In what could easily be interpreted as a blatantly vitriolic, and characteristically Celian scatological, attack on twentieth-century literary theory and criticism, *La cruz de San Andrés,* 1994 (St. Andrew's Cross), opens and closes with a pointed reminder that "the chronicle of a collapse" of the Galician López Santana family has been written on rolls of toilet tissue (*CSA* 9).[1] Matilde Verdú, one of the numerous female voices that constitute the elusive, protean narration, is equally as undaunted in her admission that she has done everything in her power to "disobey the norm" (*CSA* 221), going so far at one point as to antagonize the readers by calling them "stupid" (*CSA* 73). Given such open hostility, it is no wonder that the awarding of the Planeta Prize to Cela in October 1994 for this novel caused a commotion to which its author has grown accustomed.[2]

Using the colorful image of *las calderas de Pedro Botero* (Satan's cauldrons [*CSA* 192])—a common expression for hell—to describe the rudiments of this tale of demise, *La cruz* is an intentionally apocalyptical deconstruction of certain narrative and theatrical literary devices that come together as an end-of-century reminder of confusion that is at once iconoclastic concerning the past and a challenge for the future. In keeping with his own constancy for creative renewal, Cela boldly presses into service again the signature traits of his prose fiction: narration interfaced with and oftentimes generated in dialogue; alternating narrators with changing identities (within the same sentence or paragraph); anecdotal enigmas that become permanently imbedded in the narration; narrative consciousness that imbues the text with movement, vitality, and suspense; a compulsive thematics of death; and an underlying layer of refrain-like aphorisms that attest to a life (Cela's) that has virtually spanned the twentieth century.

Among these vintage Celian literary traits three break new ground in *La Cruz* and facilitate the hybridization of his prose fiction, thereby satisfying Cela's thirst for constant change.[3] These include the following: the preponderance of a supposed female point of view (the novel is narrated primarily by women, as we shall see); the use of icons from North American pop culture (nicknames, references to Ronald Hubbard's science of dianetics, a quote from Woody Allen, and comparisons with movie stars like Marilyn Monroe and Ava Gardner); and, last, reliance on theater as a structural blueprint for the novel.[4] In addition to facilitating all types of transference from one frame of reference to another—female to male, narrative to theatrical, Spanish to English—they also enhance a rhythmic duality that sets the tone for the narrative happenings that constitute the hermetic parameters of *La cruz* as it takes place, contrary to the rural landscape of *Mazurka,* in urban areas such as, for example, Ferrol (Franco's birthplace) and La Coruña (the capital of the province of the same name and one of the most important fishing ports and shipbuilding cities of Spain).

Based on classical five-act plays, *La Cruz* follows suit in essence and structure with regard to its own quintuple division: "Dramatis Personae," "Plot," "Exposition," "Crux," and "Dénouement, Final Coda, and Internment of the Last Puppets." As a means of further advancing the drama-driven format, measured references to Shakespeare appear throughout the narration as well as in two of the four epigraphs that introduce parts 1, 3, 4, and 5 of the novel.[5] In addition, the title calls to mind the distinctive X configuration of St. Andrew's crosses which connotes, among other things, public crucifixions used by the Romans to punish criminals, thus also evoking one of Cela's major themes of late, that being the public spectacle that is derived from executions. The presence of at least one male extradiegetic narrative voice notwithstanding, Matilde Verdú and her other female narrative counterparts' voices clearly echo the words of María Sabina, the mysterious Celian antihero of the play by the same name which Cela published around the time of Verdú's own fictive present of 1969 (the year Gimferrer has called "the twilight of Francoism" in Spain).[6] Set during the period immediately preceding Spain's emergence as a newly formed twentieth-century European democracy, following Franco's death, the almost forty-year-old Verdú and her girlfriends lived during the harshest period of Francoist rule, entering adolescence immediately following the end of the Spanish Civil War.[7] The consequences of having been conditioned by life in a "house divided" readily explain Cela's incessant preoccupation with the idea that blood is thicker than water and that violence only begets violence. Moreover, when plagued with the nationalistic and religious fanaticism of the Francoist regime's discourse regarding every aspect of Spanish life, even *familial* love is capable of assuming a side as sinister as that which Amancio (a derivative of the word *amar* [to love]) preaches to his followers, as we shall see.[8]

Although situated in Galicia, the seven López Santana family members move about in a chaos not unfamiliar to the characters of *San Camilo* and the city dwellers of *The Hive.* Seen from a late-twentieth-century perspective, these newer-generation Galicians further Cela's view of the human debacle that came of the fratricide that Spain suffered as the result of fanatical intransigence. What has changed in *La Cruz* is a widened perspective on the problem in light of those events that have drastically affected the course of history in the last twenty-five years: sexual revolution and AIDS, increased cult followings and the group suicides they oftentimes spawn, revolutions in technology and knowledge acquisition, and waning of traditional religion as an organizing principle of human conduct and behavior.

Added to the more universal spectrum of occurrences against which the López Santana family members play out their lives, however, is the importance that Galicia acquires in this novel and in Cela's recent fiction (being that his long-awaited novel *Madera de boj* [Boxwood] is supposed to deal primarily with the life of an ill-fated Galician sailor). In this regard *La cruz* is reminiscent also of *Mazurka*. The reputed bounty of Galicia's folklore, together with its geography, affords the important focal points that provide a constellation of poetic images that gauge passion and tension in the novel, most of which take their cue from common maritime topics: seagulls, shipwrecks, sailors, islands, beaches, cliffs, and storms, not to mention the wind and sea. Everything, it seems, is affected by Galicia's location on the westernmost promontory of the Iberian Peninsula: "In La Coruña a retired tobacconist dies almost every day, it's sad to see how the wind sweeps her into history, La Coruña is a city of a lot of wind, it blows everywhere, it lifts up us women's skirts and it swells men's heads, it fills them with fantasies" (*CSA* 87).

Woven into the fabric of *La cruz* are also some of Spain's most prized taboos—namely, sexuality and challenges to orthodox Catholicism.[9] While customary Celian sarcasm has as its target such Spanish "institutions" as Franco and the church, there is sustained tension between a plethora of binary oppositions that deal with the story line, themes, philosophical posturing, and narrative reliability.[10] From the two Shakespearean epigraphs that are taken from *Hamlet* and *As You Like It* to a quote from Woody Allen, and from the seriousness of the novel's title to the stark contrast of the paper upon which the chronicle was written, traditional Catholic dogma runs current with beliefs about Satan's different personae, while high culture is pitted against pop culture (the written vs. the spoken word) just as significantly as Matilde Verdú's admitted fabrications are supposed to be the truth (like her surname, which closely resembles the word *verdad* [truth] in Spanish). As a framing device for the ebb and flow of these dualities, Shakespeare's "all the world's a stage" (*CSA* 113) crosses over into narrative and converts theatrical illusion into the cornerstone of supposed narrative veracity. Matilde Verdú's mention of reincarnation (*CSA* 195) and a "paper" (*CSA* 86) given to her because it spoke of the "tremendous powers and faculties that exist" hidden inside every human being as well as her insistence upon the eradication of a chronological, historical ordering of reality lend themselves favorably to the ever-changing nature of the (at least) three people who are said to be writing "these papers" and who attest to the same with their assured first-person imprimatur (*CSA* 69).

As a further source of confusion, Cela has made his characteristic, spontaneous dialogues an integral part of the narrative discourse by way of giving the impression that Matilde Verdú is being interrogated with regard to her knowledge of the events about the López Santana family and information concerning her husband and his political affiliations, which, we are led to believe, was the reason why the couple was to be crucified on St. Andrew's crosses.[11] Once again we are presented with side-by-side oral and written versions of the events which constitute the novel and which are a stroke of technical virtuosity that bears upon the *cross*over between theater and narrative. This is made apparent when the initial incorporation of these anonymous dialogic vignettes singles out the narrative voice in question while simultaneously authorizing the *telling of the tale:*

—¿Why do you stick so closely to the letter of the word?
—I don't know. (*CSA* 10)

—Continue to introduce yourself.
—With mister president's permission. My name is Matilde Verdú, my
    mother was also called Matilde Verdú . . . (*CSA* 11)

—Good, you may retire. (*CSA* 11)

—Reflect upon the fact that killing children is less compromising and
    dangerous because they usually do not see the danger that awaits them,
    some little girls guess [at] it. (*CSA* 15)

Because of her husband's reportedly peculiar personal habits and his allegiance to the Alianza Popular, suspicion and intrigue surround Matilde Verdú and bestow an inquisitorial tenor upon her interrogation. This, in turn, arouses the reader's instinctive curiosity about why she says she and her husband were to be crucified on St. Andrew's crosses. The fact that other people supplied her with different kinds of toilet paper for her "chronicle" elicits visions of her in a type of confinement that is, nonetheless, never corroborated in the novel.[12]

Matilde also has favorite refrains, one of which speaks of her as an "ordinary woman" *(mujer vulgar)* who has no claim to fame and whose tolerance is greater than a "Turkish eunuch well fed with Karabuk bull's meat" (*CSA* 9). Her strange words link her to her predecessors, María Sabina and Mrs. Caldwell. In Matilde's case the fact that she was born to an unmarried woman at that time in Spanish history is particularly relevant. Moreover, the assumption that her mother must have been a "good woman" (because she wrote well-received biographies of the Spanish mystics Teresa of Avila and John of the Cross) substantiates Matilde's own "goodness" and the credibility of what she is relating, especially, it should be emphasized, in light of her own martyrdom/crucifixion. In addition, the ability to write (which she inherited from her mother) is manifested in the fact that Gardner Publisher Co.—through its agent Paula Fields— has agreed to publish her chronicle, thereby conferring dignity and value upon her for being an intelligent and trustworthy woman whose writerly skills merited a publishing agreement.

It must be remembered that Verdú is, however, a Celian transmitter of fictive truths. This being said, it is not surprising to begin questioning the upstanding moral fiber and the victimization she has had to endure over the years when Matilde (almost in the same breath in which she mentions the deal with Gardner Publisher Co.) lets slip two significant facts concerning her book deal: that she did not sleep with Paula Fields to get the contract and that she earned close to $600,000 for her (yet to be published) book, a detail that strongly suggests she was dealing with a North American publisher, given her reference to "dollars" (rather than Spanish *pesetas* or the British *pound*). From there on doubt grows, as she begins the narration about the López Santana family with an introduction to "her aunt Marianita" as a friend of other women who are close to the family (*CSA* 15).

Her recollections of the events of the lives of these women is intermittently interspersed with the answers she gives to authority figures—like her confessor Don Walter (*CSA* 195) and the chief officer of Franco's Guard (*CSA* 125)—and to women who literally leap forth from the story to converse with her.[13] At one point (at the beginning of pt. 2) Matilde Verdú's narration doubles upon itself as she in turn becomes the subject of the narrative voice that is acquainted with both Matilde Verdú and her good friend Jesusa Cascudo. Since Aunt Marianita is also claimed as this narrator's own relative, Verdú's assertion is contradicted to the point that the reader falls into the trap of thinking that perhaps one of the three Matilde narrators has been assigned to different parts of the chronicle. The conflicting testimony is, however, not resolved; rather, it is exacerbated when Matilde Verdú adamantly states: "I have said it twenty times, I repeat it always, my name is Matilde Verdú" (*CSA* 61). Doubts linger, though, particularly since it is easy to confuse her name with Marta's nickname, Matty. As such, her chronicle is smudgy not only because of the consistency of the different brands of toilet paper given to her so that she may continue writing but also on account of her own lack of credibility. Despite the unidentified higher narrative authority that is, in reality, in charge of transmitting to us Matilde's work-in-progress, she insists that her words do not constitute a novel (*CSA* 32).

Before actually listing the individual family members, Matilde first provides a context that bodes an ominous note for the López Santana genealogy. First to be introduced are the extended female family members who are in one way or another associated with censurable behavior, insanity, or death: her aunt Marianita choked to death while eating sugar-coated almonds in church on the fifth day of a novena to Our Lady of Perpetual Help; the aunt's friend, doña Leocadia, kept a young man named Javier Perillo; Loliña Araújo, the maternal grandmother of the López Santana clan, was one of the first to see the body of an unidentified dead man whose cadaver was washed ashore one day; Clara Erbecedo, the other grandmother, loved to invite young men to her chalet in San Pedro de Nos; her daughter, Mary Carmen (aka Vicenta), is a nymphomaniac who, like Betty Boop and Matty, has to be committed from time to time to Conjo, an insane asylum in which she is sexually abused by an attendant named Chus Chans Chao. By way of underscoring this family's idiosyncratic history, Loliña Araújo is also said to have made an excursion to Kamilyayla (*CSA* 74), a detail that runs parallel to periodic references to exotic flora and fauna of places like Kirkagac, Kinik, Iskilip, Karakasu, and Kizikaboluk, which progressively disenfranchise not only the characters but also the readers from the more familiar Spanish places of La Coruña, Ferrol, and Vigo (Galicia). This, then, is the genealogy of the López Santana family which occupies completely the pages of the chronicle: the parents, Eva and don Jacobo, and their five children: Diego (Pichi), Marta (Matty), Claudia (Betty Boop), Rebeca (Becky), and Fran (Paquito).

The story of this family heaps one dysfunction upon another, as anecdotes about all of them constitute the chronicle that is transmitted to the readers: Pichi's abusive behavior toward women; Betty Boop and Matty's insatiable sexual appetites, affairs, doomed marriages, and numerous ill-fated attempts at motherhood; Fran's homosexual leanings; Eva and Don Jacobo's eventual failed marriage; and Becky's refusal to marry, to name only a few. Fashioned somewhat after the buildup of tension in a play, the narration of the lives of the López Santana siblings, however bound for the disaster that we already know about from the onset, evolves rather uniformly from Betty Boop's and Matty's dating habits and eventual marriages, with more tangential references to their other brothers and sister Becky. Mention of Betty Boop's and Matty's wedding days is numerous (pts. 3–4), yet they are narrated retrospectively, saying not only that the last one to get married always resented the fact that she did not go first but also providing information about what occurred before the actual weddings *after* mention of the disastrous marriages is made (a detail that could very well substantiate the existence of the numerous narrators of which Matilde Verdú speaks at the beginning). Similar chronological confusion grows when decidedly proleptic information stands in direct conflict with narration about past events, such as, for example, the ending of part 4: "And [a woman] reflects: we are on the very brink of shaming ourselves about this bitter and sentimental chronicle, blood is thicker than water and here we are all going to end up vomiting blood" (*CSA* 185).

Provocative are the seemingly countless episodes of Betty Boop's and Matty's extramarital affairs and, by extension, the disasterous results of their mothering and housekeeping skills. Because of their repetitiveness, however, they are also confusing and inconsequential, it being pointless to try to maintain a clear notion of which adventures and boyfriends relate to each of the sisters. As a result, the tables are actually turned: what is purportedly the main story line resembles a cheap, dime-store novel that, curiously enough, brings to light the concealed subtexts that constitute the narrative threads that really hold everything together and command the reader's attention. Primary among these are the following: Matilde Verdú and her husband's crucifixion on St. Andrew's crosses, which she promises to recount with utmost simplicity ("a la pata la llana" [*CSA* 19]); Matilde Verdú's relationship with Pilar Seixón, a curious woman mentioned only six times in reference to her own chronicle about the López Santana family; the demonic overtones of Galician superstitions regarding different manifestations of Satan in various regions of Galicia (as they interrelate with the clandestine activities of Julián Santiso and Salustiano Balado Abeijón, two friends of the family and members of a secret organization called "The School of the Gamma-Delta-Pi Dawn [Community of the Daybreak of Jesus Christ]"); and, of course, the nature and eventual completion of the manuscript that Matilde Verdú is supposed to turn in to Gardner Publisher Co. on 1 September.[14]

While details of the happenings of the López Santana family accumulate consistently yet with fluctuating degrees of intensity from one part of the novel to another, these four subtexts follow more closely traditional dramatic (theater) development. From this enigmatic and diminutive presence (pts. 1 and 2) comes a crescendo of deafening proportions (from the third part forward) which culminates (at the end of pt. 5) in the ritualistic cult-fashion suicide of Betty Boop, Matty, Fran, Julián Santiso, and Salustiano Balado, whose spilled blood flows down the stairs that lead to Fermín Corgo's apartment, causing him to call the police. As information about the clandestine Community of the Daybreak of Jesus Christ leaks out, more prolific are the (eleven) invocations referring to the organization's leader, Amancio, particularly as his association with Julián Santiso and Salustiano Balado is revealed. Given the propensity of the López Santana children for seduction by word and deed, it becomes apparent that their numerous failed love relationships make them ripe for membership in a sect that promises to "liberate mankind [that has been] traumatized by doubt, all of us are watched by the Office of the Guardian" (*CSA* 170). Although it is never made absolutely clear, the woman who changes her name to "Adoración Espantoso Naveira" (*SAC* 130) and then to "Adoración Cordero Chousa" (*CSA* 214) is most likely Matty, an easy mark for membership in the Amancio cult. To this end, and not unlike the secret society that lures the López Santana people, Cela's use of enigmas opens the door to the bold turn of events which culminates in finally exposing what was before only felt to be an air of perversion encoded in whispers; dissonant references to strange places and breeds of fighting turkeys from Kalekapi (*CSA* 124); poisonous orchids grown in aunt Clara's greenhouse in San Pedro de Nos; and women with "very exaggerated" names (*CSA* 230), such as Mesalina and her maid, Muñeca Mecánica (Mechanical Doll).

Along similar lines the fact that Matilde Verdú is told by her interrogator (in the first two parts of the novel) that she does not have to make much of an effort to clarify confusing details because "it isn't worth the bother" (*CSA* 39), given that "nobody is listening to her even though they make believe they are" (*CSA* 63), she persists in developing her narration despite the fact that we are told by an unnamed extradiegetic narrator that her memories at times "dumbfound her" (*CSA* 46). Without ever clarifying anything else about the original source document, Matilde also makes reference to the way Pilar Seixón wanted *her* version of the chronicle to read, specifically concerning what to put in which section of the manuscript. Moreover, Matilde speaks adamantly regarding her "firm resolve about the *correction*" (*CSA* 113; emphasis added), resolutely determined to "organize her recollections and papers." There are also indications that somebody is reading Matilde's manuscript as the interrogation progresses, and questions are asked about previous narrative segments such as the query that is prompted by the image of the "island of loneliness" which is used to convey the isolation that surrounds her existence:

—That one against whose inaccessible and fierce cliffs of basalt and pumice stone crash the waves of that power that is never enough?
—Yes. (*CSA* 126)

Similar metatextual references abound as linguistic commentaries are offered concerning regional usage/register, semantics, and spelling. Wherein parts 4 and 5 begin with more philosophical queries about death (instead of anecdotal information regarding the characters), the reliability of Matilde Verdú's text-in-process departs radically from its course as she confesses that everything she has said about her mysterious husband—and the impending crucifixion—has been included simply to satisfy Paula Fields's and the publisher's demands: "My husband was not in exile not for a single day . . . I never would have married such a loser" (*CSA* 146). She goes on to "confess before all of you" that she never loved nor was loved, that she is nothing more than "an almost old woman with very bad health in whose heart forgetfulness always abided" (*CSA* 147), and, finally, that the infamous St. Andrew's cross "will continue to be a useless symbol of gratuitous pieces of nonsense" (*CSA* 209). In yet another instance toward the end of the novel someone—perhaps Matilde Verdú?—asks "Did you like the story?" (*CSA* 215), immediately after a horrific recounting of the way Betty Boop's last child was born on the streets of La Coruña. Once again the sense is that she said/wrote exactly what she knew the reading public wanted to hear. A further blend of fact and fiction is rendered by saying that the garrote that was used to execute one such Fernando Gambiño (for brutally killing his wife, Berta) is now housed in the Cela Foundation, the repository for Cela's original papers and manuscripts which is located in Iria Flavia (Galicia).

Thus deconstructed, the history of the decline of the López Santana family and the intriguing thematic motif about the crucifixion are mounted upon an image that portrays the most sacred ritual in Catholic Christianity, that being *the holy sacrifice of the Mass,* which is believed to be a reenactment of the death of Jesus Christ in atonement for humankind's original sin. Revolving around death, it is a ceremony whose core belief is that Christ's body and blood are transformed into bread and wine of which the faithful partake in the same way as the biblically narrated account of the Last Supper in which Christ's twelve disciples joined Him before his own crucifixion and death. In *La cruz* no sooner does the narrating voice identify itself (at the beginning) as the long-suffering one than attention is pointedly shifted to the "sounding trumpets" that announce the beginning of "the *black Mass of confusion,* the solemn *academic act* of the most blurred of all confusions" (*CSA* 9; emphasis added), in which the priests and priestesses don their austere blood-red, gold-trimmed "military uniforms" in order to eat of strands of "filthy" pork and contemplate the image of the face of an unshaven dead man as it appears on their towels.[15] In the background are heard:

> bells that peal out good news or sound out death according to the phases of the moon: it deals with telling a story close to the fire, the *farce* should be staged with simplicity so that the revered public enjoys itself, you have to throw rotten entrails, lungs, hearts, intestines to the hyenas so that they don't brutally beat the adolescent and sad, bitter, pale and disillusioned school-girls. (*CSA* 9; emphasis added)

Iconoclasm aside, these Goyaesque images boldly suggest an atmosphere of death, obliteration, and fanaticism while clearly linking together the three major components of *La cruz:* narrative (the story), theater (the philosophical underpinnings for the narration), and belief system (in its broadest sense). Literary critics and narratologists alike are invited to figure out what they are about to behold in the "mass of confusion." Everything proceeds, then, from the key place of theater as ritual.

As this central Catholic belief is raised to the level of metaphor, it serves as a unique structural, philosophical, and thematic point of departure for the entire narration. If the Mass is but another "representation" and "all the world's a stage," as is frequently cited, then the chronicle about the downfall of the López Santana family is also *staged,* in this case to meet the demands of Gardner Publisher Co., about which Matilde Verdú sardonically reminds her confessor:

> when I speak about the two López Santana sisters and about myself and our adventures I am lying, I was never involved in such games, nor would I ever want to be so coy, but what I am saying is true, sometimes I write in first person in order to satisfy my agent and my editor, Paula Fields as well as Gardner Publisher Co. have their prejudices and quirks . . . what is really exemplary is that they turn everything into money . . . and they are able to sell the most bizarre products of subintellegence. (*CSA* 94)

In a manner similar to the way in which Julián Santiso was able to get the López Santana brother to call himself—and believe that he was—Simón Pedro (Simon Peter) rather than Francisco López Santana, Matilde Verdú is as persuasive in trying to convince everyone about what she is saying. In reality, she *is* truthful, primarily in reference to the farcical nature of the crucifixion story.

In another more personal, yet significantly theatrical, setting that took place one night during a terrible thunder and lightening storm that knocked out all the power, she is pictured sitting half-naked in front of her mirror by candlelight, saying rather nonchalantly that, despite not having rehearsed enough, she and her husband knew exactly how to "act the part" of the ones who were to be executed, even though at times they would start laughing, something that "the good fans do not forgive" (*CSA* 130).[16] In another, less spectacular setting she narrates that she and her two best girlfriends, Betty Boop and Matty, were also good actresses, and that Betty Boop "could have saved herself from the collapse [had she] gotten up on stage," because stage lights prolong life (*CSA* 70).

Given that the stage seems to save—in a fashion similar to that of the Mass for those who partake and believe that receiving Christ's body and blood will lead to their eternal salvation—it is not surprising that the originator of the chronicle, Pilar Seixón, also plotted her document along the same axes of a dramatic/theater text, thereby insuring that it would also achieve perpetuity. For this reason Matilde Verdú resists her confessor-father Castrillón's suggestion that the episode about one of Betty Boop's boyfriends, Miguel Negreira the violinist, be put in the second part of the chronicle; again, upon the suggestion that something be said right away in the third part, she responds that "Pilar Seixón had anticipated putting it in chapter IV" (*CSA* 133), making clear that in no way is she "about to disobey her." This show of fidelity to the Seixón chronicle aside, neither Matilde nor anyone else clarifies the relationship between her version—on her own brand of writing paper—and Pilar's or the other avowed narrative voices, nor is explanation given for Matilde's original reference to the "correction" (*enmienda* [*CSA* 113]), leaving one to speculate that perhaps the third-person narrator (whose presence circumscribes all other indications of narrative authority), rather than Paula Fields of the Gardner Publisher Co., collected Matilde Verdú's "rolled" manuscript.

Pulled in different directions, Matilde Verdú (aka Matilde Lens [midwife] and Matilde Meizoso [Pichi's wife]) is also apparently reading from a preestablished "script" (*guión* [*CSA* 44]) which, most likely because of her (fictitious) involvement with her (fictitious) politically active husband, has been given to her by the police:

—Why do you adjust so much to the script that the police gave you?
—I have my reasons to do what I do, I also warn you that for now I do what I want and that nobody writes the script for me about what I have to say, about what I feel like saying. (*CSA* 44)

At one point close to the end of the novel she is told to "continue with her monotonous *melopea*" (*CSA* 213), to which she responds with words that resemble María Sabina's chanting and which further underscore the theatrics that contextualize her every utterance.[17] Not only is she responding to Pilar Seixón, her confessor, the police, and Paula Fields and Gardner Publisher Co., but she also has inherited her unmarried mother's literary creativity. Matilde is also a professional woman who, regardless of a meager salary, earns her living as a "supervisor of primary education" (*CSA* 11, 53). As for her interests, Verdú was an avid enthusiast of Rabindranath Tagore, the recipient in 1913 of the Nobel Prize in literature, an outspoken opponent of fanatical nationalism (which obstructed unity), and a prolific writer whose works combine fantasy, mysticism, and realism. Furthermore, in claiming the names of Matilde Lens and Matilde Meizoso, she respectively assumes points of view which would be natural for them; for example, since Pichi's wife never got along too well with Verdú, she would most likely have attempted to discredit her namesake, while the former Matilde, being a midwife, might have paid a great deal of attention to women, their experiences with childbearing, and how they subsequently raised their offspring. Going one step farther, however, is Matilde Verdú's subtle association from the very beginning of the chronicle with children, a connection that could also cause one to wonder if she was not being interrogated for reasons of witchcraft.

In spite, however, of her literary antecedents and the fact that for whatever reason she is the one who has been chosen to write the López Santana chronicle, Matilde Verdú bemoans the fact that she and her other female friends are never taken seriously nor have never been worthy of being included in the annals of history: "It isn't that we ordinary women have no history, men neither, we are ordinary women in spite of ourselves and we are ignorant of the most common things, what happens is that we do not know how to tell our own history" (*CSA* 10). Even though her deal with the publishing company seems to be the reason why she commits the people, places, and events of the López Santana family to (toilet) paper as well as the reason why she is being questioned, she is the source of the attention that is being paid to her and her friends. She is not at all disturbed by numerous inconsistencies in her text, one of the most obtrusive being the four different battlefronts on which she said that her grandfather died during the Spanish Civil War (Asturias, Huesca, Nules, and Valsequillo). On the other hand, she is paradoxically insistent upon being faithful to Pilar Seixón's original chronicle, agreeing solely to "come out with the painful history of a collapse which I wrap up in a nostalgic and bitter story" (*CSA* 58).

Matilde Verdú is also spared in the end. Having been smarter than her two girlfriends in not subscribing to Julián Santiso's words, she is not one of the victims of the group suicide: "here ends this chronicle of a collapse, I've also used up the last roll of toilet paper" (*CSA* 237). The irony surrounding her "survival" is that she did know "how to tell [her] own history" in a way that captivated somebody's attention—namely, Paula Fields and the people who are questioning her. And, even though this particular "history" seems forever to bear the scorn of its readers—and critics?—and the rapid disintegration of its content (given the quality of the paper upon which it was penned), her manuscript did nevertheless withstand the cataclysmic events of the "collapse" of the López Santana family and, thus, was also worthy of an outside narrator's attention, an observer who, while not a typical Celian editor-transcriber per se, witnessed Matilde's words and deeds and deemed her a "prudent teller of the chronicle of events" (*CSA* 53), thereby, one would imagine, transposing everything to us in the name of *La Cruz*.

The López Santana chronicle, then, redefines history itself, the other topic that has been the source of much of Cela's contemptuous ridicule:

History is written [based] on history books, on established [rules for] history textbooks, and it doesn't amount to more than literary fallacies . . . could you please give me a glass of water?, yes, may I continue?, yes, with permission, the worst thing about common women is not that we do not have a history, that would be the least of all concerns, the worst thing is that history drowns us in ordinariness, monotony, and routine[.] (*CSA* 200)

If ordinary men and women do indeed possess their own stories, then they also have histories to tell and to be told. What goes into them, however, seems to be as predetermined as the rules that govern the proliferation of "history textbooks," as Matilde Verdú so candidly admits in acceding to her publisher's wishes (in order to come up with something that will sell). For this reason both she and those who supplied her with paper recognize the futility of taking any of this seriously; they know that they, too, are puppets whose strings are pulled by the ever-growing mediocrity of the demands of a consumer public that more often than not determines what gets published: "rotten entrails, lungs, hearts, [and] intestines" that will appease the voraciousness of the hyena-like public.

As a fitting closure, Matilde Verdú proffers a poetic finale to her tale of dastardly deeds by way of inviting us to contemplate another distortion, this time a Galician seascape in which all the seagulls, upon seeing so many blood-

ied souls flying around, fled inland in search of safety on the "rooftops . . . trees
. . . street benches . . . everywhere," the likes of which were never before seen.
The image, together with her parting words, reinstates the rhythmic cadence of
the novel, as Galician lexicon stands side by side Castilian usage: "gaviotas a
terra, mariñeiros á merda. Aquí somos todos marineros" (seagulls on land, sailors to hell. Here we are all sailors [*CSA* 237]).[18] The contrasts are striking:
seafaring birds "everywhere" on land, sailors "to hell," and everyone else, like
the sailors, bound for a voyage on an endless sea of "*mass* . . . confusion"
(emphasis added).

Conclusion

Many people, unfortunately, still think almost exclusively of Camilo José Cela in terms of *Pascual Duarte, The Hive,* and his well-published travel book, *Journey to the Alcarria.* This affirms the "neglect" to which Pérez refers in assessing Cela criticism.[1] To approach Cela's novels in this way is myopic at best and misguided at worst. Without minimizing their (seminal) importance, *Pascual Duarte, Rest Home,* and *The Hive* are only the first fruits of a fifty-year career that was built upon an unwavering commitment to creative renewal. The novels that come after these attest to Cela's dedication to his craft. They also signal how important poetry has been to him. Although he published only one true book of poems, its legacy is *Mrs. Caldwell* and subsequent works that reverberate with a surrealism that has allowed Cela to exploit his command of Spanish in such a way as to facilitate the innovations characterizing his work. In *San Camilo* selected aspects of Cela's personal life are allowed to surface; this, in turn, creates a persona that fosters a stream of consciousness that aggressively repudiates history. No stronger evidence of this exists than the "purge of his heart" of *oficio de tinieblas 5.* Still a virtual enigma for critics, *oficio* paved the way to the pinnacle of Cela's career as a novelist.

What followed this *darker* period yielded a resurgence of literary productivity, the awarding of prestigious literary prizes—the Nacional (1984), Príncipe de Asturias (1987), Nobel (1989), Planeta (1994) and Cervantes (1995)—and the conferring of numerous honorary degrees and awards such as the Andrés Bello medal of honor which Ramón José Velásquez, president of Venezuela, conferred upon Cela in 1993 for his contribution to Iberoamerican culture. *Mazurka* is a narratological work of art. The product of a confident master writer of fiction, *Cristo* departs from familiar fictive Spanish soil and takes up again an interior monologue that challenges the myths of Tombstone and Spain's presence in America. Cela's latest works of fiction, *El asesinato* and *La cruz de San Andrés,* represent a hybridization of the novel as art form. Not only do they defy pigeonholing his works, but they are also a forum for the major issues with which Cela has struggled during his life: personal freedom (in the spirit of Mateo Ruecas) and the disastrous outcome of blind faith in fanatical belief systems (such as those espoused by Amancio Jambrina).

While it could be argued that the hermetic confines of Cela's novels are the result of having *come of age* at the height of Francoist censorship, the fact remains that Cela was a forerunner of novelistic experimentation, exposing many contemporary issues facing Western civilization. Cela was ahead of his time from the moment Pascual Duarte uttered the infamous words that bestowed upon the reader the impossible task of deciding whether or not Cela was a repentant sinner or a hardened sociopath, a debate that continues to fuel both sides of the question about personal responsibility and socioenvironmental conditioning. The questions troubling Celian characters over the years are argued passionately nowadays: the dignity and love sought by terminally ill patients; the choices facing abused children; the prejudices that drive and divide societies; and the spiritual poverty of societies run by politicians and technocrats.

Despite Navajas's assessment of the nonprescriptive nature of Cela's works,[2] they are, nevertheless, solidly lodged on an ethical foundation of insights that allow Cela to view human beings in the most basic of lights: needs, desires, and fears. For this reason the Nobel committee spoke of his as a "rich and intensive prose, which with restrained compassion forms a challenging vision of man's vulnerability."[3] Nowhere is this more evident than in works such as *Izas, rabizas y colipoterras* and *Rol de cornudos* in which provactive themes such as prostitution and cuckholdry give way to penetrating insights into a female condition that is fraught with ignorance, poverty, and a vacuous "machismo." Cela is a writer for this age. He learned well the lessons of his 1898 mentors and carries on the tradition of his compatriot Valle-Inclán, through whose *esperpentic* lens the world is refracted.

Cela does not write to appease, to satisfy, or to entertain. The shocking realism of his language emanates from characters whose humanity is more real than fictitious. The people, places, and situations that are repeated over and over again in one work after another, together with the litanies that assume prominence in his later works, thus demonstrate one simple truth: there is no escape from our common humanity. His stories cut to the quick from the onset, with no proverbial happy endings whatsoever. To paraphrase doña Rosa in *The Hive,* nothing is gained when perspective is lost, thus the delicate balance of reading Cela without losing hope, for it is precisely our ordinariness as human beings which enables us to attain greatness by participating in the heroic challenge of daily living.

Notes

Introduction

1. Shirley Mangini, *Rojos y rebeldes* (Barcelona: Anthropos, 1987), 53. For excellent studies of the Spanish Civil War, see the following: Burnett Bolloten, *The Spanish Revolution: The Left and the Struggle for Power* (Chapel Hill and London: University of North Carolina Press, 1991); Gerald Brenan, *The Spanish Labyrinth* (London: Cambridge University Press, 1943); Raymond Carr, *Spain, 1808–1939* (Oxford: Oxford University Press, 1966); Gabriel Jackson, *A Concise History of the Spanish Civil War* (London: Thames and Hudson, 1974); Stanley Payne, *The Spanish Revolution* (New York: Norton, 1970); and Hugh Thomas, *The Spanish Civil War* (London: Eyre & Spottiswoode, 1961).

2. Keeping in mind that Cela's works sometimes challenge a traditional grouping according to literary genres, they include the following: thirteen major novels, more than fifteen collections of short stories, numerous short novels, one book of poems, seven travel books, two autobiographies, at least five books written in homage to artists and writers, two dictionaries, and various other writings that defy classification.

3. *La rosa* (The Rose) is the title of the initial segment of his autobiography. It was published in 1959 and was supposed to be the first in a series of autobiographical works that were to bear the title "La cucaña" (The Greasy Pole).

4. Sarah Kerr's essay entitled "Shock Treatment" (*New York Review of Books,* 18 October 1992) provides an excellent review of these novels.

5. *Vuelta de hoja* (Barcelona: Destino, 1981), 131.

6. The following studies present an intelligent analysis of "exile literature": Paul Ilie, *Literature and Inner Exile* (Baltimore: Johns Hopkins University Press, 1980); Gareth Thomas, *The Novel of the Spanish Civil War (1936–1975)* (New York: Cambridge University Press, 1990); and Michael Ugarte, *Shifting Ground: Spanish Civil War Exile Literature* (Durham: Duke University Press, 1989). Barry Jordan's study is also significant: *Writing and Politics in Franco's Spain* (London and New York: Routledge, 1990).

7. *El asno de Buridán* (Madrid: El País, 1986), 298.

8. The writers who are traditionally grouped together as the "Generation of 1898" include the following: Azorín (José Martínez Ruiz) (1873–1967), Pío Baroja (1872–1956), Antonio Machado (1875–1939), Miguel de Unamuno (1864–1936), and Ramón María del Valle-Inclán (1866–1936).

9. Robert Kirsner, *The Novels and Travels of Camilo José Cela* (Chapel Hill: University of North Carolina Press, 1963), 9–13.

10. Spain joined the European Common Market in 1986.

11. Darío Villanueva,"Estudio preliminar," in *Páginas Escogidas,* by Camilo José Cela, ed. D. Villanueva (Madrid: Espasa Calpe, 1991), 61.

12. At the conclusion of *Memorias* Cela wryly says that, should hardening of the arteries hold off, he will write the third part of his autobiography which he will call "Turno de réplica" (Time to Reply) and in which he will chronicle down to the last detail (the names, places, dates, and verbatim quotations concerning) his struggle with those who have sought to defame and hang him publicly (347).

13. *Insula* was founded in 1946 with the bold intention of bringing together those artistic and intellectual currents that had been interrupted by the war. For the special issue dedicated to Cela, see *Insula* 518–19 (February–March 1990).

14. Camilo José Cela Conde. *Cela, mi padre* (Madrid: Ediciones Temas de Hoy, 1989).

15. Cela, *El asno de Buridán,* 52.

Chapter 1: *Pascual Duarte and His Family*

1. All references pertain to Herma Briffault's translation, *Pascual Duarte and His Family* (New York: Las Americas Publishing, 1965), hereafter abbreviated as *PD*. Her title differs from that of Anthony Kerrigan's translation of the same novel, *The Family of Pascual Duarte* (New York: Avon Books, 1964).

2. The term *tremendista* was coined by Antonio de Zubiaurre to refer to the violence, crime, and human degradation that were reflected in many Spanish novels of the 1940s.

3. This information is provided by Cela in the second part of his autobiography (*M* 341).

4. Among the plethora of studies that exist concerning these respective points of view are the following: Jorge A. Marbán, *Camus and Cela* (Barcelona: Ediciones Picazo, 1973); J. S. Bernstein, "Pascual Duarte and Orestes," *Symposium* 22 (1968): 301–18; Juan Antonio Masoliver Ródenas, "Las dos lecturas de *La familia de Pascual Duarte,*" *Insula* 518–19 (February–March 1990): 51–52; Carlos Jerez-Farrán, "Pascual Duarte y la susceptibilidad viril," *Hispanófila* 1 (1989): 47–63; Arnold M. Penuel, "The Psychology of Cultural Disintegration in Cela's *La familia de Pascual Duarte,*" *Revista de Estudios Hispánicos* 16.3 (1982): 361–78; Rafael Osuna, "Pascual Duarte: Asesino, Miliciano, Nacionalista," *Ideologies and Literature* 3.11 (1979): 85–95; and Jorge Urrutia, *Cela: La familia de Pascual Duarte* (Madrid: Sociedad General Española de Librería, 1982), 53–67.

5. To this end the well-known Cela scholar Darío Villanueva has recently published a study of the evolution of the novel from manuscript form to its first publication ("1942: *La familia de Pascual Duarte,* del manuscrito a la edición," in *Hora actual de la novela hispánica,* ed. Eduardo Godoy Gallardo [Valparaíso: Ediciones Universitarias de Valparaíso de la Universidad Católica de Valparaíso, 1994], 193–201).

6. Urrutia states that after 18 July 1936 political criminals in Spain were shot and not executed in this way (*Cela,* 66).

7. For articles that deal with this proleptic aspect of the novel, see Luis T. González-del-Valle ("La muerte de la Chispa: su función en *La familia de Pascual Duarte*," *Sin Nombre* 6 [1975]: 56–58); Matías Montes-Huidobro ("Dinámica de la correlación existencial en *La familia de Pascual Duarte*," *Revista de Estudios Hispánicos* 16 [1982]: 213–21"); and John R. Rosenberg ("Pascual Duarte and the Eye of the Beholder: Cela, Sartre, and the Metaphor of Vision," *Revista Canadiense de Estudios Hispánicos* 14.1 [1989]: 149–59).

8. For a discussion of other possibilities regarding the identity of this individual, see Urrutia, *Cela,* 58–64. Additionally, Germán Gullón speculates further about Pascual himself—rather than don Joaquín—being the narratee of his own text ("Contexto ideológico y forma narrativa en *La familia de Pascual Duarte*," *Hispania* 68 [March 1985]).

9. To be precise, this occurs at four times in the text: in describing don Jesús's house (*PD* 19); Lola's reference to the "wonderful . . . fat" eels that fed in the creek that passed through don Jesús's property (*PD* 25); don Jesús's ranch Los Jarales, where Pascual used to hunt partridges; and the advice that Pascual received from the local priest, don Manuel, about doing exactly as don Jesús did during the Mass that he was attending on the morning that Pascual went to the church to make arrangements for his marriage to Lola.

10. The term is taken from Robert Spires, "Systematic Doubt: The Moral Art of *La familia de Pascual Duarte*," *Hispanic Review* 40 (1972): 283–302.

11. Two of the most intelligent articles that have recently been written on this aspect of the novel are the following: John Kronik, "Encerramiento y apertura: Pascual Duarte y su texto," *Anales de a Literatura Española* 6 (1988): 309–23; and John R. Rosenberg, "El autobiógrafo encerrado: Pascual Duarte y su transcriptor," *Explicación de Textos Literarios* 24.3–4 (1985–86): 63–72.

12. Cela, "Al *Pascual Duarte:* Andanzas europeas y americanas de Pascual Duarte y su familia," *Camilo José Cela. Obra completa* (Barcelona: Destino, 1962), 1: 550–84.

13. Cela, "Palabras ocasionales," *Camilo José Cela. Obra completa* (Barcelona: Destino, 1962), 1: 581.

Chapter 2: *Rest Home*

1. Cela, "La experiencia personal en *Pabellón de reposo*," *Camilo José Cela. Obra completa* (Barcelona: Destino, 1962), 1: 204–8.

2. Cela, "Nota a la segunda edición," 10. These prologues include the following: a "Nota" to the first publication in 1944 of *Rest Home,* a "Nota [dated 1952] a la segunda edición," and "La experiencia personal," which was first published in *Papeles de Son Armadans* and later in 1960 as a prologue (of sorts) to the edition of *Rest Home* found in Cela's complete works *(Camilo José Cela. Obra completa).* Since the English translation used here (Herma Briffault, trans. [New York: Las Americas, 1961]), contains only

prologue excerpts, references to these documents are from the fourth Spanish edition of the novel (Barcelona: Ediciones Destino, 1965) and will be indicated parenthetically in the text. All references to the Briffault translation will also be indicated accordingly in the text.

Luis Blanco Vila looks to Cela's two periods of confinement for treatment of tuberculosis for the genesis of two of the male characters of *Rest Home*—nos. 52, whom Vila regards as the narrator, and 14 (*Para leer a Camilo José Cela* [Madrid: Palas Atenea, 1991], 35–36).

3. David W. Foster, *Forms of the Novel in the Work of Camilo José Cela* (Columbia: University of Missouri Press, 1967), 34.

4. Cela, "Nota a la segunda edición," 13.

5. The poetic qualities of *Rest Home* are far too numerous to analyze here. Among those most recognizable are the references to various aspects of nature and seasons of the year. Such technical devices as anaphora, refrains, parallel construction, and antithesis are also apparent. On a more subtle note echoes of other famous Spanish poets such as Luis de León, Calderón de la Barca, Vicente Aleixandre, and Gustavo Adolfo Bécquer are heard throughout the novel. Discernible also are surrealistic images of sorts (patient no. 14's comparison to a croaking frog) and strains of mystic poetry. Likewise, numbers 52 and 14 feature themselves poets.

6. Eugenio de Nora sees in this the precursor for Cela's later "multiple protagonist" in *The Hive, San Camilo,* and *oficio* ("Sobre *Pabellón de reposo*" [*Insula* 518–19 (February–March 1990): 55–56]). A number of critics speculate about the ambiguous principal/extradiegetic narrator of *Rest Home,* and there is consensus that at least one of the male patients in the sanatorium is the persona used by Cela to convey his personal experience with the disease (see Foster, *Forms,* 48; Gonzalo Sobejano, *Novela española de nuestro tiempo,* 2d ed. [Madrid: Prensa Española, 1975], 108–9; and John Kronik, "*Pabellón de reposo:* La inquietud narrativa de Camilo José Cela," in *Actas del VIII Congreso de la Asociación Internacional de Hispanistas,* ed. A. David Kossoff et al. [Madrid: Ediciones Istmo, 1986], 105–11).

7. Robert Kirsner discusses the horrifying aspects of the illness (*Novels and Travels,* 35), and Kronik reminds us that tuberculosis was not treated with streptomycin until 1944 ("*Pabellón,*" 106).

8. Coined and created by the Spanish writer Ramón María del Valle-Inclán, the term *esperpento* embodies aesthetic and literary formulas that are based on the optics of concave mirrors. The term was first used in Valle-Inclán's play *Luces de Bohemia,* 1920 (Bohemian Lights). Sumner M. Greenfield gives the following definition: "theoretically, the *esperpento* is based on the opinion that Spain is a grotesque deformation of European civilization, and that the tragic sense of such an anomaly can be communicated only by an aesthetic in which classic norms and heroes are systematically subjected to geometric distortions like those of a concave mirror. The result is a devastating attack on the country's institutions and

contemporary history" ("Valle-Inclán, Ramón María del [1866–1936]," *Columbia Dictionary of Modern European Literature,* 2d ed. [New York: Columbia University Press, 1980], 838).

José María Castellet refers to Cela's brand of realism as what earlier critics called *tremendismo,* that is, Cela's depictions of reality as deformation, *esperpentism,* or a type of naturalism, rather than an objective view of the same ("Iniciación a la obra narrativa de Camilo José Cela," *Revista Hispánica Moderna* 28.2–4 [1962]: 148).

9. Ilie (*La novelística de Camilo José Cela* [Madrid: Gredos, 1971]) and Kirsner *(Novels and Travels)* discuss at length this aspect of the novel.

10. Cela, "La experiencia personal," 207.

11. Kronik, in particular, notes the disparity between the nurturing atmosphere outside the sanatorium and the truncated life within its hospital walls (*"Pabellón,"* 108). All critics who have studied this work comment on its structural symmetry. Ilie explains that Cela was one of seven children whose mother had six siblings (*La novelística,* 96). It should also be noted that the number 7 connotes the obvious division of Western time into days and weeks and carries with it the biblical allusion to creation which Cela converts into death.

12. Numbers 11 and 2 sign their letters with "C." and "B.," respectively, while number 103 is called Felisa in a letter from her boyfriend. Different women's names are associated with number 40. In the first case the name Elisa is mentioned by a nurse who tells (patient no. 40) a type of fairy tale about a female character with this name. In another context number 14 romantically refers to number 40 as someone who could have been his "ideal *Mimí* . . . [or] *Margarita"* (155). The ambiguity of both circumstances, however, suggests an ironic association between three (onomastic representations of) ideal women and the dying woman in room number 40.

Specific names are used for people in the outside world and/or who are in good health. Among these are the following: Raimundo Lulio, the name a caring male nurse practitioner gives himself in jest and who, number 11 says, was dismissed because he dared use the Castilian version of Ramón Lull (1235–1315, a Catalan theologian and philosopher renowned for contributions to scholastic theology); Hortensia and Pedro, the sister and brother-in-law of number 40; Isidoro, the French gendarme who inspired the story the nurse tells number 40 (shortly before the death of the latter); and Francis James, who wrote a prayer about infant mortality.

13. See Ilie (*La novelística,* 96–99), for a discussion of the relationship between this intense self-consciousness, Thomas Mann's novel *Magic Mountain,* and the transformation of sickly patients into artists.

14. Ilie, *La novelística,* 99.

15. In this regard Kronik (*"Pabellón,"* 109) speaks of three primary techniques that are employed by Cela: fragmentation, equalization, and simultaneity.

16. Cela cleverly has number 52 say to number 37 that he would prefer not to have witnesses (she, of course, turns the picture around).

17. The epigraph does not appear in the Briffault translation of *Rest Home.*

18. The text is separated by different editorial symbols, such as a type of asterisk which indicates Cela's changes in scenes in the *Intermedio* and the appearance of the

gardener (with wheelbarrow). Ellipsis points are used to indicate a hiatus in the narration. Italics are also used for emphasis in parts of Cela's introductory "notes" to indicate the gardener's appearance and in a reference (after the Cervantine epigraph) to Claudius van Vlardingenhohen. A supposed friend of Cela, this ordained Protestant deacon is an executioner on the island of Java and has advised his Spanish friend that happiness is found only in exploring all that life has to offer.

19. Kronik (*"Pabellón,"* 106) cites the Romantic treatment of tuberculosis as a literary theme compared with the stark realism it evoked in the twentieth century.

20. "Dos meses" (two months) is repeated in the first part of the novel and ironically parallels the division of the novel into halves.

Chapter 3: *The Hive*

1. Numerous Spanish editions have come forth since 1951. Because the English translation used here (J. M. Cohen, trans. [New York: Farrar, Straus and Giroux, 1993]) does not include these prologues, all references to them are taken from the Spanish edition used here (Camilo José Cela, *La colmena,* ed. Raquel Asún Escartín [Madrid: Editorial Castalia, 1990]) and will be indicated parenthetically (as Asún Escartín) in the text. All other references to the novel are taken from the Cohen translation and will be indicated (as *H*) in the text. For a complete listing of the most important editions of *The Hive,* see Asún Escartín's introduction, 75–76.

In the order in which they appear in the Spanish edition that we are using, the prologues/notes include the following: "Historia incompleta de unas páginas zarandeadas," 1965 (Incomplete History of a Few Sifted Pages); "Nota a la primera edición," 1951 (Note to the First Edition); "Nota a la segunda edición," 1955; "Nota a la tercera edición," 1957; "Nota a la cuarta edición," 1962; "Ultima recapitulación," 1963 (Last Summing-up); and "Prólogo a la edición rumana de *La colmena,"* 1965 (Prologue to the Rumanian edition of *The Hive*).

2. In his article *"La colmena*—An Oversight on the Part of Cela" (*Romance Notes* 13 [1971–72]: 414–18) David Henn clarifies that the reference to the Teheran conference mentioned by the characters in the novel refers to late 1943 (rather than 1942, as indicated by Cela). David K. Herzberger's article ("Cela and the Challenge to History in Francoist Spain," *Ojáncano* [April 1991]: 13–23) provides a superb analysis of Cela's treatment— and debunking—of Francoist historiography.

3. Cela, "Algunas palabras al que leyere," intro., *MC,* 14.

4. Henn, *"La colmena,"* 17. Two excellent studies on the innovative aspects of Cela's narrative techniques are the following: Dru Dougherty, "Form and Structure in *La colmena:* From Alienation to Community," *Anales de la Novela de Posguerra* 1 (1976): 7–23; and Marie E. Barbieri, "El 'Final' de *La colmena,* o la ruptura con la novela tradicional," *Explicación de textos literarios* 20.2 (1991–92): 27–32.

5. Specifically, these are labeled chapters 1 through 6, with the last chapter called "FINAL."

6. Vicente Cabrera says that the narrator reports, the camera focuses, and the characters live ("En busca de tres personajes perdidos en *La colmena*," *Cuadernos Hispanoamericanos* 337–38 [1978]: 134).

7. Emilio Alarcos Llorach recalls the connection with Madrid's symbolic burial ground for the country's war dead ("Al hilo de *La colmena*," *Insula* 518–19 [February–March 1990]: 3–4).

8. Henn, "Theme and Structure in *La colmena*." *Symposium* 19:115–22.

9. Robert Spires, "Documentación y transformación en *La colmena*," *La novela española de posguerra* (Planeta/Universidad de Kansas, 1978), 96–98.

10. José and Julián are jokingly known as "Pepe el Astilla" (Pepe, the Splinter) and "la Fotógrafa" (The [Female] Photographer), respectively. The nicknames are a hallmark of Cela's unlimited and poignant onomastic virtuosity. For an astute study of this aspect of Cela's style, see Luis A. Oyarzun, "The Onomastic Devices of Camilo José Cela," *Literary Onomastic Studies* 9 (1982): 165–75.

11. Foster refers quite aptly to the Margot-Marco connection as an "illusion of objectivity" (*Forms*, 72).

12. Norma G. Kobzina, "*Bleak House* Revisited: Cela's *La colmena*," *Hispanófila* 82 (1984): 57–66. We are told that Marco, in contrast to his sister Filo, is oblivious to the number of years that his mother has been dead.

13. Spires, "Cela's *La colmena*, 873–80.

14. Spires, "Documentación," 120.

15. Among others, see the following: Paul Ilie, *La novelística*, 124–51; Kirsner, *Novels and Travels*, 57–84; Foster, *Forms*, 61–81; Spires, "Cela's *La colmena*," and "Documentación y transformación en *La colmena*"; Gonzalo Sobejano, "*La colmena*: Olor a miseria*," *Cuadernos Hispanoamericanos* 337–38 (1978): 113–26; José Ortega, "El humor de Cela en *La colmena*," *Cuadernos Hispanoamericanos* 208 (1967): 159–64; and Henn, "Theme and Structure," and "*La colmena*—An Oversight."

16. See Thomas R. Franz, "Three Hispanic Echoes of Tolstoi at the Close of World War II," *Hispanic Journal* 6.1 (1984): 37–51; and Ernest Rehder, "Ecos de Nietzsche en la novela española de posguerra: *La colmena, Fiesta al noroeste* y *Tiempo de silencio*," *Romance Notes* 27.2 (1986): 113–20.

17. José Luis Giménez-Frontín, *Camilo José Cela. Texto y contexto* (Barcelona: Montesinos, 1985), 49–65.

Chapter 4: *Mrs. Caldwell Speaks to Her Son*

1. All quotations in English come from J. S. Bernstein's translation (Ithaca: Cornell University Press, 1968) and will be indicated parenthetically in the text.

2. Cela finalizes the afterword to *Mrs. Caldwell* in the following way: "Madrid, Spring of 1947—Los Cerrillos, Guadarrama Mountains, Fall of 1952, *with long interruptions*" (191; emphasis added).

3. This prologue was written by Cela in 1952 in Navacepeda (Gredos Mountains). It appears with *Mrs. Caldwell* as it appears in *Camilo José Cela. Obra completa* (7:9–15) and in another edition of the novel (Barcelona: Ediciones Destino, 1979 [9–15]). It is not found in Bernstein's translation.

4. It is entitled "The Head, Geometry, and the Heart," is found in Bernstein's translation (195–206), and is introduced as "a translation of the author's preface to the definitive Spanish edition of *Mrs. Caldwell Speaks to Her Son,* to appear in Volume VII of Cela's *Complete Works,* now being published in Barcelona. I wish to thank Professor Dalai Brenes for his assistance in translating this preface" (195).

5. David Foster refers to "overalienation" of the reader's emotions and interest as a possible reason for the negative criticism that *Mrs. Caldwell* generated (*Forms,* 34).

4. Cela, "Nota a la segunda edición."

5. Foster, *Forms,* 99.

6. Mrs. Caldwell usually says the opposite of what one expects to hear, for example: "It is a real blessing to feel alive and in good health so as to be able to devote a few hours a day to detesting something with all one's heart" (62); instead of regretting not knowing how to swim, she states that "perhaps this ignorance of mine . . . could take me much more rapidly to the place where you are waiting for me" (73); and "tobacco . . . is good for the health. . . . If one could give a cigarette to the orphans and the needy in time . . . there would be from then on, many fewer people classified as orphans or needy to receive welfare" (105).

7. Foster, *Forms,* 98.

8. Ilie, "El surrealismo de Cela: *Pisando la dudosa luz del día* y *Mrs. Caldwell habla con su hijo,*" *Insula* 518–19 (February–March 1990): 40–42. The poets traditionally associated with the "Generation of 1927" include Vicente Aleixandre, Jorge Guillén, Federico García Lorca, Rafael Alberti, Pedro Salinas, Gerardo Diego, and Luis Cernuda, among others. Since their mentor/muse was Luis de Góngora y Argote, 1927 was designated as the commemorative date of the tercentenary of his death, hence the name by which they came to be known.

9. Patient number 14 intertwines verses of poetry (about sirens, the sea, and seashells) with his own narration about death: "and the hoarse roar of the conch-shell bearing to our mountain the S.O.S. of mariners drowning while they recall their distant sweethearts, and the shrieks of horror of the sweethearts standing on the cliff above the sea, scanning the horizon which would bring them no consolation" (*RH* 151). Number 103's beloved was, it will be recalled, a sailor: "It is painful to have to drown . . . in sadness and solitude, where float all the feelings which do not let themselves be drowned resignedly, all the feelings which impotently rebel against their fate, like those new-born kittens that take a long time to be swallowed up by the water into which the miller's cruel wife has thrown them and in which they struggle with their clumsy little legs" (*RH* 81). Number 11 compares his love to "those voyagers who fall overboard from the deck of a trans-Atlantic steamer in mid-Ocean without one piece of iron in the ship's hulk or one muscle in the captain's face or one wave of the deep green sea shuddering at that mystery which is being solved" (*RH* 63).

10. Ilie defines Mrs. Caldwell's obsessions in terms of two major preoccupations: Eliacim's death and her love for him (*La novelística,* 197).

11. Olga Prjevalinsky's analysis of his 1955 novel *The Blonde* attests to Cela's brilliant and masterful command of the Spanish language (*El sistema estético de Camilo José Cela* [Valencia: Editorial Castalia, 1960]).

12. Pastrana is located to the west of Madrid, in the province of Guadalajara. It is the cite of the palace where Ana of Mendoza (the Princess of Eboli [1540–92]) was imprisoned. Cela devotes a chapter ("Pastrana") to this locale in his book *Journey to the Alcarria.*

13. Etymologically, the name closely resembles the French *vierge* (virgin). In this context the name (Desverges) and profession are clever indictments of the "deflowering" of Eliacim by his mother.

14. Foster, *Forms,* 93–99.

15. Susan G. Polansky speaks of four narrators: Cela, Mrs. Caldwell, Sir David, and Eliacim. Because Sir David's and Eliacim's presence is defined more by their absence than their active participation in the development of the story line, it would perhaps be more appropriate to speak of them as narratees of varying degrees and perspectives. At any rate Polansky's assessment of the "initial image of . . . [Mrs. Caldwell] involved in a process of careful fragmentation" as "a metaphor of the work's total narrative structure" is perceptively accurate and well-founded ("Narrators and Fragmentation in Cela's *Mrs. Caldwell habla con su hijo,*" *Revista de Estudios Hispánicos* 21.3 [1987]: 21–31).

16. *Mrs. Caldwell* anticipates Miguel Delibes's 1966 novel, *Cinco horas con Mario* (Five Hours with Mario), in which the bereaved Carmen sits up (the night before his funeral) with the cadaver of her husband, Mario, with whom she establishes a one-sided conversation based upon the underlined portions of his Bible (which serve as headings for the novel's twenty-seven chapters).

17. Ilie, "El surrealismo de Cela," 41.

18. These chapters are, respectively, "Let's Get up at Dawn to See the Sunrise, the Majestic Sunrise over the Round Old Hilltop Where the Fragrant and Timid Little Wild Flowers Grow" and "The Assuming Young Ladies of Down, the Fresh Young Ladies of Antrim, the Merry Young Ladies of Londonderry, the Coquettish Young Ladies of Tyrone, Always So Amiable, the Smiling Young Ladies of Armagh, the Jolly Young Ladies of Fermanagh, Who Keep Those Very Beloved English Traditions, Come What May, in Ulster."

19. In this regard Foster speaks of the novel's "achronology" (*Forms,* 92).

20. Ilie and Foster agree on this point. In speaking of Mrs. Caldwell's "disorganized, meandering mind," Polansky seems to be of the same opinion ("Narrators and Fragmentation," 29). Elizabeth Morales de Eggenschwiler, however, bases all of her assumptions on Mrs. Caldwell's realiability as a narrator ("El mundo asfixiante de Mrs. Caldwell," *Hispania* 63 [September 1980]: 498–505).

21. His mother's account of Eliacim's behavior implants seeds of doubt about his response to her sexual overtures. Among these (numerous) ambiguities is the following from chapter 161 ("The Bronze Bell Which Resounds over the Mountains"): "when I am concentrating most and thinking of you, your eyes, for example, or the tone you put

into your voice to ask me to *prepare your bath for you,* or the beauty mark which you had on your neck, or *your inexpert hands" (MC* 134; emphasis added).

22. Ilie speaks of the "surrealistic epigrams" that emerge from Mrs. Caldwell's prose *(La novelística,* 205).

23. Ilie, *La novelística,* 167–87.

24. *Dictionary of American Family Names* (New York: Harper and Brothers, 1956), 32; and *The Origin of English Surnames* (London: Routledge and Kegan Paul, 1967), 31, 44.

25. *Mercer Dictionary of the Bible* (Macon, Ga.: Mercer University Press, 1990), 432.

26. Aegeus (son of Pandion, king of Athens) drowned while searching for his son Theseus, who was thought to have been devoured by the Minotaur. In addition, when Eliacim gambled he had the habit of mumbling the name Zeno of Elea (chap. 35, "The Roulette Wheel at That Seaside Resort That Resembled Paul Valéry's 'Graveyard by the Sea'"). Zeno (also known as "Zeno the Cruel") was a Greek philosopher and disciple of Parmenides. He is the author of *Sophisms* (about the arrow, Aquiles, and a tortoise), in which he denied that movement as such existed. In this regard Eliacim's full name is Eliacim *Arrow* Caldwell (emphasis added). Other aspects of classical Greece include references to Homer, Ganimedes, Tantalus, a map of the Aegean Sea, and Mrs. Caldwell's assertion that the Greek world was a model of political maturity and development (chap. 126, "Archery"). For Ilie chapter 98 ("The Maternal Instinct") is the "key" to the novel *(La novelística,* 181).

27. See Ilie *(La novelística,* 198–99), for an interpretation of the sea's impact on how Mrs. Caldwell's mind works.

28. Examples include: flies, seagulls, sparrows, crows, butterflies, spiders, scorpions, sharks, seals, octopuses, frogs, dogs, cats, cattle, bears, bulls, rabbits, etc. Chapters 60 and 60 *bis.* also bear the titles "Animals Set Free" and "Animals Set Free (another version)."

29. This concept is reminiscent of the first well-known line of verse from a poem written in 1918 by Juan Ramón Jiménez (1881–1958) which reads: "¡Intelijencia, dame / el nombre exacto de las cosas!" (Intelligence, give me / the exact name for things!), and, thus, attests to *Mrs. Caldwell's* poetic point of departure.

30. This chapter was not included in the first edition of the novel. Bernstein says it was added by Cela to the novel in its definitive 1969 version ("Cela's Mrs. Caldwell," in Bernstein's translation, xxv).

31. The dead child(ren) motif appears throughout the novel. Ilie interprets it as the manifestation of the generic mother-son theme and of Mrs. Caldwell's hatred toward Eliacim *(La novelística,* 172–75).

32. Jean-Eduardo Cirlot, *Diccionario de símbolos,* 5th ed. (Barcelona: Editorial Labor, 1982), 181–82.

33. Cirlot, *Diccionario de símbolos,* 54.

34. Ilie, *La novelística,* 167–69. Two additional points should be made in this regard: first, that many of the symbols used by Mrs. Caldwell are phallic in nature (the deer's caramel-coated horns, references to bulls, and so forth), in addition to the uncanny spatial relationship that exists between people, that is, people are frequently "encima de" (on

top of) one another in real or psychological terms; second, there are countless examples of Cela's play on such words as *polvo, leche, cuernos,* and *paja/pajarera/pájaros,* among others, all of which have sexual connotations.

35. Eggenschwiler reminds us that navigators who traversed the Aegean Sea were reputedly excellent swimmers, thereby heightening even more the irony of the entire novel ("El mundo asfixiante de Mrs. Caldwell," 504).

36. See Ilie (*La novelística,* 188–89), for a brilliant analysis of this episode in terms of its symbolism within the novel. For Cirlot fountains, particularly (in Jungian terms) when located in the middle of a garden, symbolize life (*Diccionario de símbolos,* 211–12).

37. In one of the transcriber's few intromissions in the text, he hastens to inform the reader—in a footnote—that chapter 203 ("Dawns") is incomplete because some of its pages appear somewhat burned. He intervenes again at the end of Mrs. Caldwell's last page by saying that the original manuscript contained "two blurred, and completely undecipherable pages with obvious signs of moisture, showing unmistakable signs of having spent hours and hours under water, like a drowned sailor" (*MC* 189).

38. Cirlot speaks of the garden as signifying consciousness as opposed to the confusion of the jungle (*Diccionario de símbolos,* 258).

39. The play on words is lost in the translation: "(This is understandable, Eliacim, easily understandable since everything is straining and fighting to separate us . . .)" (72). The use of the word *visto* is a derivative (past participle) of the verb *ver* (to see) and is, therefore, particularly cogent (all quotations from the Spanish version of *Mrs. Caldwell* are taken from Barcelona: Ediciones Destino, 1979).

40. David Foster, "La estética de la 'nueva novela.' Acotaciones a Camilo José Cela," *Revista de ideas estéticas* 108 (1969): 325–34.

41. Ilie makes a point of stressing Eliacim's rejection of his mother (*La novelística,* 170–75).

42. Ilie (*La novelística,* 192–93) provides another superb interpretation of this department store dream (chap. 209).

Chapter 5: *San Camilo, 1936*

1. For a succinct assessment of the innovative aspects of *San Camilo,* see Janet Díaz, "Techniques of Alienation in Recent Spanish Novels," *Journal of Spanish Studies* 3 (Spring 1974): 5–16; and Janet Pérez, "Historical Circumstance and Thematic Motifs in *San Camilo, 1936,"* *Review of Contemporary Fiction* 4.3 (1984): 67–80. *San Camilo, 1936* is Cela's first novel since 1962, when, *Tobogan of Hungry People* having received scant critical attention, some critics were predicting the eclipse of Cela's importance as a novelist in Spain.

2. Luis Blanco Vila, *Para leer a Camilo José Cela,* 157.

3. Among those most critical of *San Camilo, 1936* are Corrales Egea, Uriarte, Domingo, Gogorza Fletcher, and Ilie, while those who praise it include Tuñón de Lara, Díaz, Roberts, Hickey, Vandercammen, Echave, Ullman, Camyd Freixas, Pérez, and

Bernstein. The broad critical spectrum concerning Cela's work gives evidence of the direction that literary theory took in the 1970s. Another important factor is the tenor of the studies written by Spanish critics living in Spain in 1969 as opposed to those Spanish critics in residence in other countries, such as, for example, Tuñón de Lara (who had lived for a number of years in Paris). Additionally, non-Spanish critics provide still another point of view, of which a good example is Bernstein's assessment of the significance of houses of prostitution in Cela's works ("Confession and Inaction in *San Camilo*," *Hispanófila* 51 [1974]: 47–63).

4. Among those who have defined the novel in these terms are, respectively, the following: Madeleine de Gogorza Fletcher, *The Spanish Historical Novel, 1870–1970* (London: Tamesis, 1974), 147; Luis Blanco Vila, *Para leer a Camilo José Cela*, 174; Jo Labanyi, "Fiction as Release: *San Camilo, 1936, Reivindicación del conde con Julián, La saga/fuga de J. B.*," *Myth and History in the Contemporary Spanish Novel* (New York: Cambridge University Press, 1989), 183; and Gonzalo Sobejano, *Novela española de nuestro tiempo*, 125–37. For a recent assessment of *San Camilo, 1936* as a "Spanish Civil War" novel, see Gareth Thomas, *The Novel of the Spanish Civil War*, 212–15.

5. Edmond Vandercammen, "Cinco ejemplos del ímpetu narrativo de Camilo José Cela," *Cuadernos Hispanoamericanos* 337–38 (1978): 87.

6. Francisco López, ed., *Mazurca para Camilo José Cela* (Madrid: Gráficas P y Punto, 1986), 76.

7. John H. R. Polt's recent English translation of the novel (Durham: Duke University Press, 1991) provides a useful listing of "Characters and Other Matters of Interest" (292–300) and an excellent "guide to the reader" (xi). Although some critics find the inventory of characters to be useless, Polt's work is invaluable and astute. All references to the English translation of the novel are taken from Polt and will be indicated parenthetically in the text.

8. Maryse Bertrand de Muñoz, "El estatuto del narrador en *San Camilo, 1936*," in *Crítica semiológica de textos literarios hispánicos,* ed. Miguel Angel Garrido Gallardo (Madrid: Consejo Superior de Intestigaciones Científicas, 1986), 587.

9. Silvia Burunat ("El monólogo interior en Camilo José Cela," *El monólogo como forma narrativa en la novela española* [Madrid: José Porrúa Turanzas, 1980], 72) and Mario Merlino ("Muerte: crimen y discrimen," *Cuadernos Hispanoamericanos* 337–38 [1978]: 191) speak specifically of Valle-Inclán's influence in *San Camilo, 1936*. It should be noted that the words "droll and grotesque air" replace "*chusco y* valleinclanesco" (167; emphasis added), a translation that overlooks Valle-Inclán's significance. All Spanish quotations are taken from the fourth edition of *San Camilo, 1936* (Madrid: Ediciones Alfaguara, 1979) and will be identified in the text accordingly.

10. See, in particular: Herzberger, "Cela and the Challenge to History in Francoist Spain"; J. H. R. Polt, "Cela's 'San Camilo, 1936' as Anti-History," *Anales de la Literatura Española* 6 (1988): 443–55; Pierre Ullman, "Sobre la recitificación surrealista del espejo emblemático en *San Camilo, 1936* de C. J. Cela," *Neophilologus* 66 (1982): 377–85; Vicente Cabrera, "La instrospección del punto de vista narrativo en *San Camilo, 1936* de C. J. Cela," *USF Language Quarterly* 15.1–2 (1976): 57–60; and Angelines Echave,

"Historia e intrahistoria en *San Camilo 1936*" (Ph.D. diss., Emory University, 1980). So vehement is Paul Ilie's reprobation of the novel that a small portion of it bears repeating: "This is the novel's true obscenity: not the sexual frankness for which it has been criticized but the misplaced use made of sex in explaining political and cultural problems" ("The Politics of Obscenity in *San Camilo, 1936*," *Anales de la Novela de Posguerra* 1 [1976]: 25–63).

The following are but a few examples of Cela's merciless sarcasm: Virtudes's husband, Victoriano, has a nickname, "el Gonococo" (Gonococcus), while she herself was "Miss Carabanchel" (a poor working-class district of Madrid); comparison of the *tertulia* at Madame Teddy's to the famous Madrid Ateneo (Athenaeum [*SC* 27]) because of all the librarians and journalists in attendance; and, reference to "the Bar Zaragoza [as] the Palace of Syphilis" (*SC* 220).

11. Numerous critics have commented on this aspect of *San Camilo, 1936*. In this regard Bernstein, among others, refers to the autobiographical nature of the novel ("Confession and Inaction," 47). An example of the two different fictive present moments of narration is the reference to don Olegario's place of residence as "the Vereda de Postas, *now called* the Calle de Orense" (*SC* 157; emphasis added). Other instances of the same are found sporadically throughout the novel.

12. Numerous studies exist in which the narrator is viewed from various psychological, and oftentimes Freudian, viewpoints (such as an interpretation in terms of ego and alter ego [Cabrera, "La introspección," 57–58]).

13. David Henn, "Endemic Violence and Political Balance in Cela's *San Camilo, 1936*," *Romance Studies* 3 (Winter 1983–84): 31–46.

14. Much of the biographical information about the narrator and his friend Camilo José Cela fleshes out Cela's activities when he was twenty years old (see Bernstein, "Confession and Inaction"). In terms of narrative technique Cela's recent—second-part— autobiography (*Memorias*) is strikingly similar to *San Camilo, 1936* in terms of the collage of historical information, advertisements for products, and so forth, which is intertwined with fragments of actual autobiographical information.

15. Subtitled "a tragic farce in three acts and an epilogue" (*El carro de heno o el inventor de la guillotina,* 69), the play deals with the execution of Cam, Sem, and Jafet. See Sabas Martín, "El teatro transgresor y alucinado de Camilo José Cela," *Cuadernos Hispanoamericanos* 337–38 (1978): 211–32; and Lucile C. Charlebois, "Camilo José Cela ante las candilejas: *María Sabina* y *El carro de heno o el inventor de la guillotina,*" *Anales de la Literatura Española Contemporánea* 19 (1994): 241–59.

16. Miguel Mercader, one of the narrator's friends, reads *La lucha por la vida,* 1904 (Struggle for Life), a trilogy written by Baroja. In addition, the narrator refers frequently to writers and literary works such as Antonio Aullón Gallego's *Madrid de noche* (Madrid by Night [a guide to houses of prostitution in Madrid]), Benito Pérez Galdos's *Episodios nacionales* (National Episodes), the poets Pedro Salinas and Juan Ramón Jiménez, and other Spanish intellectuals such as María Zambrano and Ortega y Gasset.

17. The Civil War began in Spanish Morocco with the revolt of General Francisco Franco's troops, who were transported by German aircraft to the mainland of southern Spain.

18. The epigraphs read, in order of their appearance: "la inseguridad, única cosa que es constante entre nosotros" (. . . insecurity, the only thing that is fixed among us [1]); "A las tierras de Madrid/ hemos de ir;/ todos hemos de morir" (To Madrid now go we must; / All of us shall turn to dust [113]); "Señor, ¿por qué nos tienes a todos fuerte saña? / ¡Por los nuestros pecados non destruyas a España!" (What have we done, oh Lord, to kindle thus your ire? / Do not for these our sins plunge Spain into the fire!" [168]); and "¡Cuídate, España, de tu propia España!" (Beware of your own Spain, oh Spain! [281]). They are taken, respectively, from the works of Spanish (and one Peruvian) writers: Pérez Galdós, Cristóbal de Castillejo, the anonymous epic poem *Poema de Fernán González,* and César Vallejo.

19. Prjevalinsky's observations of Cela's use of reiteration in *The Blonde* is in keeping with the growing importance that this device has in his plays and works of prose fiction (*El sistema estético de Camilo José Cela,* 35).

20. The Spanish version ends in the middle of the word for "tool," *herramienta* (*herram* [*SC* 198]), thereby underscoring the mirror as tool.

21. Among the numerous critics who have cited the narrator's perception as a vehicle for the elaboration of the narrative discourse, see in particular Polt, "Cela's 'San Camilo,'" 448–49.

22. Where the word *moments* appears in the English translation, Cela uses the word *agonía* (agony, anguish, last throes).

23. For specific information about the deaths of these two men and other political figures, see Ian Gibson, *La noche en que mataron a Calvo Sotelo* (Barcelona: Editorial Argos Vergara, 1982).

24. Of importance in this regard is Herzberger's article on the demythification of Francoist history in *San Camilo, 1936* ("Cela and the Challenge to History").

25. Among the most frequent expressions of concern in the first part are the following: *estamos sobre un polvorín* (79) (we're sitting on a powder keg [63]); *vamos a acabar ardiendo* (82) (we'll wind up on fire [65]); and *el país está nervioso* (89) (the country is nervous [71]). The most common concern in part 3 is *esto no puede seguir así* (209) (it can't go on like this [178]). In essence the comments culminate in Uncle Jerome's indictment that "dentro de cada español habita un incendiario religioso" (227) (inside every Spaniard there dwells a religious arsonist [194]), alluding, of course, to the Spanish Inquisition and the purge by fire of Don Quixote's books on chivalry.

26. Erik Camyd Freixas, "El monólogo literario y 'la novela de posguerra': Miguel Delibes y Camilo José Cela," *Plaza: Revista literaria* 11 (Fall 1986): 38.

27. Thanks to Bernstein's research, we may speak of King Cyril of England as Cela's invention and therefore another example of total disdain for the historical record ("Confession and Inaction" [54]). Furthermore, Gibson tells us that not only is 14 April the date of the proclamation of the Republic in 1931, but it also marks the day in 1936

when the second lieutenant of the Civil Guard, Anastasio de los Reyes López, was assassinated by some "Reds" at a Republican parade during which the Falange placed an explosive device close to the reviewing stand (144–45).

28. See Ullman's article for an excellent analysis of this aspect of the novel ("Sobre la recitificación").

29. As a prefiguration of Cela's next novel, *oficio de tinieblas 5,* this segment of Jerome's "prophecy" bears quoting at length: "this is only a purgation of the world, a preventive and bloody purgation but not an apocalyptic one, the end of the world will be announced with very clear and unequivocal signs: children will poison their mothers in the womb with the most innocent poisons, a brew of savin leaves, a glass of arsenic tea, the most illustrious and reverential trees, the cypress, the walnut, the oak, will turn into opaque hard sponges, and the sun, instead of rising from the horizon, will rise from the bitter mirrors of wakes" (*SC* 290).

30. José Homero, "*San Camilo, 1936* o cómo escapar del espejo," *Siempre!* 6 (December 1989): 42–43.

Chapter 6: *oficio de tinieblas 5*

1. In a footnote to her translation of Francisco Umbral's essay on *oficio de tinieblas 5,* Pérez makes the following observation: "Umbral's title is an untranslatable pun which plays on the title of Cela's last novel, *Oficio de tinieblas, 5.* 'Oficio' refers both to the concept of trade, as of a writer or skilled worker, and to 'office' in the Roman Catholic sense of 'divine office'" (Umbral, "Cela: The Writer's Trade [in Darkness]," *Review of Contemporary Fiction* 4.3 [1984]: 66). Since there is no English version of *oficio,* all translations are my own and have been taken from *oficio de tinieblas 5* (Barcelona: Plaza y Janés, 1989). All references will be indicated parenthetically in the text.

2. The motif becomes increasingly significant in all of Cela's work from now on. In a long essay entitled "La comba de la novela y estrambote didáctico para escarnio de malintencionados" (The Curve of the Novel and Extra Didactic Verses for Mockery of Evil-Intentioned People) written in 1965, Cela defines in his own terms the *tremendismo* that, to his lingering consternation, critics applied to *Pascual Duarte.* In line with his appraisal of Camus's "absurdist fatalism," Cela defines *tremendismo* as the "sanguinary caricature of reality" (22) which obliges conscientious writers to call things as they see them. This, in his opinion, obliterates the maliciousness of the originators—usually his detractors—of the term (9–10).

3. Respectively, the epigraphs read as follow: "odi et amo. quare id faciam fortasse requiris. nescio, sed fieri sentio et excrucior" (Catvlli Carmina, lxxxv); "La literatura no es más que muerte" (Literature is nothing more than death. Unamuno, *Cómo se hace una novela* [How to Write a Novel], 8).

4. Cela, "Palabras a una tertulia," *Papeles de Son Armadans* 71.213 (1973): 202.

5. Reference is made in monad 1057 to Pablo Picasso's death by way of

ulpiano the stone cutter, who heard the news on the radio. The rest of the segment constitutes a surrealistic elegy to this Spanish artist, who was an admired, personal friend of Cela. Together they collaborated on a collection of short, experimental prose works entitled *Gavilla de fábulas sin amor* (Bundle of Loveless Fables), which Carol Wasserman speaks of as having a direct bearing upon *oficio* ("*oficio de tinieblas 5*: culminación de un desarrollo estilístico y temático en la obra de Camilo José Cela," Ph.D. diss., New York University, 1981).

6. The visual counterpart of this and the narrator's experience is well served by the cover design of the 1989 edition of *oficio*. Designed by GS-Grafics and Eduardo Crespo, it depicts a print by Goya called *El sueño de la razón produce monstruos* (The Sleep of Reason Produces Monsters). In the original work Goya wrote (as he did on all of these prints) that "imagination abandoned by reason produces impossible monsters: united with her, she is the mother of the arts and the source of their wonders" (Philip Hofer, ed., *Los caprichos,* by Francisco de Goya y Lucientes [New York: Dover, 1969], 43).

7. His obituary notice begins as follows: "ivón hormisdas the heretic dead on the battlefield or in the battle to end all battles died already in too many battles in eighteen or maybe in nineteen battles and he still has eleven or twelve more battles in which to die" (m. 885). The rest of the long monad evolves into a litany of specific battles—ending with Lepanto in 1571, in which Cervantes lost his arm and Spain emerged victorious over the Turks—with accompanying Latin responses such as "cordibus nostris subveni," "corporibus nostris salutem ferto," and so forth.

8. Among the dead are the following: the woman with a lift in her left foot (m. 794), the woman dressed as Pierrot (m. 844), ivón hormisdas (m. 885), the Prussian coronel (on vacation at Lake Tiberius, m. 915), the narrator's grandfather (m. 916), ulpiano the stone cutter (m. 956), Fátima the houri (m. 1007), the baron with conjunctivitis and the orange-colored mole (m. 1047), Orlando the baritone singer (m. 1081), the dental prosthesis (m. 1102), Don iluminado (m. 1140), domingo calcetín (m. 1169), verzeni the necrophyle (m. 1170), and the *tú* narrator (m. 1194).

9. Silvia Burunat, "El monólogo interior en Camilo José Cela," 77. This aspect of *oficio* warrants a careful study in line with the latent surrealism of Cela's book of poems *(Pisando)* and *Gavilla de fábulas sin amor.* The following three examples are offered as samplings of the perplexing psychic poetic images that almost consistently dominate the narrative discourse: "jean grenier was eating bifid children and foulmouthed polyglot angels until miss garibane turned him into the bishop of Salerno" (m. 528); "the elderly Danish blind people on their visit to the museums of Italy were drunk twenty-four hours a day their virgin wax-covered cadavers float during two or three weeks in great gas cylinders" (m. 727); and "the heads of hair that smell of the perfume of garden flowers or of fresh cheese are usually combed and decorated by the editors of the history from their ranks arise the town guides" (m. 996).

10. Tomás Oguiza, "Antiliteratura en *oficio de tinieblas 5,* de Camilo José Cela." *Cuadernos Hispanoamericanos* 337–38 (1978): 186.

11. In this regard attention is called to monad 1163.

12. All the inhabitants of this dwelling represent various aspects of sexual

comportment, beginning with the newborn child and accompanying family dog (first floor); the old woman who dies, her undertaker and the cook (second floor); a husband, his cousin and unfaithful wife (third floor); a married couple (fourth floor); an adolescent (fifth floor); and a homosexual couple (attic). One is again reminded of Baroja's influence on Cela, for of primary focal interest in the Tree of Knowledge is a boardinghouse.

Chapter 7: *Mazurka for Two Dead Men*

1. Janet Pérez, "*Mazurca para dos muertos:* Demythologization of the Civil War, History and Narrative Reliability," *Anales de la Literatura Española Contemporánea* 13.1–2 (1988): 84.

2. Pérez, "*Mazurca para dos muertos,*" 85.

3. In an interview with Francisco López, Cela speaks of a vengeance similar to that of the Carroupo-Guxinde which his relatives carried out against a Falangist from Carballino for having killed a family member (*Mazurca para Camilo José Cela,* 99).

4. All quotations are indicated parenthetically in the text and are taken from the following translation: Patricia Haugaard, trans., *Mazurka for Two Dead Men,* by Camilo José Cela (New York: New Directions, 1992). Haugaard's translation includes neither the map nor the vocabulary section. Additionally, numerous problematic translations exist and will be noted accordingly.

5. Basilio Losada, "Cela, novelista gallego en castellano," in *Mazurca para Camilo José Cela,* ed. Francisco López (Madrid: Gráficas P y Punto, 1986), 28.

6. Masoliver Ródenas refers to some characters in *Mazurka* as "straight out of Valle-Inclán's iconography" ("*Mazurca para dos muertos* Seen through Its Characters," trans. Janet Pérez, *Review of Contemporary Fiction* 4.3 [1984]: 93). In Cela's previously mentioned interview with Francisco López, he speaks about his common heritage with Valle-Inclán, particularly the latter's plays subtitled *Comedias bárbaras* (Barbaric Comedies), which constitute "the epic trilogy about the Montenegro family" in its natural setting of rural Galicia (Greenfield, "Ramón María del Valle-Inclán," 838). Cela also speaks about having been named an "honorary forensic doctor" for the "Forensic Report" he wrote and appended to his novel (López, *Mazurca para Camilo José Cela,* 99).

7. In translating *cruceiros* as "crossroads" (*MTDM* 16), Haugaard misses the mark, for the *cruceiros* also refer to crosses that have been erected to indicate places where people died, a practice that gives tangible reality to death and the spirit world, which are a part of Galician folklore. In this regard Robert Manteiga's essay "Das meigas, bruxas e demos: Superstition and Violence in Cela's *Mazurca para dos muertos*" (in *Actas do Segundo Congreso de Estudios Galegos,* ed. Antonio Carreño, 421–29 [Vigo: Galicia, 1991]) provides an excellent study.

8. Adega, too, plays different songs on the accordion; these include "Fanfinette," "Mon amour," and "París, París" (*MTDM* 49). Other musical instruments are also popular.

Gaudencio plays the bagpipes very well, Ramona's father was reputed for playing the banjo, and she is a pianist who entertains people with tangos and Chopin compositions. See Carol Wasserman, "A Stylist, an Institution, a Book: Cela, Censorship and *Mazurca para dos muertos* (*Review of Contemporary Fiction* 4.3 [1984]: 48) for further discussion of the mazurka "Ma petite Marianne."

9. In terms of other "outsiders" Pérez quite appropriately asserts that "there is no mention in the entire novel of fascist intervention" (*"Mazurca,"* 93). It must be noted, however, that reference is made to "an Italian regiment [that] has arrived"*MTDM* 231) as well as to "an Italian" (*MTDM* 104) who worked in "The Great Beyond," the coffin factory owned by one of the narrator's "grandparents" (*MTDM* 104), and who bore the brunt of not being a clan member by having his hind end "gummed up . . . with sealing wax then stitched . . . up with string and tied . . . to a tree near the village of Carballediña, beyond the Oseira monastery" (*MTDM* 104). By extension one is reminded of Cela's dedication in *San Camilo, 1936:* "to the conscripts of 1937 . . . and not to the adventurers from abroad . . . who had their fill of killing Spaniards like rabbits and whom no one had invited to take part in our funeral" (*SC* ix). In keeping with the outsider motif, the Chopin polonaise that Robín Lebozán asks Ramona to play on the piano constitutes a curious link with the Polish origins of the mazurka (*MTDM* 225), both of which represent something not originally Spanish and much less Galician (tangentially, it brings to mind the Polish court of *La vida es sueño,* 1635 [Life Is a Dream], in which the action of Calderón de la Barca's well-known play takes place).

10. Pérez speaks of the implicit nature of the "cabalistic significance" of the number 9 (*"Mazurca para dos muertos,"* 92). It might also be added that Cela's penchant for the number 3—whether expressing things in three's (as in the use of triple adjectives), structuring his works in tripartite fashion, or other thematic manifestations of this number (such as Policarpo's missing three fingers)—is as prevalent in *Mazurka* as in other works.

11. Too numerous for a complete listing, the following includes a representative sampling of these devices and markers. In the middle of a long narrative segment about Ramona and Robín Lebozán, the narrator is heard correcting him-or herself: "Adega's husband, *I mean,* Benicia's husband . . . and Adega—*I mean* Benicia. . ." (*MTDM* 145; emphasis added). At other times the narrator specifically addresses an obvious listener, such as, for example, what is being told about Don Isaac: "Don Isaac turned out a pansy, but that's a matter of birth and could happen to anybody, to *you* or me even" (*MTDM* 276; emphasis added). An important description of Robín Lebozán's manuscript incorporates free indirect discourse (not readily discernible in the English translation) which, this time, allows us to hear his thoughts and witness some parts of the creative process which his manuscript implies: "Robín Lebozán reads over what he has already written and corrects the occasional cacophony, repetition, or vague, imprecise word, he also changes the odd punctuation mark, *here a comma would be better than a colon, parenthesis doesn't go here,* etc., Robín Lebozán thinks that everything is on the wane, *this business of novels is just like life itself . . . remember Poe's words again"* (*M* 284; emphasis added). There are also examples of muted dialogues within other formal,

recognized dialogues, such as the interchange between a narrator and Moncho Preguizas which is spontaneously interrupted when somebody says: "Aunt Micaela never let me take her knickers off, in that respect she was very superstitious. *May I have another coffee? Thanks very much.* My cousins sometimes dance the tango" (*MTDM* 97; emphasis added).

12. At the beginning of the novel an anonymous narrator says: "In Sprat's brothel in Orense there is a blind accordion player—he must be dead by now. Ah, yes, now I remember: he died in the spring of 1945, just a week after Hitler. . . . I'm talking about in the old days; his name was Gaudencio Beira" (*MTDM* 3).

13. For an excellent appraisal of this aspect of the novel, see Pérez, "*Mazurca para dos muertos,*" 83–104.

14. This is an instance of the translation not carrying the full impact of the original wording, which in itself attests to the self-referential nature of the entire narrative discourse. Whereas the English version speaks of "their lives . . . [as being] *settled*" (*MTDM* 275; emphasis added), the original emhasizes *textual* predetermination: "los hombres tienen que conformarse con lo que el destino disponga porque está ya todo *escrito* [written]" (*MTDM* 225; emphasis added).

15. Masoliver Ródenas,"*Mazurca Seen through Its Characters,*" 86.

16. His name is not fortuitous, given its biblical implications: "one who has been raised from the dead."

17. Masoliver Ródenas, "*Mazurca Seen through Its Characters,*" 100, 149.

18. Other sanctioned aspects of Spanish life can be traced back to *The Hive.* In addition to hunger (which, among other things, forces women into prostitution) and the insanity of war, the institution that suffers the most bitter censure is the Catholic Church; for example, Gaudencio Beira is outsted from the seminary because he was going blind, and priests, besides having mistresses, are plagued with crabs. Because of its direct association with the sacredness of Easter Sunday, Mamerto's flying machine defiantly parodies Christ's resurrection from the dead: "After High Mass on Easter Sunday in the year 1935, Mamerto leant out of the belfry of San Juan, donned the wings of his flying machine and whoosh! leaped into the void, but instead of soaring upwards he plummeted down on to the ground of the churchyard. Crowds of people had turned out to watch, they had even come from as far off as Carballiño, from Chantada, and Lalín, from all over they'd come" (*MTDM* 124). The episode also resembles a scene in Valle-Inclán's play *Divinas palabras* (Divine Words), in which the sacristan, Pedro Gailo, leaps off the roof of a rural church, only to get up again after having played dead for a few minutes.

19. Masoliver Ródenas interprets the presence of sexual licence in Cela's work as "a hymn to liberty" (102), as do many other critics. *Mazurka* contains, however, an apt definition that ascribes to masturbation the important metaphorical significance of solitude and freedom (wherever it appears in Celian literature): "the masturbator must proudly proclaim his glorious, independent solitude, Machado says that a solitary heart is not a heart . . . the secret is to live with your back turned upon everything, it's a difficult state of affairs to achieve, it must be close to beatitude, there are only two possibilities: that

solitude is both desired and sought after, or that solitude is feared and is encountered against our will, in the first case it's a prize, in the second it's a price to pay, that of independence, the most prized blessing the gods can bestow upon man is that of independence" (*MTDM* 294).

20. The translation "my old man" (*MTDM* 21) does not carry the same impact as *difunto* (dead man).

21. Those who are physically the most striking are the nine Gamuzo brothers and the Carroupos, with their nine "signs of the bastard," all of whom serve as a structuring device at the beginning of the novel.

22. A most obvious parallel is the fly motif in *San Camilo*.

23. While some critics such as Masoliver Ródenas speak of *Mazurka*'s characters as having a "collective . . . [and] an individual dimension . . . [that provides] some of the keys to the book" ("*Mazurca Seen through Its Characters,*" 87), others such as Gonzalo Navajas judge them to be "unidimensional," "trivial," and virtually unimportant ("Una literatura de la ante-modernidad. *Mazurca para dos muertos* de Camilo José Cela," *Explicación de textos literarios* 20.2 [1991–92]: 14–26).

24. The episode about the narrator's grandfather is linked with that of the "saintly Fernández" (*MTDM* 79) by means of Don Modesto Fernández y González, an author who used the pseudonym Camilo de Cela. He wrote the erroneous encyclopedia article about the supposed saint and also authored *Our Grandparents' Farm* and numerous articles that were published in *The Spanish and American Enlightenment* and *Spanish Correspondence* (*MTDM* 27). So important was Don Modesto that, upon fleeing to Brazil, the grandfather gave his lover Manecha "a letter of introduction" which she was to present to the writer.

25. Even though some critics say that the gunner Camilo and Don Camilo are one and the same, it should be noted that *both* of them are present at the meeting of clansmen which is called by Robín Lebozán at Ramona's house: "*Don Camilo and Camilo the gunner,* Don Camilo is suffering from earache . . . Don Balthasar and Don Eduardo, Don Camilo's brothers, one is a lawyer and the other an engineer; Lucio Segade and his three eldest sons: Lucio, Perfecto, and *Camilo*" (*MTDM* 271; emphasis added).

26. Haugaard's translation includes a footnote indicating that, according to Cela, St. Carallán is a "fictitious saint, patron of the male sexual organs.—C.J.C." (*MTDM* 9).

27. Different critics draw distinctions between the "chroniclers" and "narrators" of the tale (Masoliver Ródenas, "*Mazurka Seen through Its Characters,* 91–93). Giménez-Frontín speaks of three narrative levels that correspond to (three) thematic units and (three) narrative voices: Robín Lebozán, Don Camilo, and the Casaldulfe Raimundo (*Camilo José Cela. Texto y contexto,* 87–95, 120); elsewhere he refers to the two novels that *Mazurka* encompasses: that of Robín and the main narrator (*Camilo José Cela,* 31). Pérez, on the other hand, does not consider Don Camilo to be a "major narrator, although his ideas are frequently cited" ("*Mazurca para dos muertos,*" 91). With this in mind we are reminded (by an external narrator) early in the novel that, "when Robín Lebozán finished writing the above, he read it aloud and then stood up" (*MTDM* 44), an observation that points to Robín's pivotal importance.

28. Masoliver Ródenas believes that Afouto's "death represents the beginning of the Civil War" (*"Mazurca Seen through Its Characters,"* 96), while Giménez-Frontín asserts that the Civil War is a chronological device that allows Cela to confront the human condition in general ("Una literatura," 16). Concerning political affiliations in *Mazurka,* the Casandulfe Raimundo hums *Cara al sol* (Face to the Sun [*MTDM* 298]) but outwardly criticizes the regime's "Official Bulletin" (*MTDM* 241). Pérez refers to his comments as "interpolated in the manner of an internal monologue" (*"Mazurca para los muertos,"* 95).

29. Many events are associated with various saints' days such as, for example, "the frogs [that] wake up after the Feast of St. Joseph" (*MTDM* 3). It is a well-known fact that Cela consults books on (Catholic) saints and frames their feast days around the lives of his characters.

30. The list provides a summary of the physical peculiarities of some of the characters whose names are disseminated throughout the novel: Moncho Lazybones, Plastered Pepiño, Gaudencio Beira, Hopalong from Marañís, Roque Borrén, Mamerto Paixón, Marcos Albite, Benito Marvís, Salustio Marvís, and Luis Bocelo. It ends with the affirmation that "Robín Lebozán Castro de Cela was declared fit for auxiliary service but was not called up" (*MTDM* 208–9).

31. Giménez-Frontín brilliantly assesses the possibilities of interpreting Cela's own participation in the war (and related critical speculation concerning the same) from a tripartite point of view through Robín Lebozán, the Casandulfe Raimundo, and Don Camilo (*Camilo José Cela,* 120–21).

32. An extensive inventory of literary texts permeates the narrative discourse. While this merits an analysis of its own, the following authors and titles are deserving of mention: don Modesto Fernández y González, *Our Grandparents' Farm;* Arnaldo Wion, *Lignum Vitae;* Ramón Cabanillas, *Vento mareiro;* Pío Baroja, *Zalacaín, the Adventurer;* Ponson du Terrail, José de Espronceda, *The Pirate's Song;* Dick Turpin, Azorín, *La guerrilla;* Rudyard Kipling, *Don Quixote;* Francisco de Quevedo, Valle-Inclán, *Winter Sonata;* José María Iribarren, *(With General Mola: New Scenes and Aspects of the Civil War); Chronicle of Aristides the Leper;* Antonio Machado, and Thomas Aquinas, *Summa contra gentiles.* There is also news about book burning at the "Craftsman's Club" (*MTDM* 173).

33. The parallel with the gardener's death cart in *Rest Home* is obvious.

34. Of his dogs is said that "Tanis Gamuzo breeds hunting mastiffs: Kaiser, Sultan, Moor, good, big, strong dogs that you can rely upon 'til the end of the world. 'With these beasts a man could go to the ends of the earth without a care in the world, when they have their spiked collars on, nothing—not even a lion—would stop these dogs'" (*MTDM* 93–94).

35. Again, the English version does not capture the significance of St. John's Night, which traditionally marks the summer solstice; in small villages it used to be celebrated by young girls searching for four-leaf clovers (in the hopes of ensuing good luck) and singing and dancing around huge bonfires, at which time suitors could openly woo their sweethearts. Haugaard's version merely reads "midsummer's night" (40).

36. There are numerous associations with bodies of water, such as the river Asneiros, in which Ramona's mother drowned (*MTDM* 69).

37. The references to rain vary from the use of the word *llueve* (it rains) to *orvalla* (it drizzles) and warrant a detailed textual analysis. Pérez refers to a "tripartite" analysis of the "rain/orvalla" segments of the novel ("*Mazurca para dos muertos,*" 100–102).

38. Haugaard's translation of "a lo mejor el fin de la lluvia es el fin de la vida" (it's great to see the rain falling without an end in sight [303]) greatly underestimates the symbolism of rain as life, for the explicit meaning refers to the fact that, if the rain ends, it will be the end of life.

Chapter 8: *Cristo versus Arizona*

1. In an article that appeared in the Spanish newspaper *El País* (14 February 1988) Cela makes clear that he uses the word *versus* as a Latin derivative, meaning "*towards and not against*" (quoted in Luis Blanco Vila, *Para leer a Camilo José Cela,* 194). All translations from *Cristo* are my own and are taken from the original Spanish version of the novel (Barcelona: Editorial Seix Barral, 1988), with subsequent references indicated parenthetically in the text.

2. Blanco Vila, *Para leer a Camilo José Cela,* 194.

3. Quoted in Blanco Vila, *Para leer a Camilo José Cela,* 195.

4. Another curious subtext dilutes biblical creation and deals with how humankind was created by animals. It deals with Bang (a lion), Fing (a brown bear), Deng (a mouse), Dahl (a red bear), Kihlie (a deer), and Sepho (a ram), among others, as they discuss what appendages and other things would best suit humans for their life on earth. Wendell says that these animals' names were added on years later (*CVA* 49), leading one to believe that this mythical treatment of creation most likely originates in folklore. Bang and his friends' conversations are interspersed throughout the first half of the novel then suddenly disappear.

5. One of the most intrusive examples of narrative-turned-dramatic text involves Father Octavio Lagares and the layman Timothy. In it Wendell literally depicts a brief scene of sexual abuse between the two men and indicates their names parenthetically according to the lines they speak, as in stage directions (*CVA* 146–47).

6. The figure of the *verdugo* (executioner) often complements this form of capital punishment. His presence is felt with varying degrees of intensity in nearly all of Cela's works of fiction and is indicative of the level of dehumanization apropos to each fictive situation.

7. While Cela has regularly woven references to drama and theater into his narratives, herein lies the genesis of *La cruz de San Andrés,* which was published in the fall of 1994 and for which he received the Planeta Prize.

8. The few critics who have written about *Cristo* speak of the years between 1881 and the 1920s in which the "action" takes place. It should be recalled, however, that

Wendell refers to the Hearst fortune and to David Duke, the Louisiana politician who became famous in the late 1980s in the United States. In a similar regard repeated allusions to (the fictitious botanist) Felice N. Orson's work entitled *Memorial* specify "chapter CLXXXVIII as being devoted to the accomplishments of Wendell's friend Gerard Ospino in his whale hunting days (*CVA* 145), thereby suggesting a curiously obtuse and coincidental encoding device that points to 1988 (in which *Cristo* was published).

9. In ritualistic fashion Wendell summarizes his customary Saturday night "maneuverings" by listing them consistently in almost block form. Though varied in length and elaboration (depending upon the context), they deal with what the two friends used to do to get ready for a night on the town (in Tombstone) and invariably culminate in the same prank: urinating on the Chinaman Wu's door. Wendell also uses numbers other than 3 and 7 in his narration; they are, for example, Zach Dusteen's five sons, the five retarded boys in the children's home, repeated references to the four evangelists, four ages of man, four types of people ("blacks, mestizos, mulattos, whites" [134]), Telésforo Babybuttock's own private ten commandments, Wendell's own ten-point confession (at the end of his manuscript), and so forth.

10. His "rebirth" is similar to that of Pascual Duarte, both acquiring a different persona because of what they say/write about themselves.

11. Wendell's use of the word *mujer* is ambiguous and lends itself to common usage in Spanish as either—literally and legally—one's wife or, more colloquially, one's *woman.*

12. The Spanish expression *sangre limpia* which Wendell uses became popular in the Spanish plays of the seventeenth century and automatically referred to the *cristianos viejos* (old Christians) as opposed to the *cristianos nuevos/conversos* (new Christians/ converts)—namely, the Jews and Moors who, deciding to stay in Spain after the fifteenth century, were forced into converting to Catholicism.

13. Examples of Zach's Latin include the following: "Deus qui unigeniti tui patientia antiqui hostis contrivisti superbiam" (*CVA* 217) and "veritatis simplex oratio est" (*CVA* 226).

14. In her essay on *Cristo* Pilar V. Rotella alludes to this interpretation by way of her study of the omnipresence of the snake and its reminder of humankind's fall from grace ("La serpiente como símbolo y estructura en *Cristo versus Arizona,*" in *Estudios en homenaje a Enrique Ruiz-Fornells,* ed. Juan Fernández Jiménez et al. [Erie, Pa.: ALDEEU, 1990], 585–92). In order to apprehend better the significance of Cela's use of the litany intertext in this novel, an analysis needs to be done of the contexts in which it is used (though this is not a suitable place to carry out a study of this magnitude).

15. She is the adulterous wife of the baseball player Bertie Caudaloso and sleeps with her brother-in-law Nickie Marrana and "the idiot Cameron" (*CVA* 174).

16. In her great magnanimity Ana Abanda knits a type of woolen cap which is designed to keep warm Anteater's one testicle.

17. Literally hundreds of places are mentioned which *span* Arizona and other states, such as, for example, Colorado, New Mexico, Texas, South Carolina, Louisiana, California, Wyoming, West Virginia, Nebraska, Utah, Pennsylvania, Arkansas, and Iowa.

They include the names of towns, streets, deserts, mountains, rivers, business establishments, cemeteries, banks, natural wonders and parks, stagecoach routes, Indian reservations, ranches and farms, and historic places like Wounded Knee. Oraibi is also said to be the "oldest nation in the country" (*CVA* 205) and the place close to which a mysterious cadaver-bearing bubble once landed.

18. This is no doubt a result of Cela's *esperpento*-orientated point of departure.

19. Four brands of tobacco are repeated throughout—Bulky Bull, Black Mary, Mad Owen, and Dusky Mule—and are easily confused with people.

20. Since he wrote *oficio de tinieblas 5* Cela repeatedly injects the idea of occupations *(oficios)* into his writing, using it as a vehicle for social commentary.

21. Tony Clints's hanging comes to mind again as a spectacular public event. Symbolically, the depravity of such a "cheap thrill" is portrayed in the novel by means of two recurring motifs: the hangman's rope—*la soga*—which Pantaleo Clinton wanted desperately to take home with him as a souvenir, and the solitary trees found in different places (like Pitiquito) where they had to be used over and over again to accommodate all the lynchings that had to be carried out for the preservation of a law-abiding citizenry.

22. The *winners and losers* theme so prevalent in this novel prefigures Cela's next novel, *El asesinato del perdedor* (1994).

Chapter 9: *El asesinato del perdedor*

1. Miguel García-Posada, "Entre Quevedo y el surrealismo," review of *El asesinato del perdedor,* by Camilo José Cela, *El País,* 4 April 1994, 10–11. Quevedo (1580–1645) was famous for his poetry (love and metaphysical sonnets and sarcastic and critical rondeaux) and the picaresque novel about the rogue Don Pablos. He was a contemporary of Lope de Vega, Luis de Góngora, Miguel de Cervantes, and Baltasar Gracián.

2. Numerous motifs, refrains, and other topics from Cela's novels appear in *El asesinato,* among which are the following: the mandrake plant *(MTDM);* the princess of Eboli, maritime adventures, and the theme of incest *(MC);* the stable as the focal point of a family dwelling *(PD);* fetuses, the *abuelita* (little grandmother), and poets such as Wences L. Wences *(odt);* African slaves and Sitting Bull *(CVA);* and references to Stalin and Hitler *(SC).*

3. About Boxwood a notice appears parenthetically in a reference to Marco Polo about whom more complete information "is given in the novel *Madera de boj,* [which is] still withheld by the censors" (*AP* 69). All translations of *El asesinato* are my own and are based upon the first edition of the novel (Barcelona: Seix Barral, 1994) and will be indicated parenthetically in the text.

The contemporary state of world affairs is reflected in a conversation about the pope's infallibility. Matías Mestre states that "the failure of Marxism does not justify savage capitalism," only to restate in the same breath that "the failure of capitalism does not justify savage Marxism" (*AP* 216).

4. Public speeches are pronounced throughout the novel and address a wide range of topics. One of the more common themes deals with the debate over government spending on programs to help society's less fortunate, a polemic that provokes bigotry and ignorance: "first they agreed that children, homosexuals, and terrorists were right, in that order; after they scorned grammatical, moral and social rules, they undermined spelling and its cradle etymology, and they sang the praises of misery, poverty, and weakness; later they looked for esoteric places of refuge, drugs, cults, nature (this isn't very clear but in all the confusion you can also figure out the truth), and at last we men armed ourselves and went back to the law of the jungle" (*AP* 215).

Opinions about the proposed titles for the novel include, for example, the following: "The Last Angel's Dance of Death" (*AP* 101), "Monotonous Love Affairs with an Ethiopian Woman" (*AP* 151), "Iconography of Queen Marie-Antoinette" (*AP* 40), "Chronicle of How the New Judge Washes His Preservatives in the Baptismal Font of St. Stanislaw Parish" (*AP* 50), and "The Marriageable Sphinx" (*AP* 104). Each one of them is followed by a brief exegesis of why the titles never materialize and, as such, warrant a careful analysis (that is not germane at this time) of their impact on credibility as a central theme in the novel.

5. The first reference to Mateo's friends includes his "five real friends": Antolín Jaraicejo Méndez, Nicolás Mengabril Artieda, Leoncio Alange Garganchón, Eusebio Corchuela Redondo, and Fidel Barbaño (*AP* 18–19). Added later to the list are four more names that constitute Mateo's "nine soul mates" (108): Benjamín Collazos Martínez, Salustio Tocino Miravete, Santos Requena Requena, and Martín Zújar Almorchón. The listings each include a profile of attributes and capabilities of the "friends." While the second set of names highlights the unreliability of the narration (first "five" best friends then "nine"), it also exemplifies the meticulousness with which Cela writes, being that the new names are added in alternating fashion to the original "five," in this way creating the illusion of a *chain* of friendship between the young men.

6. Although a certain character named Gómez is named in connection with the Aguacatala murders, the crime follows a pattern established by Cela with Doña Margot's unresolved murder in *The Hive*.

In comparison with the no-name bar and town, Cela has a field day with uncanny onomastic witticisms for other fictive spaces. There is, for example, an inn called El tiburón de estaño (The Tin Shark), a gay bar known as La ballena (The Whale), a café referred to as El tigre de cobre (The Copper Tiger), a house of prostitution called El nido circunstancial (The Circumstantial Nest), and different pubs such as El satisfecho (The Satisfied One), La pajarita de oro (The Golden Paper Bird), and La gaviota hidrófoba (The Hydrophobic Seagull). A number of these names attests to the frequent double entendres of a sexually oriented subtext.

7. Here Cela transgresses all socially accepted boundaries in designating the club as "los gozadores del ojete" (connoisseurs of the arse).

8. Mrs. Belushi is the most exotic of these women. In spite of her insatiable libidinal drives, she is sarcastically bestowed with societal acceptability because of the *title* given her through marriage (i.e., Mrs.). Less fortunate prostitutes include,

for example, Marg, Nicolasa, Blasa, Encarnita, Virtudes, and Inmaculada.

9. The questions deal with similar things: whether or not someone is ready to die, when is the best time to die, and what are the different stages of death. Serving as refrains, they are addressed primarily to anonymous individuals.

10. Pascual Duarte, it will be remembered, mentions having to go to the capital for the purpose of fulfilling his military obligations.

11. When pronounced with a Castilian accent (which, of course, characterizes Cela's manner of speech), the "New *Ciri* Post" assumes typical Celian tongue-in-cheek sarcasm, given that *ciri* is a transliteration of *theory*.

12. These first appear in an absurd conversation between two people, one of whom asks permission to douse the other with gasoline. Receiving a negative response, the same individual responds that it is perhaps better to proceed with caution, asking "to whom the Dead Sea Scrolls could matter" (*AP* 31). The short verbal exchange is framed by another common refrain that indirectly alludes to what happens when mistakes are made, in this case the female blackbird laying her eggs in a scorpion's nest: "If the female blackbird had not laid an egg in the scorpion's nest, at this point neither Estonia, nor Letonia, nor Lithuania would have declared their independence" (*AP* 143).

13. Early in the novel armed guards are described as "now" being disguised as bisons, buffalos, and ostriches (*AP* 17), a concealment that, however ridiculous, underscores the misinformation perpetuated in the Mateo Ruecas case.

14. These include the following: *Las botas de siete leguas: Viaje a la Alcarria, con los versos de su cancionero, cada uno en su debido lugar* (1948), *Del Miño al Bidasoa: Notas de un vagabundaje* (1952), *Vagabundo por Castilla* (1955), *Judíos, moros y cristianos: Notas de un vagabundaje por Avila* (1956), *Primer viaje andaluz: Notas de un vagabundaje por Jaén, Córdoba, Sevilla, Segovia, Huelva y sus tierras* (1959), and *Viaje al Pirineo de Lérida: Notas de un paseo a pie por el Pallars, Sobirá, el Valle de Arau y el Condado de Ribagorza* (1965).

15. The following is an example of the sequential incoherence of the narrative episodes in *El asesinato* (with dashes to indicate a shift in narration and/or narrative device): Claudina and boyfriend—conversation about the Last Judgment and robbing cadavers of their valuables—diseases that pine trees suffer—a proposed title for *The Murder*—the female goldfinch's mistake about laying her eggs— conversation about the Dead Sea Scrolls and dousing somebody with gasoline— the puppets of a Punch-and-Judy show—Mateo Ruecas's friend Antolín Jaraicejo Méndez's conversation with Sagrario (Mateo's mother) about getting revenge for what happened to Mateo because of Don Cosme—the "little grandmother" (*abuelita*) and her conversation with her three grandsons—Isidoro de Antillón's novel *The Necessity of Securing Citizens' Freedom with Effective Laws against the Abuses of the Armed Forces (Necesidad de asegurar con leyes eficaces la libertad del ciudadano contra los atropellos de la fuerza armada* [32]).

16. A discussion runs through the novel about whether or not the harmless thug named Gómez or Valeriano Tiburcio Mendoza murdered the Aguacatala family. The dilemma is never satisfactorily resolved.

17. Even though there is no biographical information concerning where Don Cosme studied law, someone's reference to the University of Salamanca (one of Europe's oldest and most prestigious institutions of higher learning) automatically connotes education and training and therefore casts further aspersions on professionals in general: "Salamanca . . . isn't what it used to be, now they give honorary doctoral degrees to any captain of fortune or any puppet who has converted [to Christianity]" (*AP* 178).

Chapter 10: *La cruz de San Andrés*

1. All translations are my own and are taken from Camilo José Cela, *La cruz de San Andrés* (Barcelona: Editorial Planeta, 1994), with references indicated parenthetically in the text.

2. Among the novel's first reviewers are the following: Xavier Moret, "Cela gana el Premio Planeta con la crónica de una destrucción colectiva a causa de una secta," *El País*, 17 October 1994, n.p.; Pere Gimferrer, "Camilo José Cela, hoy," *ABC*, 13 November 1994, n.p.; and Ignacio Echevarría, "Morcilla de sangre triste, *La cruz de San Andrés*, último premio Planeta, en la estela de la obra de Camilo José Cela," review of *La cruz de San Andrés*, by Camilo José Cela, *El País*, 5 December 1994, 7.

3. Moret quotes Cela as having said that an idea about retiring in 1989 (after winning the Nobel) yielded to the establishment of a personal "boxing match with himself" ("Cela gana el Premio Planeta," n.p.) in an effort to continue "proving himself" as a novelist.

4. Cela's treatment of his female characters and narrators provides an excellent opportunity for serious gender-based (and psychoanalytical) studies. These issues will not, however, be discussed here.

The preponderance of characters from North American pop culture is well suited to Cela's propensity for the use of pastiche (for current and past news items and advertisements for different Spanish products that promise to camouflage human imperfections and aging).

5. Quoted as they appear in the original Spanish version of the novel, the epigraphs read as follow: ". . . what is this quintessence of dust? Man delights not me; no, nor woman neither. Shakespeare, *Hamlet*, II, ii, 316; "All the world's a stage / And all the men and women merely players." Shakespeare,*As You Like It, II, vii, 113* (III); "My brain it's my second favourit organ." Woody Allen, (IV); "Sola una cosa tiene mala el sueño, según he oído decir, y es que se parece a la muerte, pues de un dormido a un muerto hay muy poca diferencia. Sancho, en el cap. 68 de la segunda parte del" (V) (There's only one bad thing about sleep, according to what I've heard say, and it is that it resembles death, for between a man asleep and a dead man there's very little difference).

6. Gimferrer, "Camilo José Cela." Cela's work *San Juan de la Cruz* was published as *Matilde Verdú* in 1948. Given the significance of John of the Cross as a doctor of the Church, Mystic poet, and founder of the Discalced Order of Carmelites, Matilde's

association with him is significant, particularly with regard to the perplexities of her own identity, as we shall see.

Despite the overwhelmingly female voices of *La cruz de San Andrés*, one clear example of an unquestionably male narrative voice is found in a long narrative segment in which the narrator refers to himself by way of the masculine form of the words used, that is, his being *"el único,"* (the only one [*CSA* 212; emphasis added]) who believes something that has just been related. At the end of the same paragraph, however, the narrating voice identifies itself as female in its assertion that "before the French Revolution *we* women and not the oxen tilled the land" (*CSA* 212; emphasis added).

7. Matilde says that her friend Matty is "not even forty years old, she should be about to have her thirty-eighth birthday" (*CSA* 161).

8. Relating to the preservation of a family's name and honor, the expression "la sangre llama a la sangre" (blood is thicker than water) recalls the Spanish fifteenth-and sixteenth-century concept of racial purity (commonly known as *la limpieza de la sangre*) and the Calderonian notion of avenging one's *soiled* honor (which dominated the thematics of seventeenth-century Spanish theater).

9. A source of constant consternation to church and government officials in Spain (and to Franco in particular) has been Freemasonry. *La cruz* is no exception, since it falls ideally into the thematics of the cult, in which the López Santana family members become enmeshed. References to Masonic beliefs are, as might be expected, indirect and include, for example, the following: messages from "the Supreme Arquitect" (*CSA* 65) which were traced on paper by Julián Santiso as directed by "the will of God"; "the apex of the triangle, our leader Amancio Jambrina, Amancio Villaralbo, demands blind obedience" (*CSA* 125); and, among others, the description of the "pyramidal organization" (*CSA* 174) of the "Community of the Daybreak of Jesus Christ."

10. Among the numerous examples of bitter sarcasm directed at Franco and the church are the following: Betty Boop's husband Roberto *Bahamonde* (who is ironically surnamed after Francisco Franco [emphasis added]) is an idiot and a lout; comments concerning Galicia's backwardness and Spain's inability to deal with the changes proposed by the Vatican II Council for Catholic Church reform (receiving the wafer for Holy Communion in one's hand and giving the "kiss of peace" during the Mass); and, Xeliña's retarded son, Curriño, who attends the "Father Benito Jerónimo Feijóo" school (being that the priest for whom the school was named is considered one of Spain's most enlightened men).

11. Mention by Matilde Verdú of the manner in which she and her husband were crucified on these crosses is the most significant refrain of the novel. Not only does it tease the reader into closely following the story line in order to discover how and why the couple met such a fate, but it also blurs chronological boundaries between past, present, and future, given that Matilde's allusions to the crucifixion deal with the past as well as the future, such as, for example, when she says: "they crucified us naked" (*CSA* 63) and "they *are going* to crucify my husband and me" (*CSA* 208; emphasis added). Furthermore, the astute reader begins to wonder right away how Matilde herself survived the purported crucifixion, since she is obviously alive and quite able to narrate the events

of the chronicle. Of subsequent importance in establishing a linkage with Masonic architectural allusions is also the importance Matilde places on describing the configuration of their crucifixion, that is, that they were hung "on the Herminia end, beyond the Adormideras polygon" (*CSA* 63) and "under the stone they call The Altar" (*CSA* 181). Finally, Matilde ascribes her husband's and her fate to that of the French royal family of Burgundy, with which the St. Andrew's cross is customarily associated.

12. Matilde is insistent upon bringing to our attention the brand names of this paper: *La Condesita, La Jirafa, El Gaitero Bucólico,* and *La Delicadeza Alemana.*

13. The most undisguised jump from narration to dialogue (which involves a blend of fictive characters from the narration and Matilde Verdú as narrator *and* as the object of a third-person extradiegetic narrator) is found at the end of part 3:

> Matilde Verdú invited Obdulita Cornide for chocolate and *churros,* it's a pity that the owner of the *churrería* on Franja street ended up throwing himself out of a window! and putting together a very honeyed voice and an appropriate posture she said to her:
> —You may go on, if you wish, with the chronicle of the collapse, I am bothered by some mild cervical annoyances, I don't think that it's anything but I am somewhat tired, go on.
> —As you [*formal*] wish.
> —Woman, feel free to address me as *tú.*
> —As you [*familiar*] wish. Eva continued speaking to her daughters:—I say this to you with great sadness[.] (*CSA* 141)

Nowhere is the confusion more obtuse between the women of *La cruz.*

14. Among the commonly cited references to Satan in *La cruz* are the following: Belcebú Seteventos, from Lugo whose curious wood pigeon used to lay gold coins engraved with the bust of Charles IV; Lucifer Taboadela, from Escornabois in Orense, who had thousands of shoe and cigar boxes that were filled with silkworms so he could always dress well, "as if he were a Rajah from India" (*CSA* 33); Satán Vilouzás or Licorín, from Vimianzo in La Coruña, who impregnated young girls by just looking at them; and Astarot Concheiro, from Vilatuxe in Pontevedra, whose flight could span great distances in short periods of time and who, under the guise of a woman, entered into carnal relations with other men.

15. This is a clear allusion to the pious belief that Christ, on his way to his Crucifixion on Calvary, left an indelible imprint of his countenance on a cloth that the holywoman Veronica gave him to wipe his face.

16. Attention cannot help but be drawn here to Gilbert and Gubar's image of "the woman writer's self-contemplation . . . with a searching glance into the mirror" (Sandra M. Gilbert and Susan M. Gubar, *The Madwoman in the Attic: The Woman Writer and the Nineteenth-Century Literary Imagination* [New Haven: Yale University Press, 1979], 15).

17. *María Sabina* (the play) is divided into "five *melopeas,*" which are monotone, rhythmic chants used to recite prose or poetry.

18. Once again Cela's propensity for scatology as a means of bringing things down to size is brought to bear upon the closure of the novel. In literal terms *merda* refers to excrement of all kinds and, as such, provides the nucleus for the frequently used colloquial expression "a la mierda." In all of its repugnance it is a perfect counterpart to the rolls of toilet tissue which are so much a part of this novel. The anomaly associated with the seagulls and the sailors offers a parting transgression of expected visual metaphors, very similar to the "black *Mass* of confusion" (*CSA* 9; emphasis added), from which is launched the "chronicle of the collapse" of the López Santana family.

Conclusion

1. Janet Pérez, "A Retrospective and Prospective Assessment of the Directions of Cela Criticism," *Anales de la Literatura Española Contemporánea* 16.3 (1991): 371.

2. Gonzalo Navajas, "Una literatura de la ante-modernidad. *Mazurca para dos muertos* de Camilo José Cela," *Explicación de textos literarios* 20.2 (1991–92): 24–26.

3. Stanley W. Lindberg, ed. *The Nobel Laureates of Literature* (Proceedings of a Conference on the Nobel Laureates, University of Georgia, 2–4 April 1995), *Georgia Review* (Spring 1995): 231.

Selected Bibliography

Works by Camilo José Cela

Fiction

La familia de Pascual Duarte. Burgos: Aldecoa, 1942. (*Pascual Duarte and His Family.* Trans. Herma Briffault. New York: Las Americas, 1965.)

Nuevas andanzas y desventuras de Lazarillo de Tormes. Madrid: La Nave, 1944.

Pabellón de reposo. Madrid: Afrodisio Aguado, 1944. (*Rest Home.* Trans. Herma Briffault. New York: Las Americas, 1961.)

Esas nubes que pasan. Madrid: Afrodisio Aguado, 1945.

El bonito crimen del carabinero, y otras invenciones. Barcelona: José Janés, 1947. Republished as *El bonito crimen del carabinero.* Barcelona: Picazo, 1972.

San Juan de la Cruz. Madrid: Hernando, 1948.

El gallego y su cuadrilla y otros apuntes carpetovetónicos. Madrid: Ricardo Aguilera, 1949. Revised and enlarged ed. Barcelona: Ediciones Destino, 1967.

La colmena. Buenos Aires: Emecé, 1951; Barcelona: Noguera, 1955. (*The Hive.* Trans. J. M. Cohen and Arturo Barea. New York: Farrar, Straus and Young, 1953.)

Santa Bárbara 37, gas en cada piso. Melilla: Mirto y Laurel, 1952.

Nuevas andanzas y desventuras de Lazarillo de Tormes, y siete apuntes carpetovetónicos. Madrid, 1952.

Timoteo el incomprendido. Madrid: Rollán, 1952.

Baraja de invenciones. Valencia: Castalia, 1953.

Café de artistas. Madrid: Tecnos, 1953.

Mrs. Caldwell habla con su hijo. Barcelona: Destino, 1953. (*Mrs. Caldwell Speaks to Her Son.* Trans. J. S. Bernstein. Ithaca: Cornell University Press, 1968.)

Ensueños y figuraciones. Barcelona: G.P., 1954. Republished in the enlarged ed. of *Mesa revuelta.* Madrid: Taurus, 1957.

Historias de Venezuela: La catira. Barcelona: Noguer, 1955.

El molino de viento, y otras novelas cortas. Barcelona: Noguer, 1956.

Mis páginas preferidas. Madrid: Gredos, 1956.

Cajón de sastre. Madrid: Cid, 1957.

La rueda de los ocios. Barcelona: Mateu, 1957.

Nuevo retablo de don Cristobita; invenciones, figuraciones y alucinaciones. Barcelona: Destino, 1957.

Historias de España: Los ciegos, los tontos. Madrid: Arión, 1957. Enlarged as vol. 1 of *A la pata de palo.* Barcelona: Noguer, 1965.

Tobogán de hambrientos. Barcelona: Noguer, 1962.

Gavilla de fábulas sin amor. Palma de Mallorca: Papeles de Son Armadans, 1962.

Garito de hospicianos; o Guirigay de imposturas y bambollas. Barcelona: Noguer, 1963.

El solitario, de Camilo José Cela, y Los sueños de Quesada, de Rafael Zabaleta. Palma de Mallorca: Papeles de Son Armadans, 1963.

Toreo de salón: Farsa con acompañamiento de clamor y murga. Barcelona: Lumen, 1963.

Once cuentos de fútbol. Madrid: Nacional, 1963.

Las compañías convenientes y otros fingimientos y cegueras. Barcelona: Destino, 1963.

Izas, rabizas y colipoterras. Barcelona: Lumen, 1964.

A la pata de palo. 4 volumes. Madrid: Alfaguara, 1965–67. Vol. 1: *Historias de España;* vol. 2: *La familia del héroe; o, discurso histórico de los últimos restos (ejercicios para una sola mano);* vol. 3: *El ciudadano Iscariote Reclús;* vol. 4: *Viaje a U.S.A.; o, el que la sigue la mata.* Republished in one volume as *El tacatá oxidado: florilegio de carpetovetonismos y otras lindezas.* Barcelona: Noguer, 1973.

Nuevas escenas matritenses. 7 vols. Madrid: Alfaguara, 1965–66. Republished in one volume as *Fotografías al minuto.* Madrid: Sala, 1972.

Calidoscopio callejero, marítimo y campestre. Madrid: Alfaguara, 1966.

María Sabina. Madrid: Papeles de Son Armadans, 1967. Republished with *El carro de heno o el inventor de la guillotina.* Madrid: Alfaguara, 1970.

La bandada de palomas. Barcelona: Labor, 1969.

Víspera, festividad y octava de San Camilo del año 1936 en Madrid. Madrid: Alfaguara, 1969. (*San Camilo, 1936: The Eve, Feast, and Octave of St. Camillus of the Year 1936 in Madrid.* Trans. John H. R. Polt. Durham: Duke University Press, 1991.)

Homenaje al Bosco, I: El carro de heno o el inventor de la guillotina. Madrid: Papeles de Son Armadans, 1969.

La bola del mundo: Escenas cotidianas. Madrid: Sala, 1972.

oficio de tinieblas 5, o novela de tesis escrita para ser cantada por un coro de enfermos. Barcelona: Noguer, 1973.

Balada del vagabundo sin suerte y otros papeles volanderos. Madrid: Espasa-Calpe, 1973.

Cuentos para leer después del baño. Barcelona: La Gaya Ciencia, 1974.

Los sueños vanos, los ángeles curiosos. Barcelona: Argos Vergara, 1979.

Album de taller. Barcelona: Ambit, 1981.

Mazurca para dos muertos. Barcelona: Seix Barral, 1983. (*Mazurka for Two Dead Men.* Trans. Patricia Haugaard. New York: New Directions, 1992.)

Cristo versus Arizona. Barcelona: Seix Barral, 1988.

Cachondeos, escarceos y otros meneos. 2d ed. Madrid: Ediciones Temas de Hoy, 1991.

El asesinato del perdedor. Barcelona: Seix Barral, 1994.

La dama pájaro y otros cuentos. Madrid: Espasa Calpe, 1994.

La cruz de San Andrés. Barcelona: Planeta, 1994.

Selected Nonfiction

"Algunas palabras al que leyere." *Mrs. Caldwell habla con su hijo,* 9–15. Barcelona: Destino, 1958. This essay is (published as) the first prologue to *Mrs. Caldwell.*

La rosa. Barcelona: Destino, 1959.

Mesa revuelta. Madrid: Ediciones de los Estudiantes Españoles, 1945. Enlarged ed., Madrid: Taurus, 1957.

La obra literaria del pintor Solana. Madrid: Papeles de Son Armadans, 1957.

Recuerdo de Pío Baroja. Mexico City: De Andrea, 1958.

Los viejos amigos. 2 vols. Barcelona: Noguer, 1960–61.

Cuatro figuras del 98: Unamuno, Valle-Inclán, Baroja, Azorín y otros retratos y ensayos españoles. Barcelona: Aedos, 1961.

"Al *Pascual Duarte:* Andanzas europeas y americanas de Pascual Duarte y su familia." *Camilo José Cela. Obra completa,* 1:550–84. Barcelona: Destino, 1962.

"La experiencia personal en *Pabellón de reposo.*" *Camilo José Cela. Obra completa,* 1:205–8. Barcelona: Destino, 1962.

"Palabras ocasionales." *Camilo José Cela. Obra completa,* 1:581–84. Barcelona: Destino, 1962.

"Relativo curriculum vitae." *Revista Hispánica Moderna* 28.1 (January 1962): 179–209.

Al servicio de algo. Madrid: Alfaguara, 1969.

"La cabeza, la geometría y el corazón." *Mrs. Caldwell habla con su hijo.* In *Camilo José Cela. Obra completa,* 7:363–74. Barcelona: Destino, 1969. This essay constitutes the second prologue to *Mrs. Caldwell,* which Cela included in the (definitive) publication of his novel in his complete works.

"La comba de la novela." *Camilo José Cela. Obra completa,* 7:9–30. Barcelona: Destino, 1969.

Diccionario secreto. 2 vols. Madrid: Alfaguara, 1968–72.

"Palabras a una tertulia." *Papeles de Son Armadans* 71.213 (1973): 201–5.

Rol de cornudos. Barcelona: Noguer, 1976.

Enciclopedia del erotismo. Madrid: Sedmay, 1977.

Las compañías convenientes y otros fingimientos y cegueras. Barcelona: Destino, 1981.

Los vasos comunicantes. Barcelona: Bruguera, 1981.

Vuelta de hoja. Barcelona: Destino, 1981.

El juego de los tres madroños. Barcelona: Destino, 1983.

El asno de Buridán. Madrid: El País, 1986.

Conversaciones españolas. Barcelona: Plaza y Janés, 1987.

Los vasos comunicantes. Barcelona: Plaza y Janés, 1989.

"Elogía a la fábula." (*Eulogy to the Fable.* Nobel lecture, 8 December 1989. Trans. Mary Penney. Stockholm: Nobel Foundation, 1989.)

El huevo del juicio. Barcelona: Seix Barral, 1994.

Memorias, entendimientos y voluntades. Barcelona: Plaza y Janés, 1993.

Poetry

Pisando la dudosa luz del día: poemas de una adolescencia cruel. Barcelona: Zodíaco, 1945. Revised and enlarged ed., Palma de Mallorca: Papeles de Son Armadans, 1963.

Travel Books

Viaje a la Alcarria. Madrid: Revista de Occidente, 1948. (*Journey to the Alcarria.* Trans. Frances M. López-Morillas. Madison: University of Wisconsin Press, 1964.)
Avila. Barcelona: Noguer, 1952. (Trans. John Forrester. Barcelona: Noguer, 1956)
Del Miño al Bidasoa: Notas de un vagabundaje. Barcelona: Noguer, 1952.
Judíos, moros y cristianos: Notas de un vagabundaje por Avila, Segovia y sus tierras. Barcelona: Destino, 1956.
Primer viaje andaluz: Notas de un vagabundaje por Jaén, Córdoba, Sevilla, Segovia, Huelva y sus tierras. Barcelona: Noguer, 1959.
Viaje al Pirineo de Lérida: Notas de un paseo a pie por el Pallars, Sobirá, el Valle de Arau y el Condado de Ribagorza. Madrid: Alfaguara, 1965.
Páginas de geografía errabunda. Madrid: Alfaguara, 1965.
Barcelona. Madrid: Alfaguara, 1970.

Critical Works

Bibliographies

Abad Contreras, Pedro. "Bibliografía de Camilo José Cela." *Insula* 518–19 (February–March 1990): i–viii. The most current and complete bibliography that exists on Cela to date.
Martínez-Carazo, Cristina. "La crítica frente a Camilo José Cela." *Explicación de textos literarios* 20.2 (1991–92): 33–56.

Books

Blanco Vila, Luis. *Para leer a Camilo José Cela.* Madrid: Palas Atenea, 1991. A three-part journalistic survey of Cela's life and works which includes a personal interview concerning how Cela would like his works to be read. Much of the material is taken from a seminar on Cela's latest novels given by Blanco Vila during the summer of 1990 at the Universidad Complutense (Madrid).
Cela Conde, Camilo José. *Cela, mi padre.* Madrid: Ediciones Temas de Hoy, 1989. A tongue-in-cheek personal account by Cela's son of his father's life experiences and work as a writer, with emphasis on the Majorca years and numerous anecdotes about friends such as Picasso and others.

Foster, David W. *Forms of the Novel in the Work of Camilo José Cela.* Columbia: University of Missouri Press, 1967. Seminal study of the narrative structure of Cela's novels from *Pascual Duarte* to *The Blonde,* with a final chapter on some comparisons between *The Hive* and Cela's works of prose fiction in the 1960s (in particular, *Tobogan of Hungry People*).

Giménez-Frontín, José Luis. *Camilo José Cela. Texto y contexto.* Barcelona: Montesinos, 1985. Collection of six essays taken from a course given by Giménez-Frontín at the University of Oxford on the post–(Spanish) Civil War narrative. Discussion centers about *The Hive, San Camilo,* and *Mazurka.* Excellent insight into Francoist culture and criticism (even after Franco's death). Useful chronology of Cela's life and works.

Ilie, Paul. *La novelística de Camilo José Cela.* Madrid: Gredos, 1971. Seminal study of *Pascual Duarte, Rest Home, Nuevas andanzas y desventuras de Lazarillo de Tormes, The Hive, Mrs. Caldwell,* and *The Blonde* from a (thematic) existential point of view. Insightful analyses of the surrealism in Cela's early works.

Kirsner, Robert. *The Novels and Travels of Camilo José Cela.* Madrid: Gráficas P y Punto, 1986. Chapel Hill: University of North Carolina Press, 1963. The first book-length study in English of Cela's literary production through 1959. Thematic point of view with exegeses of recurring Celian symbols/motifs. Of importance are the chapters devoted to Cela's travel books and personal experiences on his walking trips through Spain in the 1950s.

López, Francisco, ed. *Mazurca para Camilo José Cela.* Collection of essays by Cela's contemporaries and published in commemoration of his seventieth birthday. Anecdotal insight into the writer, his life and times.

McPheeters, D. W. *Camilo José Cela.* New York: Twayne Publishing, 1969. Overview of Cela's life and works through the 1960s, with an excellent chronology and seminal bibliography.

Prjevalinsky, Olga. *El sistema estético de Camilo José Cela.* Valencia: Editorial Castalia, 1960. In-depth analysis of the linguistic aspects of *The Blonde.*

Suárez Solís, Sara. *El léxico de Camilo José Cela.* Barcelona: Alfaguara, 1969. Detailed linguistic analysis of Cela's style (i.e., use of idiomatic expressions, regionalisms, dialects, adjectives, linguistic borrowings, etc.) in a variety of his works of prose fiction.

Trives, Eduardo. *Una semana con Camilo José Cela.* Seville: Gráficas Vidal, 1960. Informal account of a week Cela spent in Alicante with friends.

Zamora Vicente, Alonso. *Camilo José Cela.* Madrid: Gredos, 1962. Seminal study written in Spanish by one of contemporary Spain's foremost men of letters (and a friend of Cela). A generalist point of departure, with countless insights into themes, preoccupations, and life experiences that constitute the bedrock of future Cela research/criticism.

Special Issues Dedicated to Cela

"Camilo José Cela." Special issue of *Review of Contemporary Fiction* 4.3 (1984): 1–175.
"Homenaje a Camilo José Cela." Special issue of *Cuadernos Hispanoamericanos* 337–38 (1978): 5–330.

"Monográfico extraordinario dedicado al premio Nobel de literatura 1989." Special issue of *Insula* 518–19 (February–March 1990). Forty-six essays (in Spanish) which touch upon Cela's major works of prose, poetry, and theater. Included as well are other aspects of his life and work and a lengthy interview with Cela.

General and Comparative Studies

Abad Contreras, Pedro. "Bibliografía de Camilo José Cela." *Insula* 518–19 (February–March 1990): i–viii

A. G. "El premio Nobel dice que 'acaba una situacíon artificial, paradójica y necia.'" *El País* 29 April 1996: 19.

Abruñedo, Angeles. "Las formas de sujeto indeterminado en la prosa de Camilo José Cela." *Cuadernos Hispanoamericanos* 337–38 (1978): 240–47.

Amorós, Andrés. "Cela y los toros." *Insula* 518–19 (February–March 1990): 9–10.

Burunat, Silvia. "El monólogo interior en Camilo José Cela." *El monólogo como forma narrativa en la novela española*, 57–82. Madrid: José Porrúa Turanzas, 1980. Studies Cela's use of stream of consciousness in *Mrs. Caldwell, San Camilo,* and *oficio de tinieblas 5.*

Camilo José Cela. Nuevos enfoques críticos. Madrid, 1991. Essays that deal primarily with new perspectives on *Pascual Duarte, The Hive, Pisando la dudosa luz del día,* and shorter works of prose fiction.

Caruncho, Luis. "Camilo José Cela y las artes plásticas." *Insula* 518–19 (February–March 1990): 13–15.

Casares, Carlos. "Cela, Galicia y galleguismos." *Insula* 518–19 (February–March 1990): 15.

Castellet, J. M. "Iniciación a la obra narrativa de Camilo José Cela." *Revista Hispánica Moderna* 28.2–4 (1962): 107–50. A seminal article by one of Spain's most important theorist/critics of the postwar Spanish novel.

Cela Conde, Camilo José. "Taller del escritor." *Insula* 518–19 (February–March 1990): 17.

"Cela recibió por fin el Premio Cervantes." *El País* 29 April 1996: 1.

Charlebois, Lucile C. "The 1989 Nobel Prize in Literature Camilo José Cela." *Dictionary of Literary Biography/Yearbook 1989,* 3–17. Detroit: Gale Research, 1990.

———. "Camilo José Cela ante las candilejas: *María Sabina y El carro de heno o el inventor de la guillotina.*" *Anales de la Literatura Española Contemporánea* 19 (1994): 241–59.

Díaz Arenas, Angel. "Cela desde la teoría del relato." *Insula* 518–19 (February–March 1990): 17–19.

Fernández, Angel-Raimundo. "Los *Papeles de Son Armadans.*" *Insula* 518–19 (1990): 21–22.

Fernández Molina, Antonio. "Nota sobre Camilo José Cela y los *Papeles de Son Armadans.*" *Insula* 518–19 (February–March 1990): 23.

Foster, David William. "Camilo José Cela: 1989 Nobel Prize in Literature." *World Literature Today* 64.1 (Winter 1990): 5–8.

———. "Cela and Spanish Marginal Culture." *Review of Contemporary Fiction* 4.3 (1984): 55–59.

——— "Cela's Changing Concept of the Novel." *Hispania* 49.2 (May 1966): 244–49.

———. "Cela y los modelos novelísticos." *Insula* 518–19 (February–March 1990): 23–25.

———. "La estética de la 'nueva novela.' Acotaciones a Camilo José Cela." *Revista de ideas estéticas* 108 (1969): 325–34.

Franz, Thomas R. "Cela's *La familia del héroe,* the *nouveau roman* and the Creative Act." *Modern Language Notes* 88:375–77.

García, Angeles, and J. F. Janeiro. "Cela recibe con emoción el Cervantes sin la compañía de anteriores premiados." *El País* 29 April 1996: 18.

García Berrio, Antonio. "El imaginario novelesco de Cela y las aporías de la modernidad literaria española." *Insula* 518–19 (February–March 1990): 25–28.

García-Posada, Miguel. "El desamparo humano." *El País* 18 December 1995: 19.

———. "Más allá de las fuentes." *El País* 29 April 1996: 19.

García-Sabell, Domingo. "Las claves de Camilo José Cela." *Insula* 518–19 (February–March 1990): 29–30.

Gazarian Gautier, Marie-Lise. "Camilo José Cela." *Interviews with Spanish Writers,* 77–96. Elmwood Park, Ill.: Dalkey Archive Press, 1991.

González López, Emilio. "Camilo José Cela." In *Pascual Duarte and His Family,* by Camilo José Cela, 239–60. Trans. Herma Briffault. New York: Las Americas, 1965.

Guereña, Jacinto Luis. "La bio-poética viajera de Camilo José Cela." *Cuadernos Hispanoamericanos* 337–38 (1978): 248–71.

Hernández Fernández, Teresa. "La condicíon femenina en la narrativa de Cela." *Insula* 518–19 (February–March 1990): 35–37.

Iglesias Feijóo, Luis. "Introducción a Camilo José Cela." *Insula* 518–19 (February–March 1990): 37–40.

Ilie, Paul. "La lectura de 'vagabundaje' de Cela en la época posfranquista." *Cuadernos Hispanoamericanos* 337–338 (1978): 61–80.

Kerr, Sarah. "Shock Treatment." Review of *The Family of Pascual Duarte, Journey to the Alcarria, The Hive, San Camilo, 1936, Mrs. Caldwell Speaks to Her Son,* and *Mazurka for Two Dead Men,* by Camilo José Cela. *New York Review of Books,* 18 October 1992, 35–39.

Kerrigan, Anthony. "The Color of Seed." *Review of Contemporary Fiction* 4.3 (1984): 15–17.

Kirsner, Robert. "Camilo José Cela: la conciencia literaria de su sociedad." *Cuadernos Hispanoamericanos* 337–38 (1978): 34–50.

———. "Trauma and Tenderness in the Novels and Travels of Camilo José Cela." *Review of Contemporary Fiction* 4.3 (1984): 59–63.

Lezcano, Arturo. "Los Celas apócrifos o el metaperiodismo." *Insula* 518–19 (February–March 1990): 45–46.

Lindberg, Stanley W., ed. *The Nobel Laureates of Literature.* Proceedings of a Conference on the Nobel Laureates, University of Georgia, 2–4 April 1995. *Georgia Review* (Spring 1995): 231–45.

López Barxas, Francisco. "Entrevista Camilo José Cela." *Insula* 518–19 (February–March 1990): 80–77.

López Molina, Luis. "El tremendismo en Cela." *Insula* 518–19 (February–March 1990): 47–48.

Losada, Basilio. "Cela, escritor gallego." *Insula* 518–19 (February–March 1990): 48–49.

Martín, Sabas. "El teatro transgresor y alucinado de Camilo José Cela." *Cuadernos Hispanoamericanos* 337–38 (1978): 211–32.

———. "Los primeros pasos literarios de un 'Nobel.'" *Insula* 518–19 (February–March 1990): 49–51.

Martínez Cachero, José María. "El septenio 1940–1946 en la bibliografía de Camilo José Cela." *Cuadernos Hispanoamericanos* 337–38 (1978): 34–50.

McPheeters, D. W. "Tremendismo y casticismo." *Cuadernos Hispanoamericanos* 337–38 (1978): 137–46.

Molina, César Antonio. "Un poeta bilingüe." *Insula* 518–19 (February–March 1990): 53–55.

Ortega, José. "Antecedentes y naturaleza del tremendismo en Cela." *Hispania* 48.1 (March 1965): 21–28. A seminal essay on the misunderstood term *tremendismo.*

Oyarzun, Luis A. "The Onomastic Devices of Camilo José Cela." *Literary Onomastic Studies* 9 (1982): 165–75.

Pereiro, Xosé Manuel. "Cela consigue el Premio Cervantes." *El País* 18 December 1995: 19.

Pérez, Janet. "The Game of the Possible: Francoist Censorship and Techniques of Dissent." *Review of Contemporary Fiction* 4.3 (1984): 22–30.

———. "A Retrospective and Prospective Assessment of the Directions of Cela Criticism." *Anales de la Literatura Española Contemporánea* 16.3 (1991): 361–77.

Pope, Randolph. "*La rosa* y la poética heterodoxa de Cela." *Insula* 518–19 (February–March 1990): 57.

Pozuelo Yvancos, José María. "Cela y la tradición viajera del noventa y ocho." *Insula* 518–19 (February–March 1990): 57.

Risco, Antonio. "Para un estudio del humor en Cela." *Insula* 518–19 (February–March 1990): 60–61.

Senabre, Ricardo. "Camilo José Cela en la España árida." *Insula* 518–19 (February–March 1990): 65–66.

Sobejano, Gonzalo. "Camilo José Cela: La enajenación." *Novela española de nuestro tiempo,* 89–141. 2d ed. Madrid: Prensa Española, 1975. An entire chapter devoted to *Pascual Duarte* through *San Camilo* by one of the foremost authorities on contemporary Spanish narrative. Each novel is discussed in the context of the *novela estructural* (structural novel), which dominated narrative poetics in the two decades following the end of the Spanish Civil War.

————. "Cela y la renovación de la novela." *Insula* 518–19 (February–March 1990): 66–67.

————. "El Surrealismo en la España de Postguerra: Camilo José Cela." In *Surrealismo/ Surrealismos*. Ed. Peter G. Earle and Germán Gullón, 131–42. Philadelphia: University of Pennsylvania Department of Romance Languages, 1976.

Steel, Brian. "Two Recurring Structures in Cela's *Prólogos.*" *Revista de Estudios Hispánicos* 6 (1969):249–64.

Tinnell, Roger D. "Camilo José Cela." *Review of Contemporary Fiction* 4.3 (1984): 38–43.

Torres, Sagrario. "El otro Cela." *Cuadernos Hispanoamericanos* 337–38 (1978): 272–90.

Vandercammen, Edmond. "Cinco ejemplos del ímpetu narrativo de Camilo José Cela." *Cuadernos Hispanoamericanos* 337–38 (1978): 81–89.

Villanueva, Darío. "Estudio preliminar." *Páginas Escogidas,* by Camilo José Cela, 9–65. Ed. Darío Villanueva. Madrid: Espasa Calpe, 1991. Provides a critical, historical overview of Cela's work to the present.

————. "La intencionalidad de lo sexual en Cela." *Los Cuadernos del Norte* 51 (October–November 1988): 54–57.

Studies on Specific Novels by Camilo José Cela

Pascual Duarte

Beck, Mary Ann. "Nuevo encuentro con *La familia de Pascual Duarte.*" In *Novelistas españoles de postguerra*. Ed. Rodolfo Cardona, 66–87. Madrid: Taurus, 1976. An excellent study of textual gaps, ambiguities, and ironies that disprove Pascual's sincerity.

Bernstein, J. S. "Pascual Duarte and Orestes." *Symposium* 22 (1968): 301–18.

Busette, Cedric."*La familia de Pascual Duarte and El túnel: Correspondences and Divergencies in the Exercise of Craft.*" Lanham, Md.: University Press of America, 1994.

————. "*La familia de Pascual Duarte* and the Prominence of Fate." *Revista de Estudios Hispánicos* 8 (1974): 61–67.

Dougherty, Dru. "Pascual en la cárcel: el encubierto relato de *La familia de Pascual Duarte.*" *Insula* 365 (1977): 5, 7. Insightful discussion of Pascual's personal text of liberation as framed by the *Pascual Duarte* text.

González-del-Valle, Luis T. "La muerte de la Chispa: su función en *La Familia de Pascual Duarte.*" *Sin Nombre* 6 (1975): 56–58

Gullón, Germán. "Contexto ideológico y forma narrativa en *La familia de Pascual Duarte.*" *Hispania* 68 (March 1985): 1–8. Pascual Duarte, the narrator, within Francoist Spain.

Hoyle, A. "*La familia de Pascual Duarte:* psicoanálisis de la historia." In *Actas del VIII Congreso de la Asociación Internacional de Hispanistas*. Ed. A. David Kossoff et al., 1–11. Madrid: Ediciones Istmo, 1986.

Jerez-Farrán, Carlos. "Pascual Duarte y la susceptibilidad viril." *Hispanófila* 1 (1989): 47–63. A carefully researched anthropological contextualization of the Extremaduran culture within which Pascual was raised and achieved manhood.

Kerrigan, Anthony. "Introduction to The Family of Pascual Duarte." *Review of Contemporary Fiction* 4.3 (1984): 50–55.

Kirsner, Robert. "Cela's Quest for a Tragic Sense of Life." *Kentucky Romance Quarterly* 17 (1970): 259–64.

Kronik, John. "Encerramiento y apertura: Pascual Duarte y su texto." *Anales de la Literatura Española* 6 (1988): 309–23. Intelligent and precise analysis of the dual texts within the novel (based on a continuation of Dougherty's earlier study "Pascual en la cárcel").

———. "Pascual's Parole." *Review of Contemporary Fiction* 4.3 (1984): 111–18.

Marbán, Jorge A. *Camus y Cela.* Barcelona: Ediciones Picazo, 1973.

Marcone, Rose Marie. "Implications of the Autobiographical Form in *La familia de Pascual Duarte.*" *USF Language Quarterly* 24.1–2 (Fall–Winter 1985): 13–15.

Marín-Minguillón, Adolfo. "*La familia de Pascual Duarte* y el efecto esquizo." In *Critical Essays on the Literature of Spain and Spanish America.* Ed. Julio Baena, 171–79. Boulder, Colo.: Society of Spanish and Spanish-American Studies, 1991.

Masoliver Ródenas, Juan Antonio. "Las dos lecturas de *La familia de Pascual Duarte.*" *Insula* 518–19 (February–March 1990): 51–52.

Montes-Huidobro, Matías. "Dinámica de la correlación existencial en *La familia de Pascual Duarte.*" *Revista de Estudios Hispánicos* 16(1982): 213–21

Osuna, Rafael. "Pascual Duarte: Asesino, Miliciano, Nacionalista." *Ideologies and Literature* 3.11 (1979): 85–95. Pascual's crimes studied in a new historicist context.

Penuel, Arnold M. "The Psychology of Cultural Disintegration in Cela's *La familia de Pascual Duarte.*" *Revista de Estudios Hispánicos* 16.3 (1982): 361–78.

Perricone, Catherine R. "The Function of the Simile in Cela's *La familia de Pascual Duarte.*" *USF Language Quarterly* 24.3–4 (Spring–Summer 1986): 33–37.

Rosenberg, John R. "El autobiógrafo encerrado: Pascual Duarte y su transcriptor." *Explicación de Textos Literarios* 24.3–4 (1985–86): 63–72.

———. "Pascual Duarte and the Eye of the Beholder: Cela, Sartre, and the Metaphor of Vision." *Revista Canadiense de Estudios Hispánicos* 14.1 (1989): 149–59.

Sánchez Lobato, Jesús. "La adjetivación en *La familia de Pascual Duarte.*" *Insula* 518–19 (February–March 1990): 99–112.

Spires, Robert. "Systematic Doubt: The Moral Art of *La familia de Pascual Duarte.*" *Hispanic Review* 40 (1972): 283–302.

Thomas, Michael D. "Narrative Tension and Structural Unity in Cela's *La familia de Pascual Duarte.*" *Symposium* 31 (1977): 165–78.

Urrutia, Jorge. *Cela: La familia de Pascual Duarte.* Madrid: Sociedad General Española de Librería, 1982. A careful study of the genesis and publication history of the novel.

———. "El manuscrito de *La familia de Pascual Duarte.*" *Insula* 518–19 (February–March 1990): 68–69.

Villanueva, Darío. "1942: *La familia de Pascual Duarte,* del manuscrito a la edición." In *Hora actual de la novela hispánica.* Ed. Eduardo Godoy Gallardo, 193–201.

Valparaíso: Ediciones Universitarias de Valparaíso de la Universidad Católica de Valparaíso, 1994. An editorial history of the publication of the novel.

Vernon, Kathleen M. "*La Politique des Auteurs:* Narrative Point of View in *Pascual Duarte,* Novel and Film." *Hispania* 72.1 (1989): 87–96.

Rest Home

Kronik, John. "*Pabellón de reposo:* La inquietud narrativa de Camilo José Cela." In *Actas del VIII Congreso de la Asociación Internacional de Hispanistas.* Ed. A. David Kossoff et al., 105–11. Madrid: Ediciones Istmo, 1986.

Nora, Eugenio de. "Sobre *Pabellón de reposo.*" *Insula* 518–19 (February–March 1990): 55–56.

The Hive

Alarcos Llorach, Emilio. "Al hilo de *La colmena.*" *Insula* 518–19 (February–March 1990): 3–4.

Asún Escartín, Raquel. "Introducción" to *La colmena.* Ed. Raquel Asún Escartín, 7–73. Madrid: Editorial Castalia, 1990.

Barbieri, Marie. "El 'Final' de *La colmena,* o la ruptura con la novela tradicional." *Explicación de textos literarios* 20.2 (1991–92): 27–32. *The Hive* as "new novel."

Bueno, Gustavo. "El significado filosófico de *La colmena* en los años 50." *Insula* 518–19 (February–March 1990): 11–13.

Cabrera, Vicente. "En busca de tres personajes perdidos en *La colmena.*" *Cuadernos Hispanoamericanos* 337–38 (1978): 127–36. Study of the gypsy boy, Doña Margot, and the man who killed himself because of the odor of onion.

Deveny, Thomas. "Cinematographic Adaptations of Two Novels by Camilo José Cela." *Literature Films Quarterly* 16.4 (1988): 276–79.

Dougherty, Dru. "*La colmena* en dos discursos: novela y cine." *Insula* 518–19 (February–March 1990): 19–21.

———. "Form and Structure in *La colmena:* from Alienation to Community." *Anales de la Novela de Posguerra* 1 (1976): 7–23.

Flasher, John J. "Aspects of Novelistic Technique in Cela's *La colmena.*" *Philological Papers. West Virginia University Bulletin* 60.5 (1959): 30–43.

Franz, Thomas R. "Three Hispanic Echoes of Tolstoi at the Close of World War II." *Hispanic Journal* 6.1 (1984): 37–51.

Henn, David. "Cela's Portrayal of Martín Marco in *La colmena.*" *Neophilologus* 55 (1971): 142–49.

———. *La colmena.* London: Grant and Cutler, Ltd., 1974. An entire book devoted to various aspects of this novel from a generalist perspective.

———. "*La colmena*—An Oversight on the Part of Cela." *Romance Notes* 13 (1971–72): 414–18.

———. "Martín Marco: El desarrollo de un protagonista." *Insula* 517–18 (February–March 1990): 33–34.

————. "Theme and Structure in *La colmena.*" *Symposium* 19:115–22.

Kobzina, Norma G. "*Bleak House* Revisited: Cela's *La colmena.*" *Hispanófila* 82 (1984): 57–66.

"La miel y la cera de *La colmena.*" *Indice de artes y letras* 44.24: 21–23.

Ortega, José. "El humor de Cela en *La colmena.*" *Cuadernos Hispanoamericanos* 208 (1967): 159–64.

————. "Importancia del personaje Martín Marco en *La colmena* de Cela." *Romance Notes* 6 (1965): 92–95.

————. "Símiles de animalidad en *La colmena.*" *Romance Notes* 8 (1966): 6–10.

Palmes, Gisela. *Literatur und Film: La Colmena von Camilo José Cela.* New York: Peter Lang, 1994.

Rehder, Ernest. "Ecos de Nietzsche en la novela española de posguerra: *La colmena, Fiesta al noroeste* y *Tiempo de silencio.*" *Romance Notes* 27 (1986): 113–20.

Sala Valldaura, Josep María. "La colmena: Algunas funciones de la modalización narrativa." *Insula* 518–19 (February–March 1990): 63–65.

Sobejano, Gonzalo. "*La colmena*: Olor a miseria." *Cuadernos Hispanoamericanos* 337–38 (1978): 113–26.

Spires, Robert. "Cela's *La colmena:* The Creative Process as Message." *Hispania* 55 (December 1972): 873–80.

————. "Documentación y transformación en *La colmena.*" *La novela española de posguerra,* 94–131. Planeta/Universidad de Kansas, 1978. Important structural analysis of fragmentation, lack of chronological sequencing, repetition, and prolongation of narrative moments/episodes.

Urrutia, Jorge. Introduction. *La colmena,* by Camilo José Cela, 11–33. Madrid: Cátedra, 1989.

Villanueva, Darío. "La génesis literaria de *La colmena.*" *Insula* 518–19 (February–March 1990): 73–75.

Mrs. Caldwell Speaks to Her Son

Bernstein, J. S. "Cela's Mrs. Caldwell." *Mrs. Caldwell Speaks to Her Son,* by Camilo José Cela, xiii–xxvi. Ithaca: Cornell University Press, 1968.

Byrne, Jack. "Mother Caldwell Writes to Her Dearly Beloved Son." *Review of Contemporary Fiction* 4.3 (1984): 105–11.

Eggenschwiler, Elizabeth Morales de. "El mundo asfixiante de Mrs. Caldwell." *Hispania* 63 (September 1980): 498–505. Studies the causes of Mrs. Caldwell's dementia and posits her as a reliable narrator.

Ilie, Paul. "El surrealismo de Cela: *Pisando la dudosa luz del día* y *Mrs. Caldwell habla con su hijo.*" *Insula* 518–19 (February–March 1990): 40–42. Comparison between Cela's surrealistic poetry and *Mrs. Caldwell.*

Liddy, James. "I Must Be Talking about Mrs. Caldwell to El Rey de Son Armadans." *Review of Contemporary Fiction* 4.3 (1984): 31–33.

Polansky, Susan. "Narrators and Fragmentation in Cela's *Mrs. Caldwell habla con su hijo.*" *Revista de Estudios Hispánicos* 21.3 (1987): 21–31.

San Camilo, 1936

Bernstein, J. S. "Confession and Inaction in *San Camilo." Hispanófila* 51 (1974): 47–63.
Bertrand de Muñoz, Maryse. "El estatuo del narrador en *San Camilo, 1936.*" In *Crítica semiológica de textos literarios hispánicos.* Ed. Miguel Angel Garrido Gallardo, 579–89. Madrid: Consejo Superior de Intestigaciones Científicas, 1986.
———. "Estudio de la 'voz' en *San Camilo, 1936.*" In *Actas del VIII Congreso de la Asociación Internacional de Hispanistas.* Ed. A. David Kossoff et al., 211–20. Madrid: Ediciones Istmo, 1986. Structuralist analysis of point of view and narration.
———. "Novelas de la guerra. *San Camilo, 1936." Insula* 517–18 (February–March 1990): 10–11.
Cabrera, Vicente. "La introspección del punto de vista narrativo en *San Camilo, 1936* de C. J. Cela." *USF Language Quarterly* 15 (Fall–Winter 1975): 57–60.
Camyd Freixas, Erik. "El monólogo literario y 'la novela de la posguerra': Miguel Delibes y Camilo José Cela." *Plaza: Revista de literatura* 11 (Fall 1986): 34–43. Stream-of-consciousness techniques in two Spanish novelists, Cela and Delibes.
Díaz, Janet. "Techniques of Alienation in Recent Spanish Novels." *Journal of Spanish Studies* 3 (Spring 1974): 5–16.
Echave, Angelines. "Historia e intrahistoria en *San Camilo 1936.*" Ph.D. diss., Emory University, 1980. Studies the narrator from a Jungian point of view as antihero within the context of (the themes of) violence and otherness.
Gogorza Fletcher, Madeleine de. "Historical Novels of the Civil War." *The Spanish Historical Novel, 1870–1970,* 129–52. London: Tamesis, 1974.
Henn, David. "Endemic Violence and Political Balance in Cela's *San Camilo, 1936.*" *Romance Studies* 3 (Winter 1983–84): 31–46.
Herzberger, David. "Cela and the Challenge to History in Francoist Spain." *Ojáncano* (April 1991): 13–23.
Homero, José. "*San Camilo, 1936* o cómo escapar del espejo." *Siempre!* 6 December 1989, 42–43.
Ilie, Paul. "The Politics of Obscenity in *San Camilo, 1936." Anales de la Novela de Posguerra* 1 (1976): 25–63. A pernicious rhetorical attack on Cela's *irresponsibility* as the creator of *San Camilo.*
Labanyi, Jo. "Fiction as Release: *San Camilo, 1936, Reivindicación del conde con Julián, La saga/fuga de J. B.*" *Myth and History in the Contemporary Spanish Novel,* 178–246. New York: Cambridge University Press, 1989.
Merlino, Mario. "Muerte: crimen y discrimen." *Cuadernos Hispanoamericanos* 337–38 (1978): 188–210.
Pérez, Janet. "Historical Circumstance and Thematic Motifs in *San Camilo, 1936." Review of Contemporary Fiction* 4.3 (1984): 67–80.
Polt, J. H. R. "Cela's *San Camilo, 1936* as Anti-History." *Anales de la Literatura Española* 6 (1988): 443–55.
Roberts, Gemma. "La culpa y la búsqueda de la autenticidad en *San Camilo 1936.*" In *Novelistas españoles de postguerra.* Ed. Rodolfo Cardona, 205–18. Madrid: Taurus, 1976.

Thomas, Gareth. "Irrationalism and Anti-historicism in the Later Novels of the Civil War (1967–1975)." *The Novel of the Spanish Civil War (1936–1975),* 207–19. New York: Cambridge University Press, 1990.

Ullman, Pierre. "Sobre la recitificación surrealista del espejo emblemático en *San Camilo, 1936* de C. J. Cela." *Neophilologus* 66 (1982): 377–85. An intelligent analysis of the mirror technique/motif within the context of the Baroque tradition of the mirror and death in Spanish literature.

Vandercammen, Edmond. "Cinco ejemplos del ímpetu narrativo de Camilo José Cela." *Cuadernos Hispanoamericanos* 337–38 (1978): 81–89.

oficio de tinieblas 5

Alonso, Ricardo. "*oficio de tinieblas*: fábula íntima y funera." *Insula* 518–19 (February–March 1990): 5–6.

Díaz-Castañón, Carmen. "Re-ordenación de un caos: *oficio de tinieblas. 5.*" *Papeles de Son Armadans* 75.224–25 (1975): 187–211. Emphasis on the importance of monad 332 and a study of stream of consciousness.

Domingo, José. "*oficio de tinieblas 5,* de Camilo José Cela." *Insula* 327 (February 1974): 6–7.

Oguiza, Tomás. "Antiliteratura en *oficio de tinieblas 5,* de Camilo José Cela." *Cuadernos Hispanoamericanos* 337–38 (1978): 181–87.

———. *C. J. Cela, más un apéndice: El libro oficio de tinieblas 5.* Valencia, 1975.

Personneaux-Conesa, Lucie. "El surrealismo en España: espejismos y escamoteo." In *Actas del VIII Congreso Internacional de Hispanistas.* Ed. A. David Kossoff et al., 447–54. Madrid: Istmo, 1986.

Rato, Antolín. "Cela: Writing about Death." Trans. Lois Parkinson Zamora. *Review of Contemporary Fiction* 4.3 (1984): 33–38.

Roberts, Gemma. "Culminación del tremendismo: *oficio de tinieblas 5.*" *Anales de la Novela de Posguerra* 1 (1976): 65–83. Intelligent consideration of the protagonist as first-person monologue, the aesthetics of the grotesque, existentialism, the language of negativity, and suicide as textual self-destruction.

Umbal, Francisco. "Cela: The Writer's Trade (in Darkness)." *Review of Contemporary Fiction* 4.3 (1984): 63–66.

Wasserman, Carol. "*oficio de tinieblas 5*: culminación de un desarrollo estilístico y temático." Ph.D. diss., New York University, 1981.

Mazurka for Two Dead Men

Giménez-Frontín, José Luis. "*Mazurka para dos muertos.*" *Insula* 518–19 (February–March 1990): 31–32.

Losada, Basilio. "Cela, novelista gallego en castellano." In *Mazurca para Camilo José Cela.* Ed. Francisco López, 25–28. Madrid: Gráficas P y Punto, 1986.

Manteiga, Robert. "Das meigas, bruxas e demos. Superstition and Violence in Cela's *Mazurca para dos muertos.*" In *Actas do Segundo Congreso de Estudios Galegos.* Ed. Antonio Carreño, 421–29. Vigo: Galicia, 1991.

Masoliver Ródenas, Juan Antonio. "*Mazurca para dos muertos* Seen through Its Characters." Trans. Janet Pérez. *Review of Contemporary Fiction* 4.3 (1984): 81–104.

Navajas, Gonzalo. "Una literatura de la ante-modernidad. *Mazurca para dos muertos* de Camilo José Cela." *Explicación de textos literarios* 20.2 (1991–92): 14–26. Analysis of *Mazurka* within a postmodern context.

Pérez, Janet. "*Mazurca para dos muertos:* Demythologization of the Civil War, History and Narrative Reliability." *Anales de la Literatura Española Contemporánea* 13.1–2 (1988): 83–104.

Wasserman, Carol. "A Stylist, an Institution, a Book: Cela, Censorship and *Mazurca para dos muertos.*" *Review of Contemporary Fiction* 4.3 (1984): 44–49.

Cristo versus Arizona

Alvar, Manuel. "*Cristo versus Arizona.*" *Insula* 518–19 (February–March 1990): 7–8.

Kronik, John. "Desde Torremejía al O.K. Corral: viaje al premio Nobel." *Insula* 518–19 (February–March 1990): 43–46.

Rotella, Pilar V. "La serpiente como símbolo y estructura en *Cristo versus Arizona.*" In *Estudios en homenaje a Enrique Ruiz-Fornells.* Ed. Juan Fernández Jiménez et al., 585–92. Erie, Pa.: Asociación de Licenciados y Doctores Españoles en los Estados Unidos, 1990. Thematic analysis of the serpent motif.

El asesinato del perdedor

García-Posada, Miguel. "Entre Quevedo y el surrealismo." Review of *El asesinato del perdedor,* by Camilo José Cela. *El País,* 4 April 1994, 10–11.

La cruz de San Andrés

Echevarría, Ignacio. "Morcilla de sangre triste. *La cruz de San Andrés,* último premio Planeta, en la estela de la obra de Camilo José Cela." Review of *La cruz de San Andrés,* by Camilo José Cela. *El País,* 5 December 1994, 7.

Gimferrer, Pere. "Camilo José Cela, hoy." *ABC,* 13 November 1994: n.p. Synthetic analysis of the evolution of Cela's style since *Pascual Duarte.*

Moret, Xavier. "Cela gana el Premio Planeta con la crónica de una destrucción colectiva a causa de una secta." *El País,* 17 October 1994, n.p.

Index

177

Jafet (*El asesinato*), 112, 144
Japan, 46
Jarama River, 83
Java, 137
Jerónimo (*San Camilo*), 55, 62
Jesuits, 79, 110
Jesusa, Doña (*The Hive*), 30
Jesus Christ, 86, 95–96, 100, 123–24, 126, 150, 159, 160
Jews, 99, 115, 154
Jiménez, Juan Ramón, 73, 141
Joan of Arc, 103
John of the Cross, 120, 158
Journey to the Alcarria, 9, 130
Juan Carlos (King of Spain), 8
Julita (*The Hive*), 32, 36–37

Kerrigan, Anthony, 133
Kirsner, Robert, 6–7
Kronik, John, 8

La Coruña, Spain, 17, 84, 103, 117–18, 121, 124
Laín Entralgo, Pedro, 4
lamb, 11, 16, 90, 95–96, 100
Larra, Mariano José de, 3
Latin, 88, 93, 95, 104, 112, 146, 153–54
Lawrence, D. H., 88
Lazarillo de Tormes, 10, 11
Lebozán, Robín (*Mazurka*), 76, 79, 81–84, 149, 151
Lee, Gypsy Rose. *See* Gypsy Rose Lee
legal system, 90, 96–97, 101–3, 105, 109, 112–14
legends, 74, 103, 153
Leibniz, Gottfried W., 64
León, Luis de, 111, 135
Lepanto, Battle of, 147
lesbianism, 38, 79
letters, 21–23, 25, 42, 102
lexicon, 89, 93, 113, 138, 142. *See also individual languages.*

Ley de Responsabilidades Políticas (Law of Political Responsibility), 34
lies, 46, 65, 89, 91, 93
limpieza de la sangre (racial purity), 154, 159
linguistics, 88, 92, 112, 124
litany, 7, 9, 66–67, 72, 75, 86, 88, 94–97, 111, 131, 154
literary theory, 116, 143
literature, 4, 65, 72, 87, 103, 147, 152
Lithuania, 157
liturgy, 65–66, 71, 95
locus amoenus, 21
logic, 40, 44, 65, 67, 138
loneliness, 23, 40, 50, 110, 123
Lope de Vega Carpio, Félix, 155
López, Concepción Castillo. *See* Castillo López, Concepción
losers, 101, 113–14, 124, 155
Louisiana, 91, 111, 154
love, 7, 23, 50–51, 62, 67, 89, 96, 117, 131
La lucha por la vida (Baroja), 144
Lull, Ramón, 136
Lurueña, Santiago (*Pascual Duarte*), 13, 16

machismo, 11–12, 62, 81, 94, 106, 131
Madera de boj, 1, 101, 118, 155
Madrid, 2–4, 6, 19, 29, 31, 37–38, 53, 56, 58–62, 83, 138, 145
The Magic Mountain (Mann), 136
Majorca, 2, 8
Malcolm X, 66
malnutrition, 31, 51
Mangini, Shirley, 1
Manhattan Transfer (Dos Passos), 39
Mann, Thomas, 136
manuscript, 7, 14, 16, 21, 42, 84–85, 88, 90–91, 95, 97, 102, 123, 126, 142, 149
Marañón, Gregorio, 11
Marco, Martín (*The Hive*), 31–33, 35, 38–39

Valencia, 62

Valle-Inclán, Ramón María del, 6, 8, 74, 131, 135, 143, 148, 150, 152

Vallejo, César, 145

Vandercammen, Edmond, 53

Vatican II Council, 159

Velázquez, Ramón José, 130

Venezuela, 4, 130

vengeance, 36, 64, 74, 82, 85, 89, 148

Venus, 67

Verdú, Matilde (*La cruz de San Andrés*), 117–21

Viaje a la Alcarria, 1

Vietnam, 72

Vigo, Spain, 2, 121

Villa, Pancho, 88

Villanueva, Darío, 7–8, 64, 133

violence, 17, 20, 39, 44, 57, 105–6, 111, 117

Virgin Mary, 70, 88, 93–94, 121

Visi, Doña (*The Hive*), 31–32, 36

Vuelta de hoja, 5

Western world, 48, 90, 101, 103–4, 107, 131, 136

wheelbarrow, 21, 26–27, 136, 152

widows, 39, 75, 82

Wild West (American), 7, 87–89

witchcraft, 17, 127

witness, 25, 83, 102, 136

W. L. (*Rest Home*), 23

work-in-progress, 27

World War II, 31, 39, 51, 85, 115

Wounded Knee, South Dakota, 155

writing, 8, 23, 41, 56, 69, 75, 99, 109, 130

written texts, 23, 25–26, 56, 80, 88, 9(, 108–9

Zacarías (*Pascual Duarte*), 17

Zambrano, María, 2

Zamora Vicente, Alonso, 2